MW00831581

PELLETIER

THE FORGOTTEN CASTAWAY OF CAPE YORK

PELLETIER

THE FORGOTTEN CASTAWAY OF CAPE YORK

INTRODUCTORY ESSAY & TRANSLATION BY
STEPHANIE ANDERSON

FROM THE ORIGINAL BOOK
DIX-SEPT ANS CHEZ LES SAUVAGES.
LES AVENTURES DE NARCISSE PELLETIER
BY CONSTANT MERLAND

ETHNOGRAPHIC COMMENTARY BY
ATHOL CHASE

M
MELBOURNE BOOKS

Published by Melbourne Books
Level 9, 100 Collins Street,
Melbourne, VIC, 3000
Australia

www.melbournebooks.com.au
info@melbournebooks.com.au

Copyright © Stephanie Anderson 2009
Athol Chase retains copyright to his essay:
Pama Malngkana: The 'Sandbeach People' of Cape York

All rights reserved. No part of this publication may be reproduced,
stored in a retrieval system, or transmitted in any form or any
means electronic, mechanical, photocopying, recording or
otherwise without the prior permission of the publisher.

Title: Pelletier—The Forgotten Castaway of Cape York
Author: Anderson, Stephanie.
ISBN: 9781877096679 (pbk.)

A catalogue record for this
book is available from the
NATIONAL
LIBRARY National Library of Australia
OF AUSTRALIA

CONTENTS

ACKNOWLEDGEMENTS

I t has been one of the pleasures of working on this translation of Narcisse Pelletier's account of his life with the Sandbeach People of Cape York, or *Pama Malngkana* in their languages, that it has introduced me to many people in Australia and France who have contributed to it. I would like, firstly, to extend my thanks to members of the Lockhart River Aboriginal Community, who shared their knowledge of their language and culture and took an interest in the Frenchman who lived with their ancestors from 1858 to 1875. In particular, Vincent Temple of the Lockhart River Land and Sea Centre, spokesperson and elder of the Angkum clan; Brian Claudie, priest-in-charge of St James Church, Lockhart River; and senior women of the community, Dorothy Short, Elizabeth Giblet, Susie Pascoe and Minnie Pascoe. A number of Lockhart River informants were consulted about correct renditions of words in their languages. These include Maria Butcher, Lorraine Clarmont, Elizabeth Giblet, Ronald Giblet, Beatrice Hobson, Donald Hobson, Evelyn Omeenyo, Susie Pascoe and Dorothy Short. I owe a special debt of gratitude to Veronica Piva of the Lockhart River Shire Council for so hospitably accommodating the Guilbaud family from France and me in her home and for sharing with us her experience and knowledge of the Lockhart River Community.

The project brought together an informal group of experts. A particular debt of thanks goes to Athol Chase, without whom the book could not have been written. Athol has given me access to the results of his research over the years of his career as an anthropologist in the Lockhart River region, answered endless queries, allowed me to quote liberally from his work and has contributed the Ethnographic Commentary which provides an authoritative ethnographic counterpart to the translation, as well as his own photographs to illustrate it. Anyone reading this book will see the imprint of Athol's work throughout its pages.

I am also indebted to Bruce Rigsby, the anthropologist and linguist and major contributor to knowledge of the languages, ethnography and history of the Lamalama people and other groups in the region, who took an interest in this project from the outset and continued to play a guiding role in it throughout. David Thompson, who was Chaplain to the Lockhart River Aboriginal Community, Diocese of Carpentaria, from 1969 to 1977, and has published linguistic and historical studies about the region, has helped immeasurably in his comments and advice also from the outset, for which I owe him special thanks. My thanks go, too, to David Clarke, of the Office of Aboriginal and Torres Strait Island Partnerships Queensland and formerly Chief Executive Officer of the Lockhart River Aboriginal Council at the Lockhart River Community, the linguist and anthropologist Peter Sutton and the linguist Clair Hill for their valuable contributions to many email discussions on north-east Cape York matters.

I would like to thank Véronique Guilbaud of the Mairie de Saint-Gilles-Croix-de-Vie for introducing me to Pelletier's home town and so generously sharing with me the information she has discovered through her own researches into the subject. The anthropologist John Liep was kind enough to share with me his ethnographic expertise about Rossel Island, where Pelletier was shipwrecked in 1858, and his own views about the tragic aftermath of the shipwreck. The maps that illustrate this book were drawn up by Paul Sjoberg and I am grateful to him for the care and time he took over them. For advice on the translation itself, I greatly appreciated the assistance of Dominique Smith who made many helpful suggestions in taking on the task of reading the whole translation. James Grieve, as always, gave incisive help with various problems. For their comments on musical questions, I am indebted to Grace Koch, Anny Letouzey-Wattelet, and Sophie Landemore. Errors that remain in the translation are entirely my responsibility.

For their invaluable advice and assistance, I would like to thank Jean-Paul Bouchon, Gildas Buron, Felicity Croydon, Frédéric Delvolte, Bronwen Douglas, Thérèse Dumont, Maryse Dupé, Joan Fitzsimmons, André Hamon, Lawrie Kavanagh, Rosine Lheureux, Ingereth MacFarlane, Alan-Michel Misson de Saint-Gilles, Leo Moloney, Roland Mornet, Frances Muncey, Michèle Musy, Ron Osborne, Stéphane Pajot, Nicolas Peterson, Colin Sheehan, Robert Spilsted and Rosemary Wrench.

My thanks go to Carol Cooper, Andy Greenslade, Anne Kelly, Darrell Lewis and George Serras of the National Museum of Australia for all their help. I am indebted to Jean Stewart and Rod McLeod of the Royal Historical Society of Queensland for their assistance on a number of occasions, and I would also like to thank the Society for giving me permission to reproduce photographs of Narcisse Pelletier held in their collection as well as to include as an appendix a long extract from one of their manuscripts. Librarians at the National Library of Australia were always courteous and efficient in obtaining research material.

I wish to thank the Thomson family and Museum Victoria for their permission to quote at length from one of Donald Thomson's articles from *Walkabout*. My thanks, too, to both the Écomusée de Saint-Nazaire and the Mairie de Saint-Gilles-Croix-de-Vie for supplying historical photographs and for allowing their reproduction here. I am grateful to the artist Elizabeth Giblet for her permission to reproduce a photograph of the basket she crafted (Collection of the National Museum of Australia).

I was very fortunate to encounter a receptive and responsive publisher in David Tenenbaum and a perceptive and sympathetic editor in Marleena Forward, and I thank them for all their help.

Lastly, I would like my mother Illarra Muirhead, my brother James Anderson and my sister Jane Pearce to know how much I have appreciated their support and interest in this project. The translation and presentation of Narcisse Pelletier's story has taken time, but my husband Craddock Morton and my son Patrick Morton have encouraged me through thick and thin; all my thanks go to them both for enabling me to see it through.

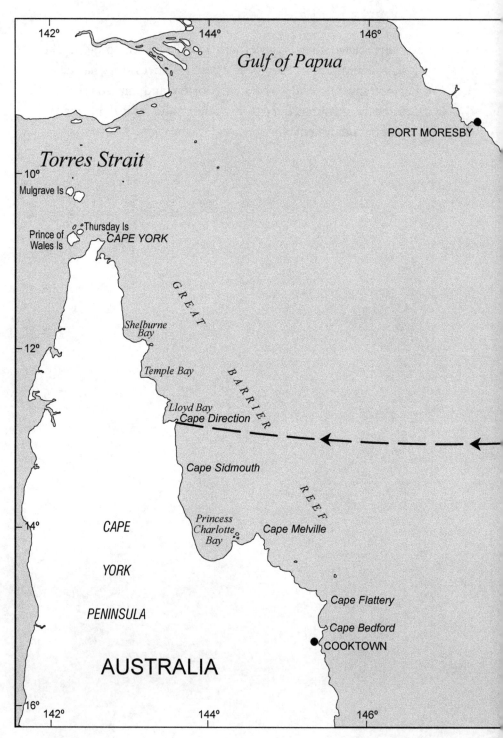

Cartographer: Paul Sjoberg

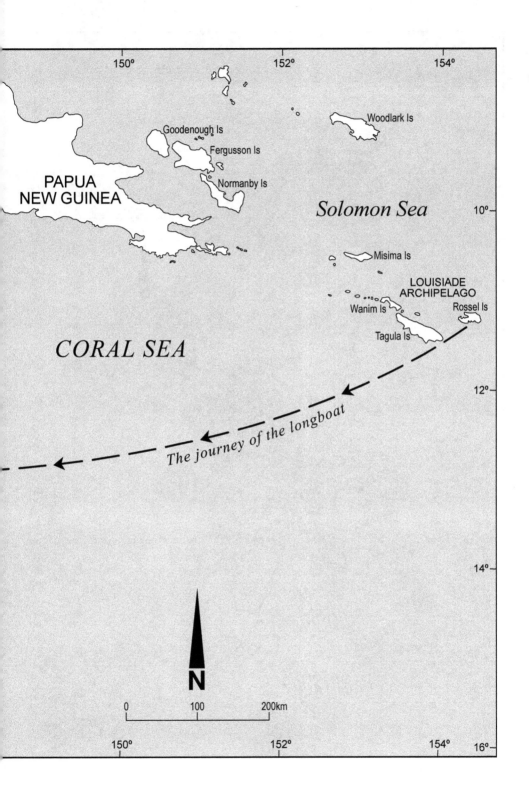

150°   152°   154°

PAPUA
NEW GUINEA

Goodenough Is
Fergusson Is
Normanby Is

Woodlark Is

Solomon Sea

10°

Misima Is

LOUISIADE
ARCHIPELAGO
Wanim Is   Rossel Is
Tagula Is

CORAL SEA

12°

The journey of the longboat

14°

N

0   100   200km

150°   152°   154°   16°

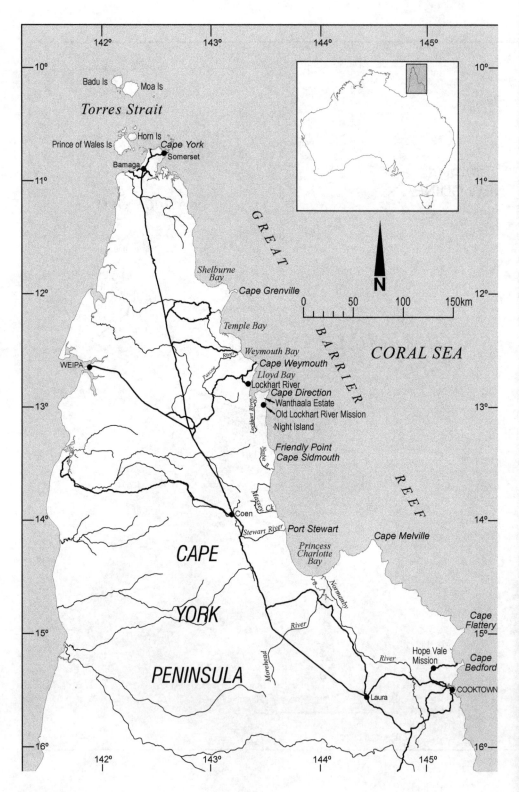

142°   143°   144°   145°

10°

Badu Is   Moa Is

Torres Strait

Horn Is
Prince of Wales Is   *Cape York*
Somerset
Bamaga

11°

G
R
E
A
T

Shelburne Bay

12°
Cape Grenville

Temple Bay

B
A
R
R
I
E
R

CORAL SEA

Weymouth Bay
River
Cape Weymouth
Pascoe
Lloyd Bay
Lockhart River
Cape Direction
Wanthaala Estate
Old Lockhart River Mission
Night Island

WEIPA

13°

Lockhart River

Friendly Point
Cape Sidmouth

Nesbit R.

R
E
E
F

Massey Ck
Coen
Stewart River   Port Stewart

Cape Melville

14°

CAPE

Princess Charlotte Bay

Normanby

YORK

Cape Flattery
15°

River
Hope Vale Mission
Cape Bedford

PENINSULA

Morehead

River

COOKTOWN

Laura

16°

142°   143°   144°   145°

N

0   50   100   150km

12

PART ONE

THE TWO LIVES OF NARCISSE PELLETIER

STEPHANIE ANDERSON

On 13 December 1875 the French ship the *Jura* sailed into the port of Toulon after a voyage that had taken her across the world to New Caledonia. Disembarking with the sailors was a good-looking young man named Narcisse Pelletier, who had boarded the ship at Noumea, in August of that year. There was nothing to distinguish him from those around him except for his very distended and pierced right earlobe. But Pelletier was a most unusual passenger. He had already known his moment of fame in Australia, having recently been found on the far north-eastern coast of Cape York Peninsula where, following a shipwreck, he had been living for the past seventeen years with a group of coast-dwelling Aborigines.

Some months ahead of his return to France, the news of Pelletier's survival had reached his village from newspaper reports. His mother, Alphonsine, who had worn mourning dress since her son's disappearance, and his father, Martin, a shoemaker, had to digest the fact that their son really was still alive. Pelletier was met at Toulon by one of his brothers who had travelled south from the village of Saint-Gilles-sur-Vie in the Vendée, now a thriving resort and fishing town on France's Atlantic coast. The two men journeyed to Saint-Gilles by way of Paris where, it seems, Pelletier had meetings with government officials, and where he was admitted to hospital. On 2 January 1876, Pelletier made his triumphal return.

The whole town had turned out to see him, a bonfire was ready for him to light and his parents were waiting for this incredible reunion. But for Pelletier, readjusting to life in France would be the most difficult part of his journey so far. Now a man of 32, he had to begin reacquainting himself with a family, a culture and a country that he had left behind in his early adolescence and had all but forgotten.

The fateful voyage that led to Pelletier's disappearance began in 1857 when he embarked at Marseilles as a cabin boy on the *Saint-Paul*, a three-mast ship bound for Sydney. The ship called at Bombay and then Hong Kong, where the captain recruited more than 300 Chinese to work on the New South Wales goldfields. In September 1858, the *Saint-Paul* struck a reef in the Louisiade Archipelago off New Guinea. Leaving the Chinese on a small island off the larger Rossel Island (now known as Yela), the captain and members of the crew, including the cabin boy, sailed in an open boat across the Coral Sea to north-east Cape York in Australia, a journey of some 1200 kilometres.

After twelve days at sea, the party landed in the vicinity of Cape Direction, where Pelletier, almost dead from his ordeal, found himself abandoned by the captain and his men. He was rescued by an Aboriginal family and taken in by their people, Uutaalnganu speakers, one of the eastern Cape York groups of coast-dwellers who describe themselves as *Pama Malngkana* or Sandbeach People. The Sandbeach People lived in a particularly rich hunter-gatherer environment, occupying the coastal beachfronts of north-east Cape York Peninsula north of Princess Charlotte Bay.[1] Pelletier grew to manhood with the Uutaalnganu and remained with them until he was found again by the crew of a pearling lugger, the *John Bell*, on 11 April 1875, and sent back to France.

Once resettled in France, Pelletier was interviewed about his experiences by Constant Merland (1808–1885), a surgeon-turned-savant who lived in the town of Nantes. Merland wrote down the story in the form of an ethnographic description and had it published to provide the young man with some income. This work, published in Paris in 1876, is entitled *Dix-sept ans chez les sauvages. Les aventures de Narcisse Pelletier*, in English *Seventeen years among the savages. The adventures of Narcisse Pelletier*. The various articles that have appeared over the years in Australian newspapers about the story of Narcisse Pelletier make no reference to Merland's book, which is now very rare. The publication in 2001 of a new edition of the work, compiled and edited by Philippe Pécot, has not changed this situation.[2]

Better known in France, Pelletier's story is still not known there entirely accurately. The linguistic and geographical distance between France and Australia in the 19th century and even later has meant that those interested in the story in Australia failed to pursue research into Pelletier after his return to France and that those interested in the story in France failed to investigate how — and even precisely where — Pelletier spent such a long period in Australia. What happened to Pelletier after his return to France is not known in Australia, while in France, even in the new edition of Pelletier's account of his adventures he is said to have lived at Cape Flattery, which is also on Cape York, but considerably further south of the region where he actually did live.[3]

Like more famous castaways or absconders such as William Buckley and James Morrill, Pelletier managed to survive in the harshest of circumstances. Like them, too, he experienced a complete and long immersion in the culture of an Aboriginal group just before European contact had started to make any significant impact on the people he lived with. In fact his 'Aboriginalisation' may have been even more profound than theirs because he was only fourteen years old when the process began.[4]

In translating Pelletier's account, I have followed the text of the original work by Constant Merland.[5] The translation is accompanied by an ethnographic commentary by Athol Chase, an anthropologist who has worked for more than 30 years in the Kuuku Ya'u, Uutaalnganu and Umpila language areas of the region of Cape York where Pelletier lived. While much anthropological and linguistic work has been carried out in this area over time, not all of it is now readily accessible. Nor has any specific ethnography that focuses on any of the *Pama Malngkana* groups yet been published. In order to make Merland's text as ethnographically and ethnohistorically useful as possible, I have annotated it with material drawn from the work of anthropologists and linguists spanning the period from the late 1920s to the present.

Of the earlier fieldworkers in the region, I have drawn especially on the writings of the talented Australian anthropologist Donald Thomson, who carried out fieldwork in eastern Cape York with coastal peoples in the late 1920s and early 1930s at Port Stewart on Princess Charlotte Bay and at Lockhart River before undertaking anthropological work in Arnhem Land and, later in his career, in the Great Sandy Desert.[6] At that time, not only were the Aboriginal inhabitants of the region virtually unknown, as Thomson reports, but the area itself was unsurveyed and without roads.[7] For Thomson, this region was a revelation. He was profoundly impressed by the seafaring people with whom he lived. He recalls his fieldwork among them as 'one of the happiest times of my life', while of his months spent recording Kuuku Ya'u ceremonial life he writes: 'Here was something quite new to me — a culture warm, virile, vital, which differed greatly from anything I knew, or had seen, in Australia.'[8] Chase, in turn, some years before studying anthropology and conducting his own fieldwork at Lockhart River, had been stimulated by Thomson's engaging articles about his Cape York experiences for *Walkabout* magazine, and remembers the 'rich picture' Thomson created of what anthropology might be — a picture his subsequent courses in British structural functionalism could not hope to match.[9]

Thomson has left a large and invaluable collection of ethnographic and linguistic material for this region in published articles, and unpublished fieldnotes, photographs and objects of material culture. (The collection is now held by the Museum of Victoria.) Given the richness of the material he amassed and the wealth of information he recorded in a comparatively short period of time, out of which two rich and classic articles emerged specifically about Sandbeach culture, it is a great loss for the ethnography of the Cape York region that Thomson was prevented from continuing fieldwork there. In the first instance he fell out with the superintendent at the Anglican Lockhart River Mission at the time, Harry Rowan, and Bishop Stephen Davies of the Diocese of Carpentaria over the performance of aspects of traditional culture such as initiation ceremonies, which the mission looked to suppress.[10] And in 1933 he protested about the treatment of Aboriginal people at Aurukun on the west of the Peninsula so that he 'became *persona non grata* on Cape York.'[11] After World War II, he attempted to return to the Aboriginal reserve lands of the area but was refused permission by the Queensland government, which controlled them.[12]

The scientists Herbert Hale and Norman Tindale actually preceded Thomson to Cape York when they made their expedition to the Princess Charlotte Bay region in 1926–7 for the South Australian Museum. They only stayed at Port Stewart — where a number of Aboriginal groups were living, including people from Umpila and Uutaalnganu lands — for a matter of weeks, but they collected useful material, particularly in relation to the daily life and technology of Sandbeach People.[13] I have also made use of their research in annotating the translation.

Athol Chase's contribution has been vital here. He has published extensively on the Lockhart River region and the groups of Aboriginal people who live there, his articles forming a unique ethnographic compendium for this area (see Bibliography). A key dimension of his writing about the *Pama Malngkana* — and in this he differs markedly from Donald Thomson, who presents a somewhat idealised or traditionalised portrait of the Sandbeach Peoples — is to situate his discussions in the context of the life these people live now in the Lockhart River Aboriginal Community, while at the same time documenting the contact history that has shaped the present situation of its members, analysing the links they actively maintain with the ideology and social patterns of their forebears and drawing on the depth of local indigenous knowledge to explore their relationship with their coastal environment in the past and in the present.

David Thompson has also published material about Lockhart River (see Bibliography). In particular, his description of Sandbeach languages (on which I have drawn frequently in annotating the translation of Merland's book) is an invaluable resource and his study of the Lockhart River Mission makes a contribution not only to the history of the Aboriginal people of Lockhart River and the Anglican mission which operated there from 1924 to 1967 but to the broader history of Aboriginal missions in Australia as well.

Where possible, I have tried to include the commentary of *Pama Malngkana* themselves, though published material recording Aboriginal speakers of the region is sparse. These voices in Aboriginal English are direct and expressive about their Sandbeach culture.

As anthropologists of the region, starting with Thomson, have pointed out, the ethnography of marine-oriented Aboriginal groups such as the Uutaalnganu is much less well known than that of desert-dwellers. Pelletier's story therefore serves to bring into focus the peoples who have lead, and to some extent still lead, this seafaring life. Athol Chase describes the distinctiveness of the Sandbeach identity:

> Beach people are 'beach people' not only because they occupied the beach strip in precontact times, but because they are the proper human exploiters of such major marine resources as dugong, turtle, fish and shellfish and the plants and animals of the littoral. They alone are the inheritors of the special knowledge of dugong and

turtles, and the bush medicines required to facilitate capture. They are people who say the proper mode of living for them involves the feel of the seabreezes on their faces, saltwater on their bodies, and the ocean vista before their eyes.[14]

If Pelletier's account is something like a time capsule describing a virtually pre-contact indigenous way of life from the inside, it should be remembered that there are significant continuities of culture and world view for Uutaalnganu people today with the lives of their forebears.

The Uutaalnganu people are commonly known as the 'Night Island people' after an island situated approximately in the middle of their coastal territory. This extends down the coast from the mouth of the Lockhart River at Lloyd Bay, north of Cape Direction, to Friendly Point, just north of Cape Sidmouth. Since 1967 they have lived at the Lockhart River Aboriginal Community, situated some 60 kilometres by sea from the centre of their homelands and just inland from Lloyd Bay. The nearby airport at Iron Range, which services the community today, was a little known but important airforce base during World War II from 1942 to 1943. Thousands of American and Australian servicemen were stationed at Iron Range, and bombing and reconnaissance missions over New Guinea and the Coral Sea took off from there in 1942. Recollections recorded from men who served in this area reveal that they found living and working in this tropical environment extremely debilitating. Many planes and crew were either shot down or lost because of the difficult flying conditions and terrain.[15]

The region in which Pelletier lived is a very remote and isolated area of Australia. It is also one of great natural beauty. From the air, islands and coral cays can be seen dotted through the turquoise waters of the inner reef. The line of beach, cut at intervals by estuarine rivers, extends in an endless white ribbon, hemming the coast and its bays. The green cover of the rainforest and woodlands spreads back from the coast and over the lowlands and ranges in a vast expanse, barely interrupted by any sign of settlement between Cooktown and Lockhart River. From the shore, the eye is drawn not out to sea — the horizon seems close — but up and down the coast. The curving outlines of blue-hazed islands, hills and headlands unfold in silhouette upon silhouette. Low mountain ranges, which form part of the Great Dividing Range, separate the narrow band of coastal lands from the interior and the Gulf country of the Peninsula to the west.

This coastal wilderness is still untrammelled by tourist development, although specialist groups — naturalists, birdwatchers and fishing enthusiasts — are drawn to the area because of the richness and diversity of its plant and animal life. South-easterly trade winds blow across the country in the dry season, while the wet season brings the north-westerly monsoons with heavy rain and the danger of cyclones.

The Lockhart River Aboriginal Community is situated 760 kilometres by road from Cairns and is only accessible during the dry season from May to November — and then only by four-wheel drive vehicles. It is made up of people from five main territorial and linguistic groups whose traditional lands lie in and around this region. These comprise one inland language group, Kaanju, and four coastal language groups, which are, from north to south, Wuthati, Kuuku Ya'u, Uutaalnganu and Umpila. The main language now spoken in the community is Cape York Creole (or Kriol), with English as a second language. It is the senior men and women at Lockhart who are the repositories of the traditional languages of their particular groups, although there are some younger members of the community who are active in preserving, maintaining and recording traditional culture and languages.

Since the government resettlement in 1969 of Aboriginal people from the site of the old Lockhart River Mission (established on the coast south of Cape Direction at Bare Hill in 1924) to their present site, the area of land gazetted as the Lockhart River Reserve has been converted into a form of tenure, the Lockhart Deed of Grant in Trust.[16] The population of the Lockhart community now numbers around 800 people, of whom several family groups retain direct links to Uutaalnganu homelands.[17] Given the siting of the community today, most residents are at a considerable distance from their homelands, which makes visits to their traditional country difficult.

In recent years, Lockhart River has seen the development of a flourishing art movement. The young artists of the Lockhart River Art Gang attract considerable attention among critics and collectors, while senior artists in the community have more recently begun to exhibit paintings, sculpture and fibrework.[18]

Uutaalnganu people today are living in very different circumstances and in a different place from their forebears when they occupied the section of coast that gave them the name of *pama yi'achi*, 'middle people', between the Kuuku Ya'u people above them and Umpila people below. We shall see that Uutaalnganu people had some limited dealings with European boats while Pelletier lived with them and, although he does not mention it, they probably had knowledge, too, from other groups of the drive into the Cape by pastoralists and then miners. But they were not yet involved in the pearling and bêche-de-mer (or trepang) industries operating out of the Torres Strait, which means that Merland's book describes the way of life of a group of coastal Aboriginal people right on the cusp of the profound changes that would be made upon their lives and their exploitation of the land and sea by a series of alien incursions. Pelletier's account of the way of life of Uutaalnganu people is the earliest ethnographic description to be written about one of the Aboriginal groups of north-eastern Cape York Peninsula. It can be compared with the model of traditional society held by Lockhart elders that Athol Chase recorded in the 1970s. This, together with other more recent ethnographic information, enables a retrospective ethnographic reconstruction of Uutaalnganu life as it was, a kind of overwriting of the outline Merland and Pelletier have left us.

Each phase was distinct and required different adjustments on the part of the coastal people, as Athol Chase describes in more detail in his Commentary. First there was the arrival of the luggermen, both European and Japanese, who operated in the area from the 1870s and recruited most of the able-bodied men to work on their boats for months at a time.[19] Then, in the first decade of the century, the entrepreneurial Hugh Giblett set up camp at Lloyd Bay and employed Aboriginal people on a seasonal basis for his sandalwood trade and trepang harvesting, an era which lasted until his death in 1923.

An Anglican mission was set up in the area in 1924 and functioned, with varying degrees of control and community acceptance according to the personality and regime of the succession of superintendents of the mission, until the 1960s.[20] The region inhabited by Sandbeach people was remote enough that child removal and the resulting Stolen Generations of Aboriginal people did not occur in the same way as in many other parts of Aboriginal Australia. However, the dormitory system of the mission in its early days meant that children were separated from their parents, and in around 1935 superintendent Harry Rowan boosted the mission population at Lockhart River by 'commandeering the children' so that families were forced to move there.[21] If early missionaries discouraged the use of indigenous languages and particular cultural practices, Chase, in his Commentary, points to the resilience of Sandbeach culture through the missionary period. In 1967, church 'intervention' was replaced by state 'intervention', the last of the 'three major intervention complexes'[22] in this area (the first being the coastal/marine extractive industries), when the Queensland government assumed responsibility for the community, imposing a highly regulated system of controls on the Aboriginal residents.[23] The stern regime that applied to Aboriginal residents in the area was paralleled by the police monitoring of certain anthropologists during this period. Both Athol Chase and Peter Sutton were subject to surveillance while working in Cape York in the 1970s, and Chase's phone was tapped by the Queensland government Special Branch.[24]

Lockhart people refer to the time before Europeans arrived as 'Before Time', and they have fixed the different phases of their contact history by distinct names: Lugger Time, Giblett Time — including Thomson Time[25] — and so on.[26] John Haviland has written of Cape York Peninsula that the 'dismantling of Aboriginal life throughout the north was cruelly effective and irrevocable. What survives is radically transformed'.[27] But the fact that in north-eastern Cape York alien penetration related to exploitation of the sea, rather than involving the takeover of land for mining or grazing, means that dispossession and displacement from homelands did not occur in the same cataclysmic way as it did for other Aboriginal people of the Peninsula and elsewhere.[28]

The concentration of groups in one site, which first occurred with missionisation in 1924 at what is now called the Old Site near Cape Direction and continued when the settlement was moved to the new site near Lloyd Bay, impeded but did not prevent access to homelands. Connection to country remains a vital force in the Lockhart community today in the formation of countryman groups, even if these groups no longer reside permanently on their estates. This basic element of social organisation relating different groups of people to specific tracts of land links the past to the present and is manifest in every important dimension of life: the formation of individual and group identity, the sharing of resources and knowledge, support networks, residence patterns, conflicts and alliances between groups and the ideology of 'right' and 'wrong' marriages.[29] Outstation movements are occurring and traditional homelands are the subject of land claims by different groups now at Lockhart.

In describing his role as Pelletier's scribe in his introduction, Merland writes: 'I shall take pains to retain the simplicity of his tale, without letting myself become too distracted by the reflections to which it might give rise, and without adding very much to it'. By and large, apart from a disquisition on linguistics and a sprinkling of classical and literary allusions, Merland sticks to his word. But given that Pelletier, although he could read and write, was a man of limited education, we can see that Merland's book reflects his scholarly background as much as Pelletier's own view of his experience. A correspondent of various learned societies, Merland was most famous for his historical work, *Biographies Vendéennes*, published in 1883 in five volumes.[30]

In his introduction Merland says that he constructed his book from notes made by Pelletier himself and from their conversations together. Those notes and Merland's papers, if they still exist, have not been found. He also drew on the report of a rescue mission to Rossel Island that was launched to recover the Chinese labourers who had been left there when the captain and his European crew made their escape. The report was written by Victor de Rochas.[31] It is a comprehensive account of the shipwreck and the fate of the captain and crew, and of the rescue mission in which the author, a navy doctor, took part. I shall return to the outcome of the mission later.

Merland provides what appears to be a reliable and unembroidered account of Pelletier's experiences and what Pelletier told him of the knowledge he had gained of Uutaalnganu life. But his presentation of Pelletier, while not extravagant, had more than merely the literary aim of establishing the bona fides of the story he was telling and its hero. Pelletier, now 32 and returned home after seventeen years' absence, needed to find some means of supporting himself, and Merland acts as his advocate in his introduction.

I believe that Merland is a straightforward reporter of what Pelletier told him. However, readers coming to Merland's book today will be struck by the antiquated flavour of his writing (which

I have tried to preserve in the translation), and his condescending attitudes towards non-European people. The style is learned but not elegant, and he uses a sprinkling of literary and classical allusions to make mocking comparisons with Aboriginal ways in an attempt at humour typical of the exotic travel genre of his day. In describing particular practices he invariably starts from the assumption that Aboriginal culture will be simple and uncivilised. This occurs right from the beginning with the title *Chez les sauvages* and continues throughout the text with Merland's very frequent use of the term *sauvages* ('savages'), first to refer to the Yela people, the inhabitants of Rossel Island, and then to the Uutaalnganu people with whom Pelletier lived.

There is no point in trying to hide this by translating his *sauvages* using another word. The power to gauge the culturally and historically specific values and attitudes expressed in such labels is lost if we substitute terms acceptable to present-day thinking — and we know that these, too, will change over time. Having said that, I hope that no offence is taken by my use of this expression in making an accurate translation of this 19th century work, especially by the descendants of Pelletier's Aboriginal rescuers who now mostly live at Lockhart River, and more generally by other Aboriginal people, as well as by the inhabitants of Yela. We can, however, gain insights into the attitudes revealed by the application of this term to non-European groups by briefly considering its usage historically, both in France and elsewhere.

Judging by the *Bulletins et Mémoires* of the Société d'Anthropologie de Paris (founded in 1859 by Paul Broca), by the time Merland was writing in 1876, the term *sauvage* was less likely to be used in French anthropological circles to refer to indigenous people, from Australia or elsewhere, than *les naturels* ('the natives') or *les indigènes* ('the indigenes'). The more likely term used by anthropologists for Australian Aborigines specifically was *les Australiens* ('the Australians'). But Merland, although a medical man and scholar, was not an anthropologist. The label he chose would have been quite normal for the time as the most common term in general usage to refer to non-European peoples from remote places. This would also be the case in the English-speaking world for the word 'savage', and indeed it was still in use by specialists as well to refer to their anthropological subjects. The term occurs frequently in Edward Tylor's classic of anthropology, *Primitive culture*, published in 1871.[32]

In Australia in this period Aboriginal people were commonly referred to as 'the Blacks' (or 'blacks') or 'blackfellows'. Ottley uses the word 'blacks' in his letter (see Appendix V), as does Hamilton-Gordon in *The Times*, although the term 'savage' appears in the title of his article, and in it he refers to Pelletier as 'the white savage'.[33] Similarly, James Morrill, another Queensland castaway, uses the words 'blacks', 'blackfellows' or 'natives' to refer to the Aboriginal people with whom he lived.[34]

Concepts such as 'wildness' are motivated by the negative opposition they imply to another term.[35] The wild, the untamed, the undomesticated, the uncultivated or the *sauvage* stand in opposition to the civilised. The pair *sauvage/civilisé* is the opposition that sustained the use of the term *sauvage* to denote little-known people in the far corners of the globe in the era of European exploration and subsequent colonisation right through the 19th century and into the twentieth. But the term *sauvage* has a long European history and was first used to describe what were thought to be the wild men of the woods of Europe itself, hence its derivation from the Latin *silvestrus*.[36] It is worth noting that while the noun *sauvage* is translated directly by the word 'savage', the primary meaning of the adjective in French is 'wild' or 'uncultivated'.

By the time of the colonial era there was little ambiguity in the way most people used the term, when the superiority of European civilisation was taken as a given, and Europeans held themselves to be racially superior in a biological sense. If any faint echoes of *le bon sauvage* remained in the French use of the term in the late 19th century, I do not think that Merland displays any primitivist leanings in his account — even if this is one reason why stories such as Pelletier's have long held such appeal. 'Primitivism,' says Hayden White, 'simply invites men to be themselves, to give vent to their original, natural, but subsequently repressed, desires; to throw off the restraints of civilization and thereby enter into a kingdom that is *naturally* theirs.'[37] Pelletier, Buckley et al were able to live out other people's dreams of a way of life that was not *policé*, an old but evocative French term for 'civilised', that was unrestrained by convention, and free. Yet of course it was no such thing: they left behind one set of social and cultural rules but could only survive by learning another. The tendency to refer to such men as Crusoes — a label sometimes given to Pelletier, while Buckley himself actually claimed to be 'the real Crusoe'[38] — completely overlooks the cultural re-education that underpinned their new existence, and the people they lived with.

My feeling is that Merland uses the term *sauvage* without even thinking about it because that is the term he has to hand, and because he starts from a perspective in which the distinction between 'savage' and 'civilised' is fundamental. In the course of the book he makes a number of comments in which his prejudice is at the fore — 'savages' are held to be emotional not rational, child-like, and to have no religious beliefs — but he allows his prejudices to be confounded as well when he is shocked that people 'living in an almost bestial state' have such respect for the dead or that sexual licence does not have free rein, that a sense of modesty is 'even more pronounced than in civilised societies'. He is adamant that the people of 'Endeavour Land' could only benefit from the imposition of his civilisation and the introduction of Christianity. But otherwise he is not as judgmental, and certainly not as derogatory, about Australian Aborigines as many professional anthropologists of his day. At this time anthropology in France had a decidedly biological and raciological focus, being dominated by the figure of the eminent doctor and researcher Paul Broca whose hardline polygenism divided humans into unequally favoured racial groupings having separate origins. Broca, and most of his colleagues, placed Aborigines at the bottom of the racial hierarchies they devised to classify human beings.[39] And by comparison with literary and popular stereotypes of Aborigines Merland's book was also less disparaging. Jules Verne's *Les enfants du Capitaine Grant* (1868), for example, gives as unflattering and ill-informed a portrayal of Aboriginal people as any one might find in this period, even as he castigates the British colonisers for their murderous expulsion of indigenous peoples from their lands.[40]

If the stark racialism of 19th century physical anthropology has now been superseded, the savage/civilised dichotomy in its application to Aboriginal Australians is tenacious. Let me give three quite different examples. W. Lloyd Warner's classic ethnography about Yolgnu people of north-east Arnhem Land, first published in 1937, displays the dichotomy in its title, *A black civilization*. Although Warner uses the word 'savage' a number of times in the text, his title in fact indicates a desire to overturn the dichotomy. Racism is blatant, though, in the chapter on Aboriginal people in Queensland that appeared in 1959 in an official centenary volume by Sir Raphael Cilento and Clem Lack commemorating the foundation of Queensland. The 'Bush Blacks', say the authors, 'were outside the ambit of any "civilization". They must be considered as nomads of the jungle or savannah or desert, comparable with the animal groups that inhabited those areas...' Pursuing the feral theme, they draw an analogy between Aborigines and dingoes: 'Like his own half-wild dogs, he could be frozen into shivering immobility or put to frenzied flight by people or things that provoked impressions of terror; or moved to yelps of delight or to racing round, or striking grotesque poses, or to expressing frantic excitement..', a train of thought that rises to a crescendo invoking 'primitive reactions' and 'ferocity'.[41] The dichotomy serves another purpose again for Patrick White in *A fringe of leaves* (1976). Basing the protagonist of his novel on the castaway Eliza Fraser, White portrays Ellen Roxburgh's Queensland Aboriginal captors as savages whose brutal ways reduce her to an almost animal state. White creates an extraordinary character in Mrs Roxburgh, exploring the shifting construction of human identity through the metamorphoses she undergoes in the course of the novel and questioning the 'civilisation' of British and colonial society by counterposing it to that of her captors. But his lurid portrayal of a barbaric indigenous world is a literary creation not based in fact.

Would Pelletier himself have used the term 'savage' to describe the people who had saved his life, taken him in and nursed him back to health and adopted him as one of their own, people whose lives he shared for so long? In Merland's book the voice of the protagonist never comes to us directly and we cannot know if Pelletier would have been happy with Merland's choice of words. We do know that he used the term in his letters to his parents after his recovery. But Pelletier, in his first letter only haltingly recovering his French, would not have had any other term in his limited lexicon to denote Aboriginal people. He would come to learn that 'savagery' was a quality attributed by others and that he was thought to have acquired it himself from his long residence in Queensland. Just as other recovered Europeans were described as 'wild white men' well into the 20th century — in fact 'wild man' is an alternative translation for *sauvage* — Pelletier would come to be referred to as *le sauvage*, and not only in the talk of his local area, but in academic publications. Merland himself did not, however, refer to Pelletier in this way.

Merland's rather surprising lack of scholarship in his approach to Pelletier's story is not confined to his use of the word *sauvage* when others were available. Even more surprising is the fact that he never refers to the place of Pelletier's residence as being situated in Cape York, or in Queensland, which had become a colony in 1859, the year after Pelletier's arrival, and he barely uses the name 'Australia'. His term 'Endeavour Land' and the erroneous location of Cape Flattery are the only geographical references he provides to his readers, together with the information that Pelletier was sent to Sydney after his recovery.

There was ethnographic literature in French that Merland could have consulted and quoted to give his readers some comparative information about Australian Aborigines. In this he seems incurious, or perhaps he was hurrying to get his book published in Pelletier's best interest. He could also have made more of comparisons between beliefs and cultural practices which Pelletier had encountered growing up in the Vendée and those he learned on Cape York since he was writing at a time when there was great interest in French folklore, with ethnographic 'facts' being collected from the different regions of France. These would have demonstrated more similarities than we might expect between the life Pelletier had left and the one he adopted.

If Merland's book contains the most complete account there is of Narcisse Pelletier's story, the story did not finish with the publication of the book. And Merland was not the only interested and sympathetic person to become a confidant of Pelletier's, which means that there are more strands to be woven into his narrative. When Pelletier was being sent from Cape York to Sydney prior to his return to France via New Caledonia, he was taken under the wing of a fellow passenger on the *R. M. S. Brisbane*, Lieutenant John Ottley (1841–1931) of the Royal Engineers, who was en route from Singapore to visit relatives in Rockhampton.[42] Part of Ottley's schooling had taken place in Paris at the Lycée Charlemagne[43] and he was therefore able to converse freely with Pelletier once he began to regain the use of his mother tongue. He says that Pelletier 'became as it were my special charge'.[44]

Just as Barbara Thompson had a sensitive and sympathetic witness and recorder of her information in the artist Oswald Brierly of the *Rattlesnake*,[45] Ottley showed an intelligent interest in Pelletier himself, in his experiences and in the way of life and language of the people with whom he lived. He collected from Pelletier a word list of about 100 words that has not yet come to light. An article he wrote about Pelletier appeared in several Australian newspapers[46] and the information he had gathered from Pelletier was used in the comprehensive report about Pelletier's story that appeared in *The Times* of 21 July 1875. The *Times* report was written by Sir Arthur Hamilton-Gordon, the first Baron Stanmore (1829–1912), also a passenger on the *Brisbane*,[47] and at the time the Governor Elect of Fiji, but it seems that he drew heavily on Ottley's information.[48] Ottley went on to have a distinguished military career in India, where he became Inspector-General of Irrigation and Deputy Secretary to the Government of India. On his return to England, he finished his career as President of the Royal Indian Engineering College at Cooper's Hill in Surrey.[49] Almost fifty years after his voyage on the *Brisbane*, Ottley, now Colonel Sir John Ottley, was contacted on behalf of the Royal Historical Society of Queensland by Henry Dodd, who had met him at Cooktown where Dodd had been the station's first telegraph operator,[50] presumably while Ottley was on that same voyage. Ottley supplied Dodd with an account of Pelletier's story, several typed pages in length, which supplies further details and more personal reminiscences than are to be found in the newspaper reports of 1875. This account is reproduced as Appendix V.

Narcisse Pelletier was born to Alphonsine Hippolyte (née Babin) and Martin Hélier Pelletier in 1844. The family, according to a relative, went by the noble name of Pelletier de Saint-Gilles but was ruined in the Revolution,[51] so Martin's occupation as a shoemaker would have signified a considerable fall in status for the family. Narcisse was the eldest of four brothers and was christened

Alphonse Narcisse Pierre though he seems always to have been called Narcisse. The village where Narcisse spent his early years is situated in the *département* of the Vendée. Renamed Saint-Gilles-Croix-de-Vie when the two communes of Saint-Gilles-sur-Vie and Croix-de-Vie, separated by the River Vie, were combined in 1967 for administrative reasons, it is an attractive town bordered by excellent surf beaches. The Vendée is famous in French history for its counter-revolutionary wars beginning in 1793 and ending in 1796, although Saint-Gilles-sur-Vie reportedly stood against the regional tide and supported the Revolution. Marcel Baudouin (1860–1941), a scholar and a native of the town, whom we shall meet again later, writes that the town had been given the name Port-Fidèle, or Port Faithful (today retained in the Quai of that name just down from the Eglise de Saint-Gilles where Narcisse was christened), at the start of the revolutionary period when names had to be dechristianised:

> It was because of the loyalty of the inhabitants of Saint-Gilles and of their constant and faithful adherence to the republican program that the town received this name, when all the neighbouring countryside was dominated by the Chouans. And the sailors of Havre-de-Vie never betrayed the Tricouleur.[52]

The population of Saint-Gilles grew from 715, according to the census of 1801, to 1140 in 1861, according to the census of the same year, while that of Croix-de-Vie went from 550 in 1801 to 763 over the same period.[53] The orientation of the inhabitants of Saint-Gilles, the Giras, was towards the sea and its occupations, as opposed to the Croix-de-Viots across the River Vie, who were farming people. In the past the rivalry between the two communities was legendary.[54] Saint-Gilles was officially established as a seaside resort in the summer of 1863 with bathing cabins erected on the beach, while the sardine fishing industry sustained a growing number of sardine canneries at Croix-de-Vie from 1850 until its rapid decline from a peak of 41 canneries in 1883.[55]

Pelletier's uncle on his mother's side, Jean Babin, was a harbour master. Naval records show that Pelletier's first voyage, lasting several months, was made aboard a small boat owned by a man named Babin, undoubtedly this same uncle. The boat's name was *Le jeune Narcisse*, so the young Narcisse, who was only eight years old at the time, seems to have made his first long sea voyage in a boat named after him. He made another such voyage aboard *Le Furet* in 1855.[56] Further voyages as cabin boy were made on the *Eugénie* and the *Reine des Mers* in 1856 and 1857, at which point Merland's narrative takes up Pelletier's career at sea. The voyage on the *Reine des Mers* was not a happy one for Pelletier, who reports that he was attacked and injured by the first mate. He left the ship at Marseilles in July 1857 in order to avoid further harsh treatment.

It was in August 1857 that he embarked on the *Saint-Paul* under the command of Captain Emmanuel Pinard.[57] The ship departed Marseilles with a cargo of wine to be delivered at Bombay and then proceeded to Hong Kong where the captain spent a month filling the ship with Chinese workers for goldfields in New South Wales, but exactly which goldfield they were headed for is not specified either by Merland or Rochas. The British colony of Hong Kong had become the departure point for labourers from the Chinese mainland, especially the province of Guangdong, who sought their fortunes on foreign goldfields. The exodus meant a thriving trade for the recruiting agents and shipowners. In 1855, for example, 32 ships carrying close to 10,000 passengers departed for Australia.[58]

The *Saint-Paul* left Hong Kong for Sydney with a complement of 317 Chinese on board. Whether by oversight or because Pinard was playing the margins, food supplies ran short and the men had to be put on half rations, though accounts of conditions on board ships ferrying Chinese to the 'New Gold Mountain' in Australia show that the ships were typically overcrowded and drastically undersupplied.[59] To quell the brewing rebellion Pinard decided to take a shorter, and more dangerous, route to Sydney than originally planned by sailing between the Solomon Islands and the Louisiade Archipelago, a long chain of island groups that trails from the south-east tip of New Guinea, rather than making a longer loop around the Solomons.

Three days of rough weather and fog made navigation through these waters a matter of guesswork. Pelletier was on watch with the first mate when the ship struck a reef lying off Rossel Island, at the eastern extremity of the Louisiades. Manoeuvres had no effect in bringing the ship off the reef. At first light the ship, now breaking up, was abandoned and all aboard were moved to a nearby island, the Ilot du Refuge, the Isle of Refuge, as Rochas called it, which faced the much larger Rossel Island. This tiny island is called Heron Island or Wolo.[60] About a kilometre from the mainland, it is 'a place of two or three acres in extent, and quite devoid of food, other than birds' eggs and shell-fish'.[61] Whatever food and provisions could be salvaged from the ship were removed as well.

Rossel Island had been named after one of the officers serving on the expedition of an illustrious French admiral, Bruny d'Entrecasteaux. The main purpose of d'Entrecasteaux's expedition was to discover what had become of the lost French navigator, La Pérouse, and his two ships (which had vanished after their departure from Botany Bay, where they had landed on 26 January 1788). In 1793 d'Entrecasteaux's ships had sailed by Rossel Island without making a landing, but in 1849 the island was described admiringly by men aboard the *Rattlesnake*, the survey ship under the command of Owen Stanley (and the ship which recovered Barbara Thompson), when they first approached it. 'Rossel is the most beautiful island we have ever yet seen, high and well wooded,' wrote one of them.[62] For those aboard the *Saint-Paul*, however, the island offered only dangers to compound the disaster that had already befallen them.

There was no water on the Isle of Refuge. When a party went to get water from Rossel Island, some of the men were attacked and killed or taken prisoner by the inhabitants. Pelletier was hit by a rock during the assault, and only he and an apprentice managed to escape, being picked up in a boat by the captain as they fled into the sea. The men on the Isle of Refuge were then threatened by a hostile mob, some swimming, some in canoes, but they warded off the attack by detonating their firearms with powder, which caused their assailants to retreat.

It is at this point that Pelletier's account of events, as reported by Merland, begins to differ from the captain's, as reported by Victor de Rochas. The captain took the decision to leave with his crew in one of the ship's boats and seek help from British settlements in Australia in the hope of mounting a rescue mission to save those left behind in the Louisiades. Given the size of the party stranded on a small unwatered island facing a hostile population not far across the water, it is hard to see what else he could have done. Pinard claimed that he consulted with the Chinese about this plan while Pelletier alleged that he left at night with his crew without informing them. He said that he himself was only included in the escape because he saw what was happening as the men were leaving and jumped on board. According to Rochas, the captain left with the eleven remaining sailors. According to Pelletier, there were nine men aboard.[63]

The journey across the Coral Sea in an open boat was a desperate one as the Chinese were left with the weapons and most of the remaining provisions. It was twelve days before the men reached land. They had covered a distance of close to 1200 kilometres with only a little flour and some water carried in seamen's boots for supplies. When these ran out they caught sea birds for food and were reduced to drinking their urine and seawater to quench their thirst.

Both Rochas and Merland, who takes his information at this point from Rochas, give the location of where the party landed as Cape Flattery, which is situated a little north of what is now

Cooktown, and was named by Captain James Cook on his voyage with the *Endeavour* on 10 August 1770. No reason is given for this being designated as the landing place; it is simply stated as fact. Subsequent publications that have appeared in French continue to name Cape Flattery as the place where the longboat first made its landing on Australian soil. However, the reports of Pelletier's recovery that appeared in Australian newspapers and in *The Times* in 1875 give a quite different, much more northerly, location for the landing place, namely First Red Rocky Point just south of Cape Direction at 13.4 degrees S., 143.32 degrees E. As the ship that took Pelletier from Somerset to Brisbane sailed down the coast, Pelletier pointed out the places where he had landed and then lived.[64] This was presumably the basis upon which First Red Rocky Point was determined as the first landing point of Pinard's party. And when Pelletier was picked up, he was found at a place on the mainland opposite Night Island, in the heart of Uutaalnganu territory. The linguistic information he gives in his account tallies with the language spoken in the vicinity of Night Island, Uutaalnganu, whereas the traditional owners of the Cape Flattery region are Guugu Yimithirr speakers. And the way of life he describes accords with Uutaalnganu ethnography. There can be no question that the two primary accounts of de Rochas and Merland and later retellings of the story in French are mistaken on this point. It must be Pinard who had wrongly identified the landing place as Cape Flattery, perhaps not surprising after twelve days in an open boat with so little in the way of supplies and a crew of desperate men. We do not know what they had with them in the way of navigational instruments.[65] Throughout his book Merland refers to the region in which Pelletier lived as 'Terre d'Endéavour' or 'Endeavour Land'. The same term had been used, without further geographical precision, in an article in the *Univers illustré* quoted by Merland, which had reported the recovery of 'Pierre Pelletier'.[66]

Rochas says that water was found during this first landing, but little food, so the boat continued travelling southwards for several days hoping to reach an English settlement. The men stopped at night, usually on small islands, rather than risk encounters with mainland inhabitants. Merland's account differs here, and describes the men spending several days in the same vicinity on land and at sea, with the search for water being their paramount concern. He also mentions an encounter with a large group of Aborigines who first of all encouraged the men to approach but then fired their 'arrows' at them.

The two accounts again differ, and more crucially, when it comes to the question of how Narcisse Pelletier came to be left behind. Rochas says that discipline was lacking in this demoralised bunch and when they again had to land to get water, all made off as they pleased to pursue their search. 'When, towards evening, they gathered at the longboat, one individual was missing from the roll call, it was the cabin boy; they called to him, they looked for him, but they did not find him and the next morning they again took to sea.'[67]

Merland describes how Pelletier, still nursing his injuries from the attack at Rossel Island, had difficulty in keeping up with the men when the captain ordered them to go back to the first place they had found water. When he reached the waterhole the men had drunk it dry. They told him to stay there until it filled up again. Pelletier waited but no water came, so he went off in search of the men but was unable to cross a tidal river that now blocked his access to the stretch of beach where the boat was waiting. He returned to the waterhole where there was still no water. He fell asleep and when he awoke the tide was lower and he was able to get back to the landing place. But there was no sign of the men and the boat had gone.

Merland accepted Pelletier's version over that given by the captain to Rochas. Sir John Ottley recalled how bitter were Pelletier's feelings towards Pinard. He writes:

On one point I was quite satisfied — namely that it would be an exceedingly evil day for his old captain, should he ever ever [sic] have the misfortune to come across the cabin boy he had deserted so many years before. Pelletier never disguised his intention of killing him if he ever had the chance.[68]

Perhaps the captain was only too happy to sail off without him. But he may also have been justified in assuming that the boy was lost and continuing on his way with the remaining men given the precariousness of their situation. The *Times* account notes that Pinard, when recovered later, told of the crew's ordeal but did not report his 'abandonment' of Pelletier.

Whatever the truth of the matter, this was the beginning of the boy's new life. Pelletier, suffering from hunger, thirst, exposure, the wounds he had incurred off Rossel Island and cuts to his feet from the coral, was found by three Aboriginal women who went to tell their husbands of their discovery. By this time his hold on life must have been very tenuous. Taken in and cared for by this group, he was adopted by one of the men, whose name was Maademan. Pelletier was given the new name of 'Amglo'. He was then taken to meet the larger group of thirty people, the 'Ohantaala' — a word identified as referring to the *Wanthaala* estate[69] — with whom he would spend the next seventeen years. He became accustomed to their food and took on their customs until finally, as Merland, with heavy symbolism, presents it, he was divested of the last sign which distinguished him from his companions: they took his clothes from him while he was bathing and tore them up to make head bands.

It is at this point, when Pelletier has lost the last vestiges of his former life, that Merland's narrative changes:

So there he was, he, too, in the primitive state. It is no longer the cabin boy Narcisse Pelletier who will be the subject of our discussion but Amglo, citizen of the tribe of Ohantaala. His personality will often recede into the background as we turn to the description of the customs, habits and beliefs of tribes among whom civilisation has not yet penetrated.[70]

Merland switches easily to the role of armchair ethnographer. The next eight chapters each treat aspects of the way of life of the 'tribe of Ohantaala': social organisation, language, beliefs, treatment of illnesses, mortuary practices, bodily decoration, dances, conflict, punishments, subsistence activities and crafts. Athol Chase will comment in more detail about the correspondence between this account and Uutaalnganu ethnography, but it is worth mentioning here that the information provided by Pelletier and assembled by Merland portrays a way of life before sustained European contact that broadly concurs with present understandings of past conditions on the part of both residents and anthropologists. The curious thing about the account, though, is its silence on some crucial dimensions of Uutaalnganu culture and society and its downplaying of others, a question I shall return to later.

Merland's decision to provide an ethnographic description rather than to explore how Pelletier himself experienced his new life means that in these chapters, which form the major part of the book, there is little in the way of narrative. It is as if Pelletier himself is in suspended animation as his years of residence with Sandbeach People pass. Merland uses the tense known as the ethnographic present throughout this presentation. The only names apart from Amglo to appear in this part of the book, and then infrequently, are those of Pelletier's adoptive father, Maademan, and of his close companion, Sassy, a boy of his own age who was a cousin to him in his new family. So there is no emergence of particular characters and personalities, no life histories, no real sense of the periodic dramas that must have punctuated the day-to-day and seasonal routines.

Merland takes the narrative up again in the final chapter of his book to describe how Narcisse Pelletier was found again and returned to France. During the time that he lived with Uutaalnganu people Pelletier had observed ships sailing along the coast. This coincided with the period when the pearl shell and bêche-de-mer industries were being opened up in the Torres Strait and the coastal waters of Cape York, industries that relied on indigenous labour,[71] as Chase will describe in his ethnographic commentary, though Uutaalnganu people and other groups in the area were not yet working on the luggers during the time of Pelletier's sojourn. This followed fairly rapidly though; indeed, by 1908 Lloyd Bay was one of Cape York's major recruiting bases.[72] It is clear from Merland's account that some exchange was already being conducted between the people of the region — he reports on their fondness for biscuits and tobacco and coloured cloth — and passing boats. Pelletier told Ottley that the people he lived with were afraid not of white men 'but of white men's guns'.[73] But he himself had only once observed Europeans on land. He had been kept well away from them on that occasion, and from any boats, even though others of his group would go off to meet them for trade.

Merland says that the vigilance of Pelletier's hosts relaxed over time and they no longer feared that he would try to escape, nor did he want to. But the lugger traffic was only going to increase, for good and for ill,[74] and Pelletier was found by one of the boats pushing down into the region from Torres Strait where the pearl shell and trepang industries were now well established. In February that year Christopher d'Oyly Aplin (1819–1875), the Government Resident and Police Magistrate at the settlement of Somerset, on the tip of Cape York, in his report on the pearl fisheries of Torres Strait, listed the proprietor John Bell as having ten boats and 75 men based at a fishing station at Jervis Island, now Mabuiag, in the Torres Strait.[75] On 11 April 1875 one of these boats, the *John Bell*, captained by Joseph Frazer, was lying at anchor off Night Island. When a party from the ship was sent to the mainland to get water, they came across a group of Aborigines and noticed that a white man was among them. On learning of this, Captain Frazer sent his men ashore again with objects to barter in exchange for the man. And, according to Merland, on this occasion Maademan actively encouraged Pelletier to trade with the sailors. The sailors persuaded him to board the boat, but he always maintained that he was taken off against his will. He had not resisted because the sailors were armed. Sir John Ottley was insistent about this. He recalls:

> As a matter of fact Narcisse Pelletier subsequently explained to me that the men of the John Bell had quite misunderstood the position of affairs. It was true that the blacks were unwilling that he should be carried off, but it was equally true that he himself had no desire to leave the tribe.
>
> Unfortunately he knew no English and was unable to talk to the seamen — moreover he gathered that if he did not sit still or if he attempted to escape they would shoot him. In short his view evidently was that instead of being rescued he was kidnapped on the 11th April 1875.[76]

Merland's account of what happened immediately after Pelletier's recovery lacks both personal information about Pelletier and some ethnographic details that are contained in the Australian newspaper articles published in 1875 about his story. The first official report about the matter was made to the Colonial Secretary, Arthur Macalister, by Aplin from Somerset, where Pelletier was taken by Captain Frazer. Aplin reports Pelletier's discovery — he included a copy of the statement made by Frazer but it has not been conserved with the original letter — and the information he had managed to obtain from him despite the fact that he still had only 'partially recovered' the use of his native language even though 'he had not forgotten how to write his name'. Pelletier had told Frazer his name, the name of his village and the names of his parents and two younger brothers (the youngest was not born when he embarked on the *Saint-Paul*). He had told him of the shipwreck and the voyage with the captain and crew.

Some details in Aplin's report do not square with later information, possibly because of the language difficulties. He says, for example, that the boat that left the Louisiade Archipelago carried seven men and was making for New Caledonia. He describes how Narcisse Pelletier was abandoned by the captain and found by Aborigines:

> He says the boat was short of water, and the Captain put into a bay on the coast for the purpose of obtaining water — that he (Narcisse) got out of the boat and laid [sic] down under a tree and fell asleep, and was left behind by the Captain — that for three days he was alone in the neighbourhood of a water-hold [sic] & subsisted on what fruits and berries he could find. That the first blacks who came to him were 2 men and 3 women, who fed him with cocoanuts, & that they took him to the tribe after 6 days' walking.
>
> He states that the name of the tribe is Macadama, and his name amongst them 'Anco', that they treated him very kindly always but would not allow him to communicate with any vessels that were passing —[77]

Pelletier was stranded at Cape York in late September or early October, during the dry season. For coastal people this was a time when the large numbers who had gathered together in the wet season camps, confined to a very limited area by the weather, were able to split into small groups that travelled more widely for food gathering and ceremonies.[78] So Maademan's group of five could have been some distance from their main camp. Given that this report was produced only a month after Pelletier's recovery, the names mentioned are significant. Ottley in his account to Dodd gives the group name as 'Muckuddumah', a more phonetic rendering of 'Macadama'. The name 'Anco' is closer linguistically to Uutaalnganu than Merland's 'Amglo'.[79]

Aplin mentions Pelletier's body markings and piercings and ends by stating that he has arranged for his passage to Brisbane by mail steamer and trusts that the French vice consul will arrange for his return to France 'where he is desirous of going'.[80] The report is a short one and makes no comment about Pelletier's behaviour as a guest at the government residence. But from then on Pelletier was 'a living curiosity', in the words of the Australian correspondent for *The Times*, and curiosity was explicit in everything that was written about him. 'The position of a nine days' wonder must be a difficult one to fill satisfactorily,' wrote the correspondent. 'The position of showman will be lying in wait for him.'[81]

The Times presents Pelletier, during his stay at Somerset, as unsettled and saying little. This characteristic would be a recurring theme in his reacculturation, except in his relationship with Ottley:

> For some days after his arrival he sat the greater part of the day perched on the rail fence of a paddock 'like a bird,' as an eye-witness describes it, casting quick, eager, suspicious glances around him on every side and at every object which came within his view, rarely speaking, and apparently unable to remember more than a few words of his own language ...[82]

Pelletier, however, had the opportunity to hear and speak French with two people at Somerset. The first was a Lieutenant Connor of the Royal Navy who was mentioned in the *Times* report as a fluent speaker of the language and thanks to whom 'a good deal more was extracted from the savage'. The second was a French cook who had less success with Pelletier, according to the notebooks of William MacFarlane,[83] an Anglican missionary whose career was spent in the islands of the Torres Strait from 1917 to 1933.[84] MacFarlane heard of Pelletier's story from a man named Johnny Maori who had worked in the bêche-de-mer trade but was at Somerset, in association with the native police, when Pelletier was brought there. MacFarlane wrote about the story for *Cummins and Campbell Monthly Magazine* in 1948, basing his account partly on information he had obtained from Johnny Maori. MacFarlane claims that when he was brought in by the *John Bell*, Pelletier was 'fastened so that he could not escape' and that he subsequently made a number of escape attempts while he was at Somerset.[85]One of the reports made soon after Pelletier's recovery, which appeared in the *Sydney Evening News*, noted that he had tried to escape after arriving there.[86]

Another piece of information from the period at Somerset, but relating to Pelletier's life with the Night Island people, is to be found in a letter to Joseph Mullens, the Foreign Secretary of the London Missionary Society, by an earlier missionary of the same name, Samuel McFarlane. The London Missionary Society was at that time using Somerset as the base for its missionary activity directed not at Cape York itself, but at the islands of the Torres Strait and from there into New Guinea.[87] McFarlane describes the recovery of Pelletier in a postscript to his letter, imparting similar information to that provided by Aplin and Ottley. He adds, however, that Pelletier had 'left two children behind'.[88] This revelation is not surprising given the length of time he spent there — his fathering no children might be more so — but it needs to be viewed with some caution.

Another piece of corroborating but not conclusive evidence about Pelletier being a father occurs in Herbert Hale's diary of his field trip with Norman Tindale in the Princess Charlotte Bay area in 1926–27. Hale noted that:

> Several of the children have remarkably light, almost ginger, hair. There is a rumour among the white people here to the effect that a Frenchman lived amongst the Pt Stewart blacks very many years ago, & one might imagine the cast of features & the light hair of some of the people to be due to this visitor. [89]

And Marcel Baudouin, whose interest in Pelletier I shall come to presently, notes that Pelletier told a confidant that he had three children.[90]

It might be assumed that Pelletier's long-term residence among Uutaalnganu people, especially if he had left any children, would still be commemorated in oral history. Hale's note shows that even in the late 1920s oral history among the white population was sketchy in its details. While Lockhart people today are familiar with Pelletier's story, his life with their ancestors has not been passed down as part of their oral tradition. In the 1970s Chase checked with the elderly men and women in the Lockhart community to see if they had heard of Pelletier but there was no knowledge of him.[91] The tenuousness of the link to the past in terms of transmission of memory is shown in his statement that his informants 'represented the last people who could have heard [from their parents] first-hand accounts of the coming of the miners and the luggermen'.[92] Chase comments further on Pelletier's absence from the Uutaalnganu record in his ethnographic commentary.

Merland sheds no real light on the matter when he comes to discussing Pelletier's betrothal (see Chapter 3). Maademan had arranged a marriage for him with a girl from a neighbouring group. When he left she was only seven years old, and she had taken an aversion to him because of his white skin. Since 'the union was still one in name only', he stated, perhaps pre-emptively, that Pelletier was free to marry, and that his fiancée need have no fear that upon his death 'children from the north of Australia will come and fight with hers over the inheritance he has left'.

In the newspaper articles and his letter to H. J. Dodd, Ottley has supplied a more detailed psychological profile of Pelletier than we gain from Merland. To European eyes his appearance was remarkable:

> When discovered, Narcisse was stark naked, like the rest of his tribe, his body burnt by the sun to a rich red color, and having a glazed appearance; his breast adorned with raised lines of flesh, of the thickness of a pencil, while the lobe of his right ear was ornamented with a piece of wood about half-an-inch in diameter and four inches long.[93]

In his letter to Dodd, Ottley describes Pelletier as being 'about middle height, broad shouldered, and evidently immensely powerful'.[94] And the photographs of him, which he sent with his letter, and which are reproduced on the covers of this book, 'show that he had a really splendid head and … a very determined look'.[95]

Ottley was also struck by Pelletier's incredibly acute eyesight. He tells of how Pelletier, as they were steaming down the coast, pointed out some tiny specks on an island in the distance, well beyond the range of 'our most powerful glasses', and identified them as the canoes of an enemy group, which he named. Only when the boat drew much closer could it be verified that the specks were indeed canoes. Those on board concluded that even though Pelletier affirmed that there were no chiefs where he had lived, he had been 'quite a personage in his tribe' on account of his strength (he claimed that while his companions were strong, he was stronger) and other remarks he dropped.[96] On the other hand, strong swimmer that he apparently was, he said that his companions surpassed him in the water.

Ottley was favourably impressed by Pelletier's intelligence, which he assumed from the rapidity with which he regained his French:

> … he was a marvellously apt pupil for before we parted he was not only discoursing volubly in French but had also to a great extent recovered his knowledge of reading and writing and had acquired as well a certain number of English words in addition.[97]

The newspaper reports note that he was reading a novel on board the *Brisbane* supplied to him by Lieutenant Connor, could count to 100 and had drawn 'some excellent sketches' of the animals he had hunted.[98]

There were quite naturally problems of adjustment for Pelletier in this early phase of his reclamation by white society. Ottley and Hamilton-Gordon recorded some that they observed. There was surprise that someone who had lived without clothing for so long seemed to feel the cold badly now that he was wearing clothes again. Pelletier shivered frequently while on deck, sought to escape the draught and was 'certainly never comfortable in his clothes'.[99] Along with his 'considerable intelligence' he displayed:

... a childish dependance [sic] and imitativeness of others. That anything is done by *les autres* is sufficient to induce him to attempt it himself. He is generally good humoured, though with occasional fits of apparently causeless sulkiness; he frequently coughs violently, and his habits of crouching about here and there are still those of a savage.[100]

The cultural dislocation that Pelletier was experiencing in these first months must have been extreme. It is no wonder that some of his movements appeared strange and that he was moody. And his dependence and imitativeness seem an entirely sensible reaction: how else would one behave when dropped, quite alone, into what to him was now a completely foreign culture? The only way to relearn European ways was to copy them, as he would have had to copy Uutaalnganu ways when first he was taken in by Maademan and his family. His sensitivity to appearing different is shown by his concluding, after a couple of days on the *Brisbane*, that he should have the lobe of his ear, distended from the wearing of an ear plug, cut off. He felt that it 'was not "the right thing" in civilized society', even though he also expressed his admiration for Uutaalnganu men who had even longer earlobes.[101] The distension is still obvious in the photographs taken of him, but it is not known whether he ever proceeded with his intention. In the photograph taken by one Peigné, a carte de visite photographer in Nantes, which forms the frontispiece to *Dix-sept ans*, Pelletier is wearing some sort of ear plug.

Ottley recalled, too, being inconvenienced by the fact that Pelletier had no sense of private property. 'Coming down to my cabin he used calmly to annex anything that struck his fancy and shewed his annoyance when I took things from him and locked them up in my trunks,' he writes.[102] If this showed something about Pelletier's conception of property, it also showed his trust in Ottley: Pelletier would not have acted as if he believed that 'we ought to hold things in common' unless he had felt reasonably secure in the relationship with his mentor.[103]

That trust, however, did not, in Ottley's view, extend to Pelletier showing him complete candour about his experiences. In the newspaper reports, Ottley (if these are his words) comments about the 'meagre' quality of Pelletier's account, reasoning there that this was 'partly because he has still some difficulty in expressing his ideas in French, and partly, possibly, because there is not much to tell'.[104] The first part of this explanation is implausible given Ottley's other comments about Pelletier's linguistic aptitude; the second part is patently not the case. In fact, Ottley looked at the matter quite differently when reflecting on Pelletier's reticence in his report to Dodd. He talks about the hurdle he had come up against when collecting from him a vocabulary of the language he had spoken. He writes:

> I was not very successful as I only managed to record about 100 words for by the time I had secured these Pelletier professed to have forgotten the remainder. The theory was that he could not hold two languages and that as his French came to the surface so did the native language sink out of sight and memory. … I am inclined to think that he had definitely made up his mind to give us no more information regarding the tribe and the language.[105]

He recalls a similar problem when Pelletier was asked about cultural matters, saying that 'he was extremely reticent when we pressed him for interesting details as to their customs[,] manners and beliefs'. When, for example, Sir Arthur Hamilton-Gordon asked Ottley to interrogate Pelletier about the occurrence of cannibalism, he 'gave very vague replies, that left us under the impression that he knew more than he chose to confess and wound up the conversation with the final remark that "ce n'est pas joli" [it isn't pretty] which we took to mean that it was not a subject that he cared to discuss'.[106]

The interesting question here is not whether cannibalism was or was not practised — in Merland's book there is one instance of cannibalism that refers to an incident in the past with the feel of legend about it, and once Pelletier is threatened with it — but the fact that Pelletier, at this early stage of his return to European society, was already avoiding talking about certain things. Audiences expect great things of those who have had the experience of 'crossing cultures',[107] but those expectations tend to be disappointed. There are various reasons for this.

Once 'brought in', men like Pelletier or William Buckley had to re-establish themselves and cease to be, as they were seen to be, 'white savages' or 'wild white men'. The frontier, colonising or civilising mentality of those who greeted them back into the European world, and the suspicion of cultural difference which must have been palpable, would have discouraged them from giving chapter and verse of their life with Aboriginal people. Pelletier, for some time after his recovery, was completely dependent on the goodwill and charity of those around him for his survival. He was a foreign national and displaced person and someone had to bear the expenses he was incurring. Aplin presumed that the French vice-consul would reimburse the government for Pelletier's passage on the *Brisbane*.[108] And the *Brisbane Courier* reported that a subscription had been set up for him on board the ship with the intention that the funds be sent to France via the consulate 'for the furtherance of his interests'.[109]

There was not 'nothing to tell' about Pelletier's seventeen years in Queensland, rather the experience and knowledge of another cultural world somehow to convey. And, whatever Pelletier was able to articulate or felt free to divulge, it was Merland, lacking any psychological or ethnographic insights or techniques, who had to elicit the information and convey it. Sympathetic as Ottley and Merland were, the task of going deeply into Pelletier's inter-cultural experience and knowledge, and revealing it from the inside, required the kind of intimate, extended conversation that Ottley, during a short voyage, was not in a position to undertake and that Merland gives no evidence of engaging in with Pelletier. According to Baudouin,

Pelletier did in fact confide in one man, a certain Morineau who was a sailmaker, but it seems that Morineau has not left behind any record of their talks. Pelletier, notes Baudouin, told Morineau of his adventures, 'which are not those published by Dr Merland'.[110]

Merland does not attempt to describe what Pelletier experienced in sloughing off his old life and taking on the new one. The account makes it appear unproblematic, a gradual transformation from cabin boy to Aboriginal man; Narcisse became Amglo (or Anco or Ankum) and that was that. But it may be that the process of becoming a cultural insider makes it impossible to retain an insider's perspective while attempting to articulate what that means to outsiders, in the same way that it is impossible to see both images of a two-way optical illusion simultaneously. The very nature of being a human being, that is a cultural being, means that Pelletier as Amglo was one person and another as Narcisse, before and after his time in Queensland.

Edouard Garnier, who wrote a musical appendix to Merland's book, and like Merland had interviewed Pelletier in the year after his return, comments directly on Pelletier's taciturnity, assuming that his Aboriginal hosts themselves were little given to conversation. 'Pelletier, who — like all those who have lived alone for a long time or with beings who converse rarely — is not very communicative and has given me very few details about his refrains,' he writes. In fact, communication, or the lack of it, was indeed an issue with men whose experience resembled Pelletier's, but not for the reason Garnier gives.

William Buckley was reportedly a man of exasperatingly few words, who deterred the best efforts of the many inquisitors who sought him out.[111] James Morrill spelt out how he felt about falling victim to the curious since rejoining colonial society in a 'Note' introducing his story. He puts forward satisfying that curiosity, together with the need for income, as his motive for publishing it:

I have so many invitations to wait on persons for the purpose of narrating my past sufferings, which were painful enough to pass through, without calling them to remembrance day after day, at the wish of anybody who may desire it; and the invitations rather increasing than otherwise. I have deemed it desirable to put on record my experiences in this brief sketchy manner ...[112]

If these are Morrill's own words, he seems to have found no difficulty in expressing himself when he chose to, but Edmund Gregory, who recorded his story, describes him as 'very shy' and 'not very communicative', taking quite some time to regain the use of English.[113] But whatever slice of their experience had been extracted from Morrill and Pelletier and Buckley, how could the resulting publications, none of them voluminous, possibly reflect its texture and totality? Reflecting on this years later, Gregory blamed himself for a missed opportunity:

When recalling the original hasty compilation of fragmentary facts, and thinking of the additional historical and ethnological value that might have been given to this narrative at the time it was written, I earnestly regret not making a special effort to exhaust Murrells' store of rare and instructive knowledge, of which I am painfully conscious I have only touched the mere fringe, and so take all available advantage of an opportunity that, once departed, can never again return.[114]

Morrill wrote in his 'Note' that 'I may possibly if I am spared very much extend this small pamphlet'. But the opportunity did not arise as he died only two years after taking up residence in the town of Bowen.

Buckley's and Morrill's narratives, like Pelletier's, leave the reader wishing to know more about their narrators and about the people whose lives they shared for so long. The information that has been obtained from them suggest that they were all observant, quite aware of the culturally different environments in which they lived rather than passive consumers of them, and well incorporated, especially in the case of Pelletier and Morrill, who were both younger than Buckley when they were found and rescued by Aboriginal people. We should bear in mind, too, as Peter Sutton points out,[115] that reflection on our selves and lives is historically and culturally specific: it would not have come naturally to people of the 19th century Vendée that Pelletier had left as a child and rejoined as an adult, or to the Uutaalnganu people with whom he lived on Cape York.

The fact that these men all became thoroughly conversant in Aboriginal languages may have compounded the problem of expression. To learn an Aboriginal language is to learn the code which defines a person's place in the human and natural world and guides their behaviour in these intimately connected realms. Where there were no cultural equivalents in English, or French in Pelletier's case, for aspects of their experience, then these things would simply not have been given expression, either because they could not be easily translated, or because the men knew that there was a gulf of understanding between the indigenous worlds they had come to know and the world into which they had returned. Insistent questioning, especially from an uncomprehending inquisitor, is more than likely to be met with irritation or surly silence. Moreover, putting any experience into words changes it, if not diminishes it, and we are left with the unavoidable impression in reading Pelletier's account that, as with Buckley's and Morrill's, what we have from them in print are very much concertinaed versions of what they had seen, learnt and lived.

For a host of reasons, there cannot be an encyclopaedic castaway testimony. As a point of comparison, Barbara Thompson is quite voluble in the account she gave to Oswald Brierly on board the *Rattlesnake* after her recovery in 1849. Unquestionably, the ethnographic information that resulted from their conversations was richer and more extensive than that extracted from Buckley, Morrill and Pelletier. Thompson had lived with Kaurareg people on Muralag (Prince of Wales Island) in the Torres Strait for five years, much shorter than the exiles of her male counterparts. But as well as her personal strengths, one reason for the quality of the information she provided was, as David Moore identifies, the quality of the relationship Brierly established with the young woman.[116] His interest in what she had to tell him, and his persistence in questioning, were more conducive to her describing what she knew than the comparable situations that occurred between Buckley and John Morgan, Morrill and Edmund Gregory, or Pelletier and Constant Merland. But Moore's research also shows that Thompson had not, understandably enough, fully grasped all the elements of the culture in which she had lived. One significant aspect of the culture for Kaurareg women, namely female initiation, she did not mention at all.[117] Perhaps if she, too, had remained for considerably more years with the Kaurareg, she may have been less amenable to sharing her experience.

In Pelletier's case there is no mention of the religious dimensions of Sandbeach culture such as Stories (spirit people, totemic ancestors or 'Culture Heroes'[118] who are the equivalent of ancestral Dreamtime figures in other parts of Australia) and story places, *puulaway*, totemic sites in the landscape these ancestors created and named; beliefs about the Old People, spirits of the ancestors who return to their homelands when they die; and the *bora*, or initiation ceremonies, which link clan territories and their story places to the realm of mythic knowledge and Law.[119] In fact, Chase points to the 'marked secularity' of coastal peoples' culture in this respect by comparison with other Aboriginal groups on the Peninsula: clan groups claimed descent from a human, not a totemic ancestor, and were not identified with a particular totem.[120] Story places were associated with particular clan groups simply by virtue of their location on their estates. But this does not explain the fact that such places are not even mentioned by Pelletier.

The concepts of the sacred, *kuntha*, and taboo, *kincha*, still today significant determinants of correct behaviour,[121] are not mentioned either. If on the one hand Pelletier did not divulge information which he judged unacceptable to European ears, on the other he may well have felt constrained, in his Uutaalnganu identity, as the Aboriginal person, or *pama*, he had become, about imparting secret and sacred knowledge. It is unlikely that a boy who was adopted by a clan member, grew to manhood and was betrothed would not also be inducted into Uutaalnganu ways as an initiated man. During his fieldwork in the region, Donald Thomson found that the realm of belief and special and secret knowledge was not freely talked about by the Kuuku Ya'u, a language group contiguous with Uutaalnganu people.[122] This would be so by definition, but it makes Pelletier's reticence quite explicable. A similar reticence may well have applied to the subject of sorcery, an aspect of life that is alluded to in Chapter 3 in Pelletier's account of his punishment for infringing a food taboo (see below) but not referred to directly, much less described. All of this suggests his continuing adherence to the belief system of the Uutaalnganu.

Nevertheless, Ottley and Merland are emphatic about the complete lack of religious beliefs of Pelletier's group.[123] If Pelletier's silence on the matter obviously contributed to this conclusion, it also reflects European thinking of the time. The notion of the common humanity of all human groups was still a subject of debate in scientific circles with polygenists positing multiple origins of human races against the monogenists who staked their belief in a common origin. The supposed absence of religious beliefs among particular peoples was one of the criteria invoked by polygenists to deny them a common origin with Europeans and rank them as racially inferior.[124]

If the lack of detail Pelletier provides about religious ideology is explicable, the almost offhand manner in which the activity of dugong hunting is raised (see Chapter 9) is really puzzling. Surrounded by myth and ritual, dugong hunting was, is, an activity requiring great skill and courage on the part of the dugong men, the *pama watayichi*, as well as involving the crafting of an array of tools — harpoons and ropes — and the outrigger canoes, as Chase describes in his Commentary. Renowned dugong hunters were men of high status. Donald Thomson's classic article 'The dugong hunters of Cape York' about the neighbouring Lamalama people not only provides a wealth of information completely lacking in Merland's chapter on hunting, but reads like a hymn of praise to the heroic men who took to the sea for the hunt.[125] Whether it was Pelletier's failure to convey its significance, or Merland's failure to grasp it, it is a pity that such a core activity was not given more attention since the marine activities and technology of coastal people is one of the distinguishing features of their way of life.

Similarly, Pelletier gives only the most rudimentary account of his social universe when the core of life in Uutaalnganu society — one's identity and behaviour to others, one's rights and obligations — derived from a widening hierarchy of identifications based on genealogical and geographical closeness. This went from the patrilineal descent group, or estate group, and the estate at the centre, to more and more distant links, such as having related dialects and sharing initiation ceremonies.[126] This central element of the life of the forebears of the people who today make up the Lockhart Community remains operative, constituting 'a social intellectuality' which constitutes and contextualises identity and informs social rules and behaviour.[127] For Lockhart people today their continuing investment in this aspect of their model of pre-contact society is integral to their lives, whereas language and material culture are pragmatically seen by most to be replaceable without this affecting their sense of identity.[128] It may have taken a social anthropologist to elicit complex information about kinship and marriage, group membership and identity from Pelletier, but its absence means that a crucial dimension of life as lived is missing, as indeed it is from Buckley's and Morrill's accounts as well.

An understandable but equally regrettable gap relates to women. This was due to the angle from which Pelletier experienced Uutaalnganu society, one in which gender lines were sharply drawn.[129] The role of an adolescent boy and young unmarried man would have given him little access to the world of women and girls. Chase points out that physical closeness between brothers and sisters ceased after puberty, and adolescent boys slept in their own camp.[130]

The other side of the communication coin applies to what Pelletier was able to tell Uutaalnganu people about his life as a boy from a coastal village in France. If there were many differences between eastern Cape York and Saint-Gilles, and their respective inhabitants, then the seafaring orientation of both was a significant point in common. But little sense of any cultural exchange on Pelletier's part comes through in Merland's rendering of the story.

Pelletier had suffered a succession of traumatic experiences before being rescued by Maademan's family. He then found himself living with people whose language and culture was utterly foreign to him, and severed from any link to family and home. Perhaps relief at being rescued after escaping death a number of times mitigated his distress. And his survival depended upon his integration not resistance. But it is hard to imagine that no lifelong psychic imprint was left by these ordeals.

The *Times* article gives a brief and conventional account of the adaptation process:

> When first found by the blacks he says he was very unhappy and often thought of his father, mother, and brothers, and longed to get away. In the course of time the recollection of them became less vivid and less painful, and he ultimately completely identified himself with the tribe.[131]

Ottley, in his report of 1923, gives more details about Pelletier's recollections of home. He writes:

A really singular feature of his case was the apparent impossibility of linking him up in any way with his early life in France. For instance he admitted he not only had a father and mother but also several brothers and sisters and yet when it was suggested to him that he would like to see them all again his invariable reply was 'they are all dead for it was so long ago.'[132]

This strange logic, which Ottley says was unassailable by argument, poignantly expresses the links between time and memory, distance and attachment. According to Ottley, Pelletier had lost any notion of religion and 'his early life and all that it meant had apparently been completely wiped off the slate of his memory'.[133] Whether or not this was so, it was clear that Pelletier had lost the use of the words to summon it up.

Pelletier was relayed from Somerset to Sydney on the *Brisbane*, which had, with déjà vu, started its journey in Hong Kong with a large consignment of Chinese to work on the Palmer River goldfields. The mail steamer's route took it from Hong Kong, to call at Singapore, Somerset, Cooktown, Townsville, Bowen, Keppel Bay and Brisbane, and then on to Sydney. From shipping notices it is possible to track the *Brisbane*'s voyage down the east coast from Somerset. Pelletier travelled steerage but the saloon berths were occupied by a number of distinguished passengers, or men who would go on to distinguished careers, who provide snapshots of colonial history. Boarding at Somerset with Pelletier was Commander George Heath,[134] whose work in implementing navigational lighting for the waters of the Inner Reef had no doubt contributed to the ever-increasing shipping traffic and marine activities in the area, and who, coincidentally, had seen the recovery of another castaway who had been rescued by Aboriginal people, namely Barbara Thompson, when he served on the *Rattlesnake*. An Hon. Finch-Hatton was a passenger, with Lionel Knight Rice. Rice and the two Finch-Hatton brothers, Henry and Harold, in partnership held cattle leaseholds in the Nebo district south-west of Mackay in the 1870s and 1880s.[135] Since Harold Finch-Hatton arrived in Queensland on another ship of the Eastern and Australian Company, the *Somerset*,[136] the brother aboard the *Brisbane* must have been Henry, later Earl of Winchilsea and the father of the pilot Denys Finch-Hatton, made famous by Karen Blixen. Accompanying Sir Arthur Hamilton-Gordon to Fiji was George Ruthven Le Hunte, appointed as his private secretary, who went on to become Lieutenant-Governor of New Guinea (one of his reports about the Rossel Island affair will be quoted later), and Governor of South Australia.[137] Sir Arthur himself was already a celebrity in colonial Australia, with large portraits of him appearing in the illustrated papers on his arrival in Sydney and then in Fiji, and newspaper articles devoted to the challenges facing him in his vice-regal appointment.

A Chinese passenger sufficiently noteworthy to be mentioned in the *Brisbane*'s passenger lists was a woman — 'Mrs Lee Gong and servant' — who met with much attention on her arrival at Cooktown because the Chinese men who toiled in the Australian colonies normally served their time alone, although she was the wife of a merchant. One of the articles published about her in the local papers reported that she was 'curiously gazed upon by a large crowd of Europeans, all eager to push forward to see her tiny feet, painted lips and eyebrows, crowned above with a magnificent head dress'.[138]

The *Brisbane* departed Somerset on 14 May 1875, arrived at Cooktown on 16 May where 340 Chinese were landed,[139] reached Townsville on 18 May, Keppel Bay on 20 May and Brisbane on 21 May. A public notice in the *Brisbane Courier* announced Pelletier's 'distinguished arrival'.[140] The steamer finally docked in Sydney on 25 May.

After the tiny settlement of Somerset, the city of Sydney, where Pelletier had been destined on the *Saint-Paul* so many years ago, must have seemed quite dauntingly cosmopolitan. The French consulate was in the heart of the city.[141] Here he began on the next stage of his journey home when delivered into the care of its consul, Georges-Eugène Simon, and, for the second time in his life, to assuming a completely new identity, this time as Narcisse Pelletier, a Frenchman. Simon, an agronomist, diplomat and once a Sinologist of some note,[142] has provided the next detailed report about him, revealing another attempt to make sense of the man Pelletier had become with the Aborigines.[143] Simon interviewed Pelletier several times and the results are curious. While Simon observed his subject closely and sympathetically, he seems, though a compatriot, to have elicited a good deal less conversation and less information from him than Ottley. As we have seen, even before Ottley started conversing with Pelletier in French on the *Brisbane* and reported Pelletier's rapid progress in regaining his native language, Pelletier had spent time at Somerset with Lieutenant Connor, a French speaker. Indeed, the missionary Samuel McFarlane could write from Somerset of Pelletier, just a month after his recovery, that his language was 'coming back to him much quicker than it did to the 'Claimant'!'[144] Yet the consul, who did not meet Pelletier for at least another fortnight during which time Pelletier had been conversing with Ottley, judged that he was still struggling badly with French.

It seems that the process of re-engaging his memories of home, which Simon pushed along, caused Pelletier bewilderment and anxiety, and his ability to converse stalled. He may also have been ill at ease with Simon and in the official setting of the consulate. And perhaps he felt more pressure about speaking French with a fellow countryman. At their first meeting, which lasted more than two hours, Simon says that Pelletier, while he had written down some French words, had not recovered the use of French. Whatever the reason for the block, Pelletier, as Simon presents him, exhibited considerable emotional suffering during their interviews, by turns astonished, stammering, anguished and excited when Simon recalled to him things about his early life.

I told him the name of his village and I then witnessed quite some of the strangest and most painful spectacles, I think, that one might see: this wretched man made extraordinary efforts to remember; he wanted to speak to me and all that came to his lips were inarticulate sounds. He felt that I was not able to understand him; one might have thought that he himself did not have much idea of what he was saying or wanted to say. His face and his eyes expressed a terrible anxiety and anguish, and something like despair which was painful. I suffered with him and almost as much as him. Sweat was breaking out on my brow as on his. Involuntarily I remembered the tale of Hoffman's of the man who has lost his shadow and his image. I would have done anything to give him back then and there his identity, which clearly he was trying to grasp hold of again.[145]

Simon's descriptions of Pelletier's gestures suggest that he tried to grasp physically what eluded him mentally. He put his hands to his ear like a horn when trying to understand, and when trying to respond 'he put one hand above his eyes and looked into the distance, as if he would have liked to discover the person to whom he had to reply. With the other arm he made great gestures to call him, to make him come closer.' He then summoned up the words 'Oui, là-bas', 'Yes, over there', which he kept on repeating whenever Simon spoke to him.[146] It was eight days before Simon felt that Pelletier could speak French reasonably well again, if hesitantly, though we know that Ottley, who had clearly gained his trust, had no trouble conversing with him in French.

There is pathos, too, in a part of Simon's report that shows something of how the Pelletier family had experienced the long years since the disappearance of their eldest son. Even though in 1862 the Minister of the Navy and Colonies had approved payment to his beneficiaries without the need for formal proof of his death,[147] and Merland says that Pelletier's mother wore mourning clothes for seventeen years, his parents must never have given up all hope of finding him alive, or at least of finding out the fate that had befallen him. When meeting Pelletier for the first time, Simon remembered that he had, filed in his boxes, letters from a family in the Vendée who, for eighteen years, had written to the consulate seeking news of their son. Simon proceeded to take out one of the letters and on reading the signature asked Pelletier if this was his name. Pelletier looked astonished (presumably at the letter bearing his surname, rather than the mention of the name which as we know he had told Captain Frazer right at the beginning), nodded that it was, but was unable to read the letter.

Merland says that Simon had Pelletier photographed while he was in Sydney. The photographs were probably taken by Alexandre Henri (also known as Alexander Henry) Lamartinière, a photographer who produced carte de visite portraits, and with whom the more famous Charles Kerry became a partner for a time.[148] The *Sydney Morning Herald* of 9 June 1875 reported that they had 'received from Mr A. H. Lemartinière [sic], photographic artist, copies of a photograph of Narcisse Pelletier', and that the photographs, now in the plural, were 'in the style of the photographic art'. The photographs that Ottley sent to Dodd are of a still bearded Pelletier, one showing him bare-chested and the other dressed in what Ottley describes as 'the slop clothes served out to him', but both posed in the carte de visite style. Ottley does not say how he came by them, but we know that he finished his journey at Rockhampton, so if his photographs are those taken by Lamartinière, which seems most likely, they would have to have been sent to him subsequently. These two photographs sum up this pivotal period for Pelletier, making him a Janus-faced figure. The door to his Uutaalnganu life had not quite closed behind him, while the European style dress he now wore signified the new phase he was entering.

We have seen that Pelletier was photographed again in Nantes by Peigné, now clean-shaven, but again bare-chested so that his cicatrices are displayed, and wearing a nose and ear plug. A drawing, probably based on a photograph, again of a bare-chested

Pelletier, who is turning his head slightly so that his pierced and distended earlobe is on view (but minus the ear plug), reached France very quickly because it was used to illustrate an article which appeared about the story in *La Presse Illustrée* in August 1875.[149] Very similar sketches of Pelletier have been published in Australian newspapers but the original artist and the place where the drawing was first published are still to be discovered.[150]

Pelletier spent more than a month in Sydney where Merland notes that he 'became the object of general curiosity' and met up with quite a number of his compatriots. He then travelled to New Caledonia and from there left on the *Jura*, for the journey back to France, departing 7 August 1875. Although the French consul had related that the writing that Pelletier did in his presence all ran together, with a letter he wrote to his parents being meaningless and not able to be sent, in fact Pelletier had written one letter to his parents from Somerset and proceeded to write two more, one from Noumea while he was waiting to board the *Jura* and one from Rio de Janeiro. Merland included the letters as an appendix to his book. They are likewise reproduced here at Appendix II, together with a transcription of the French and an approximate translation, although the translation cannot capture the idiosyncratic grammar and spelling.

Brief as they are, there is a clear development of expression and correctness from the first letter to the third, the second and third being written in impressively neat and flourishing handwriting. The tone of all three is, though, very childish, as if Narcisse, in thinking of his parents, has remained arrested at the age he was when he left, or has even regressed, and is turning to them for sympathy after all those years away. In the first letter he tells of the shipwreck, being abandoned and then found by the Aborigines. In the next he warmly and conventionally greets his parents and brothers but adds 'if you are living', still doubtful about it. The only thing he mentions about the whole of his stay is the fact that he had a poisoned leg, caused, he believed, by poison being applied when he was sleeping as a punishment for infringing a food taboo, an episode which is recounted in Chapter 3. And in the final letter he complains that he does not get on with the petty officers, notes that he eats with the sailors on rations and says that 'they' —it is not clear whether he is referring to the officers or the sailors — have shown him no sympathy for the suffering he has experienced. The letter, with an elaborate curlicued signature, and a further claim on his parents' attention, is signed 'Pelletier Narcisse Pierre Naufragé', that is 'Pelletier Narcisse Pierre Castaway'. One thing that has changed is his portrayal, either to himself or for his parents, of the Aborigines' treatment of him. In the first letter he reports that they gave him food and drink and did not hurt him. In the later ones, written when he is now firmly back with Europeans, he says how much he has suffered with them.

The journey home was uneventful and made easier for Pelletier because one of his travelling companions was a young soldier named Charles Marchand who was from Saint-Gilles. Marchand was able to tell him that his parents were well when he had left on military service, and helped him to rekindle his memories of home. A further report about Pelletier emerges from this voyage. It is a medical report written by the doctor on the *Jura*, who devotes more than one closely written page to Pelletier, a good part of it focusing on the ulcer on his left leg which proved impervious to the gamut of lotions and potions he used to try to get it to heal.[151] He confirms the other reports that Pelletier was taken on to the *John Bell* 'almost by force'. And he concludes by noting that 'Lepelletier', as he refers to him throughout, 'is endowed with above average intelligence, he writes very well, does some rough drawings taught him by his friends the savages and devotes himself to quite complicated arithmetical sums'.[152]

By the time Pelletier was sailing homewards on the *Jura* his family had received his first letter written from Somerset. They had trouble believing it was not some sort of hoax but they soon had confirmation that their son had been found again when they read the report published in the *Bulletin français*, which included an extract from the *Times* article about his recovery. In the years he had been away France had made the transition from the Second Empire under Emperor Napoleon III to the Third Republic, suffered defeat in the Franco-Prussian war of 1870, and passed through the violent period of the Paris Commune in 1871. The *Jura* arrived in Toulon on 13 December where Pelletier was met by one of his brothers. The brothers proceeded to Paris and stayed there until after Christmas. Pelletier was admitted to the Beaujon Hospital on 22 December and discharged on 28 December.[153] It would be interesting to know what else happened during this time, Merland saying only that there were people keen to meet Pelletier and that he returned with some assurances about his future. These, presumably, were government officials who had to consider questions about liability — might Pelletier sue for being abandoned on Cape York? — and his future.

Merland published his book that same year and ended his account on the high note of the celebrations that attended Pelletier's homecoming. But the fairly scant information about what happened to him subsequently points to the fact that it was not easy for him to take up his life again in the country of his birth and that he may not have been particularly happy or settled. Again reminiscent of William Buckley, who was offered the chance to be in a travelling show but declined when he discovered he was to be exhibited as 'the huge Anglo-Australian giant',[154] Merland says that Pelletier 'firmly refused to take to the stage'. Whatever he had been promised in Paris, Pelletier lost no time in seeking work from the Minister for the Navy and the Colonies, petitioning him from Nantes on 25 and 26 January 1876 about employment.[155]

It was probably during this visit that he made the acquaintance of Constant Merland and collaborated with him on the story of his adventures in order to earn some income. How much money *Dix-sept ans* made for Pelletier is not known. Despite its simple presentation — a relatively slim volume paperbound in a buff cover — the price of the book as printed on the cover was two francs, a not inconsiderable sum. As a comparison, a subscription to one of the French weekly papers which announced Pelletier's story, *La Presse illustrée*, cost ten centimes an issue in 1875 and three and a half francs for a six month subscription. But the book was hardly a runaway success because it had only one edition, and given its rarity now it cannot have been a very large one. Merland was serious about selling it, though. He contributed the first two chapters as an article called simply 'Narcisse Pelletier' to *La revue de Bretagne, de Vendée et d'Anjou*. A note from the editor promotes the book, saying that the 'two chapters will certainly inspire in our readers the desire to own this account, whose purpose is to procure some income for the man whose astonishing adventures it makes known'.[156]

Pelletier was more successful in his petition. The job he sought was that of lighthouse keeper and the petition was passed on to the Minister for Public Works. Local knowledge has it that Pelletier became the lighthouse keeper of the Phare de l'Aiguillon near Saint-Nazaire on the northern side of the estuary of the Loire, although the accounts which report this give no information as to when he began his employment there and when it finished.[157] But if they are correct, he did not stay in that job. In 1880, Pelletier, who was then aged 36, married Louise Désirée Mabileau, a seamstress, who was 22. The marriage certificate gives his occupation as 'garde de signaux', signalman. The couple lived very near the entrance to the harbour of Saint-Nazaire where he worked. They did not have any children. Pelletier died on 28 September 1894 at the age of 50 at his home at 20 Grande Rue. His father was dead, but he predeceased his mother. The death certificate gives his occupation at this time as a clerk at the harbour. His confidant, Morineau, attended the funeral. When he died his widow bought a concession for a double plot. The grave is in the Cimetière de la Briandais, one of the cemeteries of the town. Louise Pelletier subsequently remarried and moved away from Saint-Nazaire.

In all that has been published about Pelletier, the only hypothesis as to the cause of his death is to be found in a local newspaper, the *Journal des Sables*, in 1954, in an article devoted to his story written in the patois of the Bocage.[158] It was said, apparently, that Pelletier had died because a spell had been cast upon him by a black sorcerer when he had been taken away by the English. But the journalist concludes that he may have died of 'nurasténie', *neurasthénie*, that is, nervous exhaustion or depression.

In one dossier that was written about him from first-hand experience, Pelletier received a bad press from specialists who might have been expected to show him more understanding. The French consul's report on which I have already drawn was published in 1880 as supporting evidence for a thesis put forward by Charles Letourneau in the *Bulletins* of the Société d'Anthropologie de Paris, which presents Pelletier as the man 'who forgot his language among the Australians'.[159] Letourneau had no interest in Pelletier's extended encounter with Aboriginal people — a rare enough opportunity then for a French anthropologist — but in the question of whether language was a natural fact or a cultural fact. Citing famous stories of experiments in which children were separated from society to see if they would eventually generate language by themselves, he introduces Pelletier's experience as one brought about by chance but 'of the same order' as these.[160] Describing how the French consul observed the slow reawakening of the memories of Pelletier's early life, Letourneau argues that this 'extraordinary fact would be sufficient to prove the extent to which the mental state of the civilised man is still artificial, the extent to which, to be maintained, it needs to be supported by the social environment'.[161]

Letourneau takes no account of Pelletier's successful integration into an Aboriginal society and his acquisition of its language and culture, but concludes, in effect, that the environment in which he had lived was not a 'social environment', or not a social environment for a 'civilised man'. That living with a group of Aboriginal people was like living without language was an assumption Letourneau shared with an editorial writer of the *New York Times* who compared Pelletier's case to that of Kaspar Hauser, the German boy who had claimed to have spent his childhood alone in a cellar.[162]

Simon's report constitutes the major part of the article. It is followed by 'discussion' among the anthropologists who attended the session in which Letourneau presented it. The ethnographer Ernest Hamy reports that a correspondent of the society, one Monsieur Bureau, almost certainly the ship owner and linguist Léon-Jacques Bureau (1836–1900) of Nantes, more alert, it seems, to the ethnographic and ethnolinguistic value of Pelletier's experience, had drawn up an Aboriginal vocabulary from him. There is no indication how long this document is, and it too has not come to light, Bureau's papers, including the dictionary he compiled of the Breton dialect of Bourg-de-Batz, having been dispersed.[163]

Dr Arthur Chervin, a physical anthropologist with a special interest in stammering, concludes the discussion with this comment about meeting Pelletier at the Beaujon hospital:

> I have to say that this individual has left me with a rather sad impression: he was very mistrustful, sly and probably a liar; and besides, not very intelligent, but speaking French perfectly well.[164]

Chervin's dismissiveness of a man whose life experiences lay far outside the norm says more about his own sensitivity than it does about Pelletier. He did not, for example, even canvas the obvious possibility that Pelletier was suffering from any regret at having left his antipodean life and that homesickness — for his second home — had taken hold. Or that his emotions had been anaesthetised first by his ordeals and now by the need to readapt to a more constraining way of life impossibly far from the land and people to whom he had come to belong. Or that he may have been heartily sick of interrogations by the professional or curious.

There was one local scholar, Marcel Baudouin (1860–1941), a prolific writer in the fields of medicine and prehistory, who took a particular interest in Pelletier's story, gave lectures about it and published newspaper articles on the subject as well as one scholarly article in the *Bulletins* of the Anthropological Society of Paris. His interest was no doubt sharpened by the fact that, as a boy of 15, he had been home on holidays from his *lycée* in La Roche-sur-Yon and had witnessed the homecoming of Narcisse with the bonfire in the Place du Baril, the square opposite the house of the Pelletier family.[165]

One of the Society's interests had been in cases of children apparently raised in the woods by animals and brought back into human life. We saw that Letourneau's article about Pelletier's recovery had been concerned with the innateness or otherwise of human linguistic ability, but while he had referred to experiments in raising children without language he did not mention the famous, and tragic, case of a boy named Victor, known as the *enfant sauvage*, the wild child, of Aveyron.[166] However, when a lost medical report by the equally famous Doctor Pinel concerning Victor had come to light again after more than a century, it was published in the same year as Baudouin's article in another anthropological journal, the *Revue d'anthropologie*.[167] Baudouin takes up the theme and calls Pelletier the '*enfant sauvage* de Vendée', the wild child of the Vendée. But he stresses that Pelletier's case is not comparable to Victor's and that this wild child who 'having left for the virgin Forest and the Life of freedom *sound of mind*, came back from it in as excellent *intellectual health* as if he had lived in the Bocage of the Vendée here in the twentieth century!' Pelletier's alleged state of mind proved, he suggests, 'that the *Neolithic mentality* was not as distant as one believes today from that of most of our modern peasants of Savoy, the Auvergne, Brittany etc!'[168]

Baudouin's view was that Pelletier had been badly wronged in the employment found for him as a lighthouse keeper. He wrote that this had in effect exchanged one form of 'torture' for another, that he was in a 'gaol' on the ocean waves and that what this man deprived of society for so long — as if there could be no such thing with people of 'Neolithic mentality' — had really needed was to be placed in government offices in the heart of Paris.[169] A singular voice among French writers on Pelletier was Aristide Roger who, in an article headed 'The capture of Narcisse Pelletier', based on the report in *The Times*, seriously considers the question of whether Pelletier might rather not have been found again at all and might one day choose to return to Australia because of the close attachments he may have left behind.[170]

It is clear that different people formed different impressions of Pelletier. He impressed Ottley as lively and intelligent, a healthy young man of some promise, and Merland as honest, observant and well deserving of support to help him get established. The doctor on the *Jura* praised his abilities, while Dr Chervin, who met him not long afterwards, found him to be a person with no redeeming features to speak of. The French consul, Simon, struggled to get very much out of him at all.

The oral history of the region that has found its way into general accounts has played up the gruff persona of Narcisse Pelletier, a man who was difficult to work with, who hated being called by his nickname 'le Sauvage', was quizzed about being a cannibal, and who looked longingly out to sea from his vantage point on the harbour.[171] It is said, too, that relations with his family were uneasy, and that he was exorcised by the priest of Saint-Gilles after his return to expunge the heathen beliefs that had replaced the Catholic teaching he had received in his boyhood. An exorcism, if it was performed, would have signified an official expression of condemnation of Pelletier's former life and been quite damaging to his morale and sense of equilibrium. But since he left no direct descendants, and since those who knew him are now dead, there can be no way of really knowing the truth of such reports or how he lived out the years that remained to him. If there is any truth in local anecdotes about him, then the same anecdotes suggest that those around him had little understanding of him or of his experience. It was quite outside their horizons; there was no one at all who could share Pelletier's knowledge of Uutaalnganu society as an insider. The inability to find common ground with his peers, and their inquisitiveness and mockery, would have added to whatever psychological problems Pelletier experienced in readjusting to life in the Vendée.

But oral history is not necessarily reliable. Wouldn't the most likely response of a man in Pelletier's position be one of ambivalence, appreciating some aspects of his refound French life but desperately missing people and things in the life he had left behind? And his feelings may well have fluctuated from day to day, month to month or year to year. The reports about his recovery certainly suggest that his emotions were very labile in the early days of his reacquaintance with the world of Europeans. If the shutters did come down later we are lucky that Merland met Pelletier so soon after his return and was able to gather as much information from him as he did. But he still remains something of a ghost in his own story and our difficulty in hearing his true voice through the different reports, articles and books about him is something like another version of Eugène Simon's attempts to reach him, and his attempts to respond, at the consulate in Sydney.

Australian popular history has imagined a happier end to Pelletier's story than the facts allow.[172] In several articles it has been suggested that Pelletier returned to Queensland in 1881 (the year after he married), where he was seen at Cooktown, and caught a lugger up the coast to Cape Direction to rejoin his fellow tribesmen.[173] One thread of the story has it that a French-speaking man was living with Aboriginal people in the region of Staaten River on the western side of the Peninsula and well to the south of Pelletier's haunts. A couple of sandalwood cutters claimed to have seen the man several times and, in 1885, reported it to the police at Cooktown. He apparently had scribbled words in French on newspapers taken from their camp. Then, in 1916, a prospector called Owens had an encounter with a copper-coloured, white-bearded man who was in the company of three Aboriginal men. The man replied to Owens' greeting in what Owens thought was French, gave him some fish, and again the following day left a supply of fish on the creek bank in return for a bag of sugar the prospector had left for him. Owens did not see him again.[174] *Smith's Weekly*, which made this first report, followed it up the following year and reported more recent sightings of the apparently French-speaking old man living with Aborigines; the fact that people who had seen the man believed it was Pelletier; and even that one prospector, James Rodney, claimed to have seen Pelletier when he returned to Cooktown in 1882 before he rejoined his old companions, and had talked to him in 1886 near the Coleman River when he stated his intention 'to spend the remainder of his days with blacks, whom he had learned to love better than people of his own race'.[175] The speculation that this 'Mystery Man of Staaten River' was Pelletier, who had by this time been dead for more than a quarter of a century, was in fact what prompted Henry Dodd, in 1922, to make contact again with Sir John Ottley whom he had met almost fifty years before. Ottley, who clearly had heard nothing more of Pelletier after their voyage on the *Brisbane*, did not discount the possibility that he had returned to Cape York because of his reluctance to leave in the first place, but he was rightly dubious about the story on factual grounds.

One sideline to the Pelletier story concerns the infamous Swiss fraudster Louis de Rougemont, whose real name was Henri Grin.

De Rougemont made a career for himself as a writer, lecturer and performer (the latter even after he was exposed) on the basis of a concocted past as a castaway who had lived with Aboriginal people in north-western Australia and central Australia.[176] According to his biographer, de Rougemont had devoured Pelletier's story at one sitting.[177] Not only can we assume that Pelletier's story therefore fed into de Rougemont's fabricated persona, but it could be that the publicity generated by the discovery of his faked adventures dampened enthusiasm for more sustained research in Australia into Pelletier.

I have already touched on the French image of Pelletier, which was built on the reports of those who had met him at Saint-Nazaire. Pelletier's story is commemorated in his home town of Saint-Gilles-Croix-de-Vie and there is a long avenue that follows the River Vie named after him, the Promenade Narcisse Pelletier. The house to which his parents welcomed him back, just near the church of Saint-Gilles, is still there, but there are no Pelletiers now living in the town — his death certificate records that Pelletier's mother was living at Les Sables d'Olonne when he died, and it seems that none of her three other sons stayed there. But a link remains as there are still inhabitants of the town who are related to her family, the Babins. The subject of Narcisse Pelletier continues to be a matter of active discussion and research by professionals and interested amateurs. One resident of Saint-Gilles-Croix-de-Vie told me that Pelletier's story had inspired wanderlust in previous generations of the town's inhabitants, among them his aunt, who had migrated to Australia as a young woman on the strength of it.

Merland concludes his introduction plainly but perceptively when he writes: 'We can see that as well as the interest that Pelletier's story presents there is, too, the interest attaching to the man himself.' The French writers Joseph Rouillé and Jean-Paul Bouchon have responded to these twin facets without undue sensationalising. Joseph Rouillé, an historian of Saint-

Gilles-Croix-de-Vie, has retold Pelletier's story as a narrative based closely on Merland's book, having undertaken research in Australia in the 1960s but not pursued the question of where Pelletier actually resided for his seventeen years in Queensland.[178] A lucid factual version of the story and reflections on the person of Narcisse Pelletier and the limitations of Merland's account are contained in Jean-Paul Bouchon's *Un mousse oublié: Narcisse Pelletier, Vendéen.*[179]

A recent novel to appear in French about Pelletier is Maurice Trogoff's *Mémoires sauvages.*[180] Told in the first person, the novelist's pretext is that an older and wiser and now more articulate Pelletier wishes to revisit his experience and settle the debt he owes to his Ohantaala companions before he dies. The novel stays fairly close to Merland's account but the 'savage memories' of the title points to how the author slants the dramatic incidents he invents to enliven his story. One of these is the massacre of a landing party from a passing ship, which is executed not by the Ohantaalas but by the wholly fictitious Calakaïtes. The cannibal feast that ensues has a true Boy's Own bloodthirstiness. Trogoff gives Pelletier a love interest in the character of Coquillage who valiantly tries to save him as he is being taken away from her shores.

The cannibal theme has also been manufactured in the new edition of Merland's book, which appeared in France in 2001. The editor has repackaged the story to situate Pelletier in a cannibal tribe when his account does nothing to substantiate the existence of the practice while he lived with Uutaalnganu people. The title now becomes *Chez les sauvages. Dix-sept ans de la vie d'un mousse vendéen dans une tribu cannibale 1858–1875* or *Among the savages. Seventeen years in the life of a cabin boy from the Vendée with a cannibal tribe 1858–1875*. The book includes as an appendix a section from the Norwegian naturalist Carl Lumholtz's work, *Among cannibals*, based on his researches in the Herbert River region, south of Cairns. The extract focuses on Lumholtz's questionable reporting of cannibalism, and constitutes a gratuitous addition that has no bearing on Merland's book.[181]

The cover of the book compounds the misfit of material. It displays cut-out colour-tinted images of an Aboriginal man and woman. There is no explanation of who these people are or where the images came from. In fact the photographs were taken in Paris in 1885 by Prince Roland Bonaparte, a great nephew of Napoleon, whose scientific interests included ethnology and photography. The subjects of the photographs were members of a group of Aboriginal people from Palm Islands and Hinchinbrook Island, nowhere near Cape Direction, or even Cape Flattery as it appears uncorrected in this new edition, who had been taken from their land by the impresario Robert Cunningham and toured around America, England and the Continent as performing savages, as well as being examined by anthropologists.[182] Narcisse Pelletier's story is remarkable enough without needing to be dressed up, and falsified, as a tale of survival amid Aboriginal savagery. The sober tone of Merland's account is the antithesis of such treatment.

Pelletier's story, when it became known, revived that of the *Saint-Paul*, wrecked off Rossel Island. Indeed that story is probably better known because the fate of the Chinese has been discussed in newspapers, magazines and scholarly books and journals. We can take up the thread again when Captain Pinard and his men sailed off from Cape Direction without their youngest crew member. The source for this account is an article by Victor de Rochas, which appeared in 1861 in *Le Tour du Monde*, an illustrated journal that informed and entertained its readers with well-researched articles from the four corners of the globe. Pinard told the story of the shipwreck and its aftermath to Rochas, presumably in the course of the rescue mission to Rossel Island in which Rochas participated. Merland relies on this account in the first chapter of his *Dix-sept ans*, though as we have seen he challenges Pinard's version of events in relation to Pelletier and the information given to the Chinese as the European crew left in the longboat.

The men first of all sailed south in the hope of reaching British settlements but after several days they changed tack — the wind was against them (the season being that of the south-easterly trade winds) — and headed north. One man died the day after they left Cape Direction. On 5 October they pulled into a small island to spend the night. When they awoke the next morning the men found that their boat was gone. They were taken prisoner by Aborigines and ferried across to the mainland. Another man died that day. The remaining men were looked after but kept captive until they were rescued a few days later by Captain MacFarlane on the *Prince of Denmark*, who responded to their signals when they saw his ship offshore bearing the English flag.[183]

Rochas gives the location of the place where the crew of the *Saint-Paul* were recovered as near Cape Grenville at 12⁰ S. latitude. The *Sydney Shipping Gazette* reports that 'Captain Pennard, of the St. Paul, and eight of his crew were picked up on the 15th October [1858], inside Sir Everard Home's Group [now Home Islands].'[184] This location means that the captain and his crew had made their landing on an island in the territory of Wuthati Aboriginal people, who today form part of the Lockhart River Aboriginal Community. The report states further that 'Captain Pennard speaks highly of the peaceable disposition of the blacks, and of the service which they rendered him and his crew while they were among them.' Rochas reports that the men were fed when there was food for all, meagre rations or nothing when food was lacking. He gives the following description of their way of life:

> The tribe of which our compatriots were prisoners was made up of about eighty individuals, inhabiting huts made of leafy tree branches. These Australians do not move very far from the shore and live on fish, turtles, which are very abundant on the coast, shellfish, wild fruits and roots. They do not cultivate any plants; the sugar cane whose stalks they eat grows naturally.

The women appear to have a great influence among them, a remarkable thing and quite extraordinary among savages. — Each morning a matron, who appeared to be invested with authority, woke up the camp, and calling each individual by their name, allocated them their task. This task consisted for each of them of going in search of foods, according to their abilities and the direction which had been assigned to them.

These savages did not prove to be very cruel, and although our compatriots had to submit to some ill-treatment, and one of them even succumbed after the blows he received in an escape attempt, the calamity and the memories of Rossel Island had made them so long-suffering that they were almost pleased with the *hospitality* of the Australians[185]

The captain of the schooner negotiated with the Aborigines for the release of the prisoners and succeeding in recovering the boat as well. Rochas says that the men were put to work collecting turtle shell as they made their way to New Caledonia so that they did not arrive at Port-de-France until 25 December.

A rescue mission was then mounted very quickly, with the *Styx*, a warship under the command of Ship's Lieutenant Grimoult,[186] departing for the Louisiades from Port-de-France on 27 December. On 5 January 1859 the *Styx* arrived at Adele Island, which lies slightly south and to the east of Rossel Island, where Pinard thought the shipwreck had taken place. No sign of the *Saint-Paul* could be seen there, and subsequently its bowsprit and stern were sighted on a reef close by Rossel Island. The Isle of Refuge was sighted next. An officer landed and found the remnants of a tent, two corpses buried under pebbles and a large quantity of burnt shells.

The next day the captain found a mooring inside the reef and boats were launched with armed men to search for the Chinese and the inhabitants alike. They came upon six men in outrigger canoes who fled into the mangroves leaving their boats. Continuing on their way, they came upon a man standing waist-deep in the water who gestured to them. The man, one of the Chinese, 'threw himself into the arms' of Captain Pinard. The first words he uttered, in English, were: 'All dead!' He told his rescuers that only four other men were alive, one of whom was thought to have been a Prussian crew member, the master carpenter. Rochas gives no explanation for why this man was not included in the escape group. The Chinese man said that he had been adopted by one of the chiefs, and when the landing parties came next to a village the inhabitants tried fruitlessly to induce their captive to return to them.

They then reached the mouth of the stream where Pinard had set up a camp before coming under attack from the inhabitants. Writes Rochas: 'There a horrible spectacle presented itself to our gaze. Piles of clothing and Chinese pigtails (we know that there were more than three hundred of them) marked the place where the wretches had been massacred.'[187]

According to Rochas, the story obtained from this man, further amplified in Sydney with the services of an interpreter, was that the Chinese had remained on the Isle of Refuge for as long as they could, having devised a means of trapping rainwater and living on shellfish. But when they had used up this supply of food from the nearby beds, some of the Chinese responded to the invitations of the Rossel Islanders to go with them to the mainland. Rochas spares no detail of how these men were killed. The little island was too far for their cries to carry there, and the view was blocked by trees: 'It was in this way that more than three hundred men were able to be massacred successively without resistance.'[188] Soon after the rescue, the *Sydney Morning Herald* published an account from this same man, which differs slightly from Rochas's in the description of how the Chinese were dispatched.[189] He is quoted as saying that the Chinese were herded together at night and taken off by day in groups of four or five who had been selected to be killed and eaten, being beaten all over first, a detail included by Rochas. He claimed to have seen ten of his companions killed. The nationality of the European man is here given as Greek.

Following their gruesome discovery, the members of the *Styx* exhibition engaged in negotiations with the Rossel Islanders to find the other men but nothing came of it. The French were convinced that a general call to arms was being made as conch horns were sounded during the night and fires lit near their mooring place. The following day there were skirmishes in which shots fired by the French may have led to several deaths. Rocks were thrown by the islanders but did not result in serious injury to any of the French. Strict orders had been issued to the mission by the authorities in New Caledonia against making attacks, but the commander's thoughts had now turned to reprisals. About twenty men landed and set light to one of the villages they had visited, which was now deserted. They returned to their boats with clothes belonging to the Chinese that had been stored away in the huts. The *Styx* then set sail for Sydney. Rochas describes his disappointment at the results of the mission and the limited reprisals for the 'bloody horrors' that had taken place, where the French had been restrained by lack of manpower and the injunction against mounting an attack.[190]

In November 1865 the *Port Denison Times* carried the report that two further Chinese from the *Saint-Paul*, Tam-Tam and Barqué,[191] had been recovered from Piron Island[192] in the Louisiade Archipelago by Captain Edwards[193] of the schooner the *Bluebell*, after seven years apparently spent being traded between islands.[194] Edwards had delivered the men to Somerset and they were then taken on to Sydney in the *Salamander*. These men confirmed the story of the massacre by degrees of their compatriots although they stated that an initial group of twelve men was selected for 'a monster feast' following a sustained attack by a group from a neighbouring island, which had been successfully defended by the Rossel Islanders. This is not a detail mentioned anywhere else and given that the stories of the Chinese men had to be obtained largely via interpreters there is room for a degree of misunderstanding and error, first in what they said, and then in what was subsequently reported about what they said. Not only that, but the reporting shows a voyeuristic interest in the gory details of the event, so the probability that the accounts are embroidered to feed the frissons of the readers is high. Nonetheless, the accounts deriving from two separate rescues, seven years apart with no communication between the first man and the next two, both describe the other Chinese as having been killed and eaten.

The weight of opinion has been to accept the testimony of the three Chinese survivors that the 'cannibal feast' on Rossel Island (as it inevitably came to be called[195]) did in fact take place. Because cannibalism is such a contentious issue for anthropologists, I shall quote in some detail from those who have expressed views about the fate of the Chinese following the wreck of the *Saint-Paul*. In this I have drawn largely upon information collated by W. E. Armstrong, who worked as Assistant Anthropologist to the Papuan government in the early 1920s after studying psychology and then anthropology at Cambridge.[196] His ethnography, *Rossel Island*, based on two months' fieldwork, was published in 1928. Armstrong provides excerpts from a number of different reports that refer to the incident, no doubt because the incident still aroused interest. Indeed, a later anthropologist on the island, John Liep, writes that the *Saint-Paul* saga 'gave Rossel, and probably the whole New Guinea area, an evil reputation among the white population of the Pacific'.[197]

Sir Alfred Haddon, under whom Armstrong had studied at Cambridge, devotes the first half of the introduction he wrote for Armstrong's book to the *Saint-Paul* incident. In summarising Armstrong's conclusions about why the massacre occurred, he writes:

> Rossel Island, or Yela, was first discovered about 160 years ago, but it passed into oblivion until some 68 years ago when a French sailing vessel, *St Paul*, was wrecked there on her way to Australia with 327 Chinese coolies on board, who were seeking their fortunes in the

gold mines of Australia. All but two or three of them were killed and eaten by the Rossel islanders, and one was rescued by the *Styx* in 1859. Many years later I heard that this man subsequently had got into trouble somewhere in South Australia, but on learning about him, the magistrate let him off on account of his terrible experiences in Rossel. The sensational account of the fate of the Chinese has more than once been denied and later reaffirmed, and now Mr Armstrong gives us all the available evidence and this disputed incident may be regarded as settled finally. Mr Armstrong points out that cannibalism is the necessary adjunct to the funeral rites of a chief, though he also suggests that there may have been other occasions for the practice. At all events, it seems pretty clear that at the time of the shipwreck of the *St Paul*, a certain 'chief' named Muwo was a wild disorderly person, and the dumping of this cargo of live stock came very opportunely for him and seems also to have been the means of aggravating his craving for anthropophagy. It was, to say the least of it, unfortunate that the shipwreck took place when that particular man was powerful, or the fate of the Chinese might have been very different.[198]

Armstrong devotes a chapter of his book to 'death and cannibalism' on Rossel Island, in which he describes the customary practice of the ritual killing and eating of a chosen victim in the context of the death of a chief.[199] He had been 'much puzzled with the discrepancy' between this practice and the reports about the *Saint-Paul* until his informants told him about the insatiable and megalomaniac chief Muwo.[200] He writes:

> Fortunately for the natives, the *St Paul* was wrecked on Rossel early in Muwo's career, and most of his victims were Chinamen. I was told that most of the Chinamen were eaten by Muwo, and perhaps it was partly due to Muwo that they received such exceptional treatment. Perhaps it was the supply of Chinamen which first allowed Muwo to satisfy his passion for human flesh at all adequately, and the using up of this supply which led him to terrorise the island subsequently, and defy convention by eating his own kind on other than the appropriate occasions defined by custom.[201]

Armstrong evinces no doubts about what he has been told about Muwo but it defies belief that one man, no matter how greedy for human flesh, or even one man and his acolytes, could have disposed of so many men by eating them in a period of a few months.

Sir William MacGregor (1846–1919), first Administrator and later the first Lieutenant-Governor of British New Guinea, whom Armstrong quotes in detail from his Annual Reports on the colony, had been privy to no such information some years earlier and doubted the veracity of the story. This is what MacGregor concludes about the wreck of the *Saint-Paul* and its aftermath after his third visit to the island in 1892, prompted by the murder by Rossel inhabitants of a Frenchman, Lucien Fiolini. During the visit Armstrong probed the memories of the senior men on the west and south of Rossel about the events of 1858. What they told him concurred with the information he had previously received on the north coast. He writes:

> The native account of it is that the Chinese landed and obtained water, sugar-cane, cocoanuts, and all the food they could find, and then left in boats or rafts, proceeding northwards, the only direction they could well take at that time of the year in such craft. The natives described how they were afraid to go near the wreck after the people left. When they got up near to it someone suggested that the foreigners were hiding in the wreck to catch and kill them, and they turned back and did not actually enter the wreck for some days after the Chinese had left. I told a native that it had been said they killed and ate all the Chinese. His reply was that he supposed some white man must have seen skulls in their houses and thought that these were from people that they had eaten; but these skulls, he stated, were those of their own people. It is their method of disposing of the dead to keep the body until the flesh falls off and disappears, then to keep the bones in or near their houses. ... Probabilities are altogether in favour of the native account. The natives are the mildest, quietest, and most inoffensive in the Possession. I have no proof whatever that they are cannibals. The tribes all along the

southern coast are very small communities, and by no means of a warlike disposition. Their only weapon seems to be the spear. I have seen only one club on the island. There is no tribe on the island that could not be conquered by fifty Chinese armed with stones, which abound everywhere on Yela. A rough stone is but little inferior to the Yela spear as an offensive weapon. Three hundred Chinese could undoubtedly have conquered the island with such weapons as they could pick up. But the natives seem to think they had some firearms. In consideration of all these circumstances it seems to me incredible that the 326 Chinese were killed and eaten at this island, and I therefore accept the native account as being correct. They are well acquainted with the main facts. There is no village on the south coast that does not contain iron from this ship, and some of her blue enamelled plates and dishes.[202]

MacGregor makes no reference to Rochas's report, which might have given him a different perspective on the events. He may well have heard a brief version of the story in 1875 as he was appointed that year to a medical post in Fiji by the incoming Governor, Sir Arthur Hamilton-Gordon,[203] who referred to the fate of the Chinese in his report in *The Times*, but not to the mission of the *Styx*.

In 1901 the Chinese were mentioned briefly, with similar doubt about what had befallen them, in another report on Rossel that appeared in the *Annual Report on British New Guinea* after a visit to the island by George Le Hunte, the Lieutenant-Governor (and fellow passenger with Pelletier on the *Brisbane* a quarter of a century before), and another official. Le Hunte wrote:

> With regard to Europeans, the natives have for a long time been inoffensive, and they repudiate the story of their having eaten the Chinese who were shipwrecked off the island in 1858 — a supposition of those that left them there. The Rossel Islanders say that the Chinese made a raft and went away.[204]

The contact history of Rossel Island is intimately bound up with two brothers from Queensland, Frank and Harry Osborne, who arrived there in the early 1900s and set up a copra plantation. The family also became involved in the bêche-de-mer and trochus trade. Harry's sons Hugh and Ron remained on the island until 1964, running the plantation and a freight vessel that operated along the coast of New Guinea and outlying islands.[205] Hugh Osborne said that enquiries made in 1903 by his father and uncle led them to conclude that little was remembered about the *Saint-Paul* incident 'except that there had been a massacre many years earlier'.[206]

In 1911 the Lieutenant-Governor, J. P. H. Murray, made a tour of inspection of Rossel Island and, like MacGregor, obtained information about the *Saint-Paul*, though it quite contradicted the latter's. He writes:

> Various old men were seen who said that they remembered that the Chinese survivors of the *St Paul* were eaten, but they were all too young at the time to have taken part in the feast. The interpretation was not clear enough to enable me to obtain a clear account of the manner in which the Chinamen were enticed off their island. The ordinary way of preparing them, I was informed, was to cut them up and disembowel them, and to cook them on stones covered up with leaves.[207]

Two articles that appeared in 1959 in the *Pacific Islands Monthly* revisited the *Saint-Paul* affair and endorsed the occurrence of a massacre and cannibalism. But in 1960 the whole edifice was challenged when the *Bulletin* devoted its front cover and a feature article to the *Saint-Paul* story under the heading 'The case of the shipwrecked Chinaman: a hundred year old hoax'.[208] The author, Olaf Ruhen, starts by claiming that the events involving the *Saint-Paul* 'changed Australian history', what it revealed being so shocking that 'it delayed the annexation of New Guinea for a quarter century'.[209] He examines the testimony of the first Chinese man and finds it filled with inconsistencies, cites MacGregor's scepticism about the occurrence of cannibalism, and then speculates on possible reasons for what he takes to be a confabulated story. The explanation he favours is that the Greek man left with the Chinese, 'probably a Levantine of some sort', had not got on with the captain who had left him behind, and had instituted a reign of terror in which the Chinese man found by the *Styx* and the few others remaining alive on the island but not found had colluded to 'kill and eat, or at least kill and rob the luckless castaways who were not on his side'.[210] There is an Australian precedent for this theory in the story of the aftermath of the wreck of the Dutch East India ship *Batavia* in the Abrolhos Islands off the midwest coast of Western Australia in 1629 when a murderous regime was instituted by one of the ship's company, Jeronimus Cornelisz. However, the rescue mission in that case found not only the tyrant alive but many survivors left to tell the tale of what had befallen them.[211]

John Liep's opinion about what actually happened after the wreck of the *Saint-Paul* is especially valuable because of his close acquaintance with Rossel Islanders over many years. Liep is doubtful about Armstrong's explanation of aberrant cannibalism involving Muwo, who was living not in the north of Rossel, where the massacre would have taken place, but in the south-west of the island. In the 1970s Liep had in fact been told the same story about another big man named Loanga, who lived on the north coast, but in this version Loanga's magic was held to be so powerful that he was able to deflect the bullets of the Chinese, who were said to be armed. The fact that different versions of the story had evolved on the island suggests to him that the event of the massacre was already at Armstrong's time being absorbed into legend.[212]

Liep believes that a massacre did take place and that it happened for explicable and mundane reasons of survival and competition for resources:

> There is no direct evidence that the Chinese were actually eaten, although this is what Armstrong was told in 1921, and what is still believed on Rossel today. Certainly 300 refugees would pose a threat

to the available food resources of an island with a population of, say, 2,000. On the other hand, a couple of hundred men would have sufficed to dispatch the Chinese, who must have been starving and demoralized. They were left on a tiny islet (Heron Island) about one kilometre from the coast without fresh water and with provisions which, at most, could last them a week. According to Rochas they were taken to the mainland by the Rosselese in canoes a few at a time. It is, therefore, most probable that the massacre took place. The Rosselese were practising cannibalism amongst themselves and they probably regarded the castaways as a windfall — like the great whales which sometimes stranded on the reef and caused a rush of canoes from many parts of the island and much feasting.[213]

According to Liep, pacification and the eradication of cannibalism occurred rapidly after 1892 in the wake of Fiolini's death. Police patrols and arrests were instituted in response to homicides and the power of the 'big men' was seriously weakened by the advent of government authority and the police presence as its agent.[214]

A *Batavia*-type scenario cannot be excluded, but the weight of evidence supports the theory that a massacre resulting in cannibalism, as claimed by the three Chinese survivors who were recovered, did take place on Rossel Island. If there was a massacre, then John Liep's explanation for why it occurred brings this event back from the realms of surreal horror to the plane of a dreadful but comprehensible concatenation of tragic circumstances. After accounts of the shipwreck and its victims came to be published, the books and newspapers that raked over the *Saint-Paul* incident show that curiosity about this tragedy continued for many years, but its mechanics will never now be known.

✳

Narcisse Pelletier's odyssey, with its intriguing tangents, leads us through a succession of cross-cultural encounters in the world beyond Europe during the second half of the 19th century. Unfolding during a feverish period of Western economic expansion across the globe, its various episodes reveal the impact of international trade and European colonisation on big cities and remote localities alike in Asia and the Pacific, and on the lives of the individuals caught in the slipstream. Narcisse Pelletier was one of them, but an irony of his extraordinary story is that its aftermath, his reunion with his countrymen, first at the French consulate in Sydney and then on his return to Saint-Gilles, only added to the ordeals he had already had to face.

The French word *pays*, 'country' (or 'region' or 'village' or 'home') figures in the expression for homesickness in French, *mal du pays*; similarly, the French adjective *dépaysé* is used to describe someone who is out of their element, ill at ease at being away from their familiar surroundings. We can imagine Pelletier's disorientation, first on returning to his family in France, now strangers to him, and then on commencing his employment as a lighthouse keeper at the Phare de l'Aiguillon on the estuary of the Loire. The sentence in Kuuku Ya'u, '*Ngayu puuya mitimiti ngaachiku*', sums up the feelings that must have overcome Pelletier at times. It can be translated as 'I am feeling sad for home'.[216] Pelletier's return to Saint-Gilles was of course the second exile from home and country he had experienced in his 32 years. The original place of exile was now home, and the homecoming presented a new estrangement

Pelletier's story suggests that cultural identity is malleable in a child or young adolescent — he was able to take on the persona of Maademan's adoptive son as if this were all he had ever known — but relatively fixed in adults. James Morrill's period of residence with Aboriginal groups in Queensland, mainly Bindal people, in the region between Townsville and Bowen, equalled Pelletier's. He was only 21 when he was shipwrecked, but he was nonetheless a grown man. The famous words Morrill uttered on meeting two shepherds after being so long away from European society — 'Do not shoot me, I am a British object'[217] — indicate that he still retained in some part of him his sense of identity as an Englishman. Another shipwreck victim, Barbara Thompson, had been with the Kaurareg from the age of 16 (she was then already married) to the age of 21. Taken on board the *Rattlesnake*, she was asked if she would like return to the Kaurareg or go to Sydney; she replied, 'I am a Christian'.[218] There is no report of any such expressions of identification as a Frenchman in Pelletier's case. On the contrary, Merland could not put it any more simply in his final chapter when he writes that, after seventeen years, Pelletier 'was no longer a Frenchman, he was an Australian'.

The sense of feeling at home, of belonging, is based on deep attachment to the place and people you know and value. On reading *Dix-sept ans* we get the impression that Merland grasped something of what this meant to Pelletier in his second life as one of the *Pama Malngkana*. Strong elements of what had come to be important to Pelletier come through in his narrative. The bountiful but hazardous environment of the Cape York Sandbeach and hinterland looms large in this: the thrill of the dugong chase, for example, or hunting down an emu; the seasonal fruits he feasted on, like the red Wongai plum; the birdcalls he heard when moving through the bush; the lurking dangers, physical and supernatural; the look of the seas and the sky; the tools he used and crafted — we shall see that Pelletier was an expert maker of spears; the battles in which he took part to settle or rekindle feuds with neighbouring groups (twelve by his account); the great gatherings with dances and songs extending long into the night; the kin he relied on and the way they mourned their dead; his *kuyan* moiety and the Sandbeach language he now spoke. This was the life Narcisse Pelletier lived with his Uutaalnganu clan on Cape York.

Among the line-up of scholarly gentlemen who interviewed him in France, it was only Merland who produced a record of any substance about Narcisse Pelletier's adopted country and people.

We owe other early and invaluable accounts of Aboriginal life to Frenchmen as well, explorers such as Bruny d'Entrecasteaux, Nicolas Baudin and Dumont d'Urville, and the scientists who travelled with them. But Merland's account is based on the recollections of one who stayed much longer than these earlier French visitors to Australian shores, and as a participant not an observer. It opens a rare ethnohistorical window on to the way of life of an Aboriginal coastal people just prior to the sustained penetration of Europeans into their world. It also makes a significant addition to the narratives of European men and women who were rescued by Aboriginal people and remained to reside with them. And it serves to record and recognise a man who, having survived life-threatening experiences as a fourteen year-old boy, recast his identity on Cape York Peninsula to grow up as one of the *Pama Malngkana*, coping successfully with the rigours of their existence and enjoying its satisfactions.

PAMA MALNGKANA:
THE 'SANDBEACH PEOPLE' OF CAPE YORK

ATHOL CHASE

The account of Narcisse Pelletier's seventeen years among Aborigines of coastal north-eastern Cape York Peninsula (from 1858 to 1875) is less well-known than that of other Europeans who lived among the 'savages' in Australia, for example James Morrill, Thomas Pamphlett and William Buckley. Pelletier's 19th century experiences of life among Cape York Peninsula Aboriginal people come to us in a little-known French account as published by Constant Merland in 1876 after his discussions with Pelletier in France. This work has not been translated into English until now. One reason for this, perhaps, is that Queensland's self-proclaimed Aboriginal expert and popular journalist, Archibald Meston, firmly declared in a newspaper article published in1923 that the Pelletier story was a fiction. (I return to Meston's article later, as he is one of the few who made enquiries in the Night Island area regarding the Pelletier story in the early days.)

There could be another reason for its neglect, to which I shall also return later. This is connected with what I see as a reluctance on Pelletier's part to publicise his experiences with Aboriginal people of north-eastern Cape York. After all, he had spent his most formative years there with them from the age of fourteen to 31, and his departure was not of his own choosing.

Even a cursory examination of the evidence today makes it clear that Meston was quite wrong and that Pelletier did indeed spend a very long time in this part of Cape York with Aboriginal people. More particularly, he spent his seventeen years among these coastal hunter-gatherers in a region in which there has been much subsequent anthropological work. The linguistic and other ethnographic information given by Pelletier to Sir John Ottley and later to Merland is sufficient for us to be quite confident about the particular section of north-eastern Cape York Peninsula where Pelletier spent his seventeen years of residence, and to recognise Merland's reportage as the earliest historical account of Aboriginal life in this particular region. What details the Pelletier account does provide are supported by later anthropological investigation from the 1920s onward. In order to gain a better understanding of what Pelletier tells us via the voice of Merland, it will be useful for the reader to know something of the north-eastern Peninsula where Pelletier was located, and of the people who inhabited that area at the time of Pelletier's stay.

Cape York Peninsula: environment and climate

The Peninsula lies within the tropic zone, its tapering finger of land extending some 600 kilometres north to the Torres Strait. At its midpoint, roughly in the area of Pelletier's stay, it is some 200 kilometres wide, with a dramatic variation in landform and vegetation from its eastern Pacific shore to the Carpentarian shoreline in the west. Off the east coast lies the Great Barrier Reef, and at this midpoint location the coral rampart of the main Barrier Reef is about 40 kilometres offshore, with the inner reef waters studded with shallow fringing reefs, small sand cays and islands. These waters are extremely rich in fishes, rays, large meat-producing marine animals like the dugong and green turtle, and a very wide variety of reef and estuarine shellfish. The land itself provides a wealth of edible plant species, as well as a wide range of edible birds and land animals, native bee hives and freshwater fishes and reptiles.

The coastal strip here is complex, with river and creek mouths disgorging seasonal waters from the mountains behind. The land environment has complex mosaics of vegetation ranging from mangrove forests and swamps, riverine vine forests, dense scrubs on the old prograded dune systems, to extensive forests and grasslands on the coastal plains behind the littoral. The steep mountain ranges lying some ten kilometres or so behind the coast are densely clad in rainforest. This highly varied habitat of land and marine environments, all within easy reach from the central zone of the beach line for the coastal Aboriginal groups with their dugout canoes, provided a wealth of resources across the dramatically changing seasonal range. Together with other tropical coastal environments elsewhere in the Peninsula and in Arnhem Land, this was possibly one of the richest and most varied environments for hunter-gatherers anywhere in the world.[1]

Cape York Peninsula lies within the monsoonal belt of northern Australia. There is a heavy annual rainfall, nearly all in a limited part of the year, and this is followed by a lengthy dry season. The mid-Peninsula region of the east coast lies at about 13 degrees south latitude, and most (about 1770mm) of the annual average total of about 2000mm falls within the period from December to April. While there are always occasional small showers brought in by the south-east trade winds in the dry season, it is the north-westerly monsoon, presaged by dramatic storms, which fills the waterholes and rivers, and floods the many coastal swales and swamps. This massive seasonal deluge drives an annual calendar of plant regeneration, subsequent avian migrations (ducks, geese, Torres Strait Pigeons) to feed off the fruitings, and fish migrations to raid the shrimp that are attracted to the rich muddy coastal waters resulting from the disgorgement of many creeks and rivers.

The Peninsula's landform varies considerably from east to west. From the Pacific shoreline inland, a narrow coastal plain extends some ten kilometres to the foothills and slopes of the mountains of the Great Dividing Range, here reaching a maximum height of some 500 to 600 metres. These ranges and hills fall off to the west at about the Peninsula's midpoint, and the land slopes gently with little profile until it reaches the Gulf of Carpentaria. Resulting from this landform are the short, twisting and swiftly flowing rivers on the east coast, and the long, sinuous and wide rivers flowing into the Gulf. Much of the interior, in contrast to the east coast, consists of few variations in environment, with the major contrasts in vegetation found along the river edges, and in the rain-shadow of the eastern ranges.

We can see from this brief description how Pelletier managed to survive, in the physical sense at least, on the east coast. He had found himself in a place of very considerable resource richness throughout the year and, apart from the vicissitudes of the wet season, one with a generally benign climate.

North-east Cape York Peninsula and its Aboriginal peoples

The general area where Pelletier lived with Aboriginal people is a coastal strip of the Peninsula about 60 kilometres long between Lloyd Bay in the north and a point somewhere around Cape Sidmouth to the south. This area consists of the territories of three linguistic groups, all of whom spoke closely related dialects. These were (and are), from north to south, the Kuuku Ya'u, whose territory extends from the Olive River region south to the Lockhart River mouth in Lloyd Bay; the Uutaalnganu (known in Aboriginal English today as the 'Nightisland' people) whose territory extends from the Lockhart River mouth in Lloyd Bay south to Friendly Point; and last of all, the Umpila, whose territory extends south from Friendly Point to a point south of Massey Creek. Inland, in the upland region to the west of these groups, is the Kaanju language area and its people, with whom the coastal people occasionally intermarried, and who traded with the coastal groups for various artefacts such as items made from shells, stingray spines (for spear points) and other marine products.

These coastal groups were collectively known in the dialects as *Pama Malngkana* ('people of the sand beach') or *Pama Kaawaychi* ('people of the east'). They were strongly marine-oriented in their habitat and economy, and most of the year was spent camped right behind the beach in the fringing scrubs and thickets. As well as sharing similar dialects these groups had a very similar general culture including a shared ritual life based on a series of related origin myths. These myths provided the charter for the all-important secret male initiation ceremonies performed every few years.

The **Pama Malngkana:** *society and economy*

What we know today of the traditional lives of these coastal peoples has come largely from ethnographic reconstruction of their pre-contact existence by anthropologists. Before we look in more detail at the culture and society of these people it is useful to review the basis of our current knowledge. The accounts Pelletier provided to Ottley and Merland represent the only information that is available from the very cusp of contact in this region before serious inroads were made into Aboriginal lives, and they give us some indications as to how correct the later anthropological reconstructions have been. The fieldwork studies by anthropologists all took place from the late 1920s onward, a time when contact with Europeans was well established and when Aboriginal peoples were already very significantly affected by it.

The pioneering anthropological work in this area was carried out by Donald Thomson in the late 1920s and early 1930s. Thomson, originally a naturalist, made his initial base at Port Stewart, at the mouth of the Stewart River in 1928, working with Umpila and Lamalama peoples who occupied a fringe camp at the river mouth. He returned in 1929, travelling overland to the Lockhart River Mission near Cape Direction (in Uutaalnganu territory) where he studied the secret ceremonies of the Kuuku Ya'u. He carried out further investigations in 1932–33 in central and western Cape York Peninsula, after an initial return to Lockhart River. Thomson wrote prolifically on the Lamalama, Umpila, 'Yankonyu' (Thomson's name for what is referred to here as the Uutaalnganu)[2] and Kuuku Ya'u peoples, and a full listing of his publications and summaries of his pioneering work can be found in Thomson's *Kinship and behaviour in North Queensland*[3] and in *Donald Thomson: the man and scholar*, the volume of papers resulting from the Donald Thomson Centenary Anniversary Symposium held in 2001.[4] We are concerned here primarily with his writings on the groups and territories of the Umpila and their northern coastal neighbours, the Uutaalnganu and the Kuuku Ya'u, who, with some other groups, collectively make up the *Pama Malngkana*. These writings provide the first detailed information on the kinship and descent structures operating in this region, and of the heavily marine-oriented lifestyle that, through use of outrigger canoes, provided a significant portion of the meat foods for these peoples.

Donald Thomson never lost his biological interests, publishing on Papuan influences in Australia in plants and animals, and indeed on what he saw as a similar alien cultural intrusion into the world of the *Pama Malngkana*. He was fascinated by what he believed to be the southerly sweep of Papuan cultural influences in the male initiation ceremonies of the Kuuku Ya'u, and upon their tribal structures and mythological accounts and sites. There are significant commonalities in plant and animal species across this area of the Peninsula and New Guinea to its north. Thomson observed that there were Melanesian influences upon the Aboriginal ceremonies and their artefacts, and evident as well in various other artefacts like the crocodile-mouthed drum. For Thomson, these showed a past cultural influence from Melanesia sweeping down the coast as far as Princess Charlotte Bay, and this paralleled the remarkable overlap in biota between New Guinea and the northern Peninsula. While contact across the Torres Strait must certainly have occurred, the overlaps are seen in a more complex way today, rather than as a simple southward sweep.[5]

Thomson was the first anthropologist in Australia to use a biological approach to give a clear account of what today are recognised as ecological dimensions among Aboriginal people,[6] and he saw the strong focus on the marine habitat by these people as a key element in understanding their culture. Hale and Tindale are also pioneers in the general region, though their work in the late 1920s focused further south on the islands of Princess Charlotte Bay, and very briefly, with some coastal people at Port Stewart.[7]

Thomson's early work among the *Pama Malngkana* was followed in the 1960s by some specialised sign language research by LaMont West (who published nothing, but left some field notes and a large quantity of film)[8] and by Wolfgang Laade. This was followed from 1970 onward by my research among the coastal Umpila, Uutaalnganu and Kuuku Ya'u peoples,[9] and by the linguistic and anthropological work of David Thompson. Research in the more southerly region associated with the Lamalama peoples has been carried out from the 1970s onward by Bruce Rigsby and Diane Hafner, and they have published extensively on them.[10]

My early work in the 1970s focused upon the social dimensions of the Lockhart River community and the links to 'country' among the various family groups. This involved very detailed mapping of sites and boundaries throughout all the coastal estates of the groups, when senior men and women took me back to their homelands. These field visits also allowed reconstruction of the way these estates provided economic and social bases for families in the pre-contact past, as well as in contemporary times. A summary of these investigations and recordings can be found in the thesis that resulted from this work[11] and in other published papers referred to elsewhere in the translation.[12] David Thompson has provided pioneering linguistic work on the languages here and upon other cultural dimensions of the Lockhart community, including the spiritual aspects of the initiation ceremonies.[13]

Family groups and ownership of country

The arrangement of family groups and their particular territories along this coast is generally similar throughout all the dialect groups making up the *Pama Malngkana*, and indeed it reflects a pattern found in many parts of Australia. The pattern is one of a small family group (possibly about 30 in number) being intensely connected through mythic associations to a particular tract of land and sea within a larger dialect area. This grouping is sometimes referred to in the literature as a 'clan' or an 'estate group'. We can note out of interest that in this regard Pelletier refers to his 'tribe', the 'Ohantaala', or what we have now identified as the *Wanthaala* estate group, as having about 30 members (see later).

In our area of concern this group territory or estate consists on average of about seven kilometres of coastline, with the territory extending seawards to the outer Barrier Reef (here, as we have noted, some 40 kilometres or so offshore) and inland until it reaches the crests of the coastal ranges — a distance of roughly six to ten kilometres behind this Uutaalnganu coastline. The Umpila/ Uutaalnganu coastline can be seen to be divided into a fairly regular series of these estates along its length. There are ten estates in the Uutaalnganu coastal strip and seven along the Umpila coast; as a fairly general guide I have estimated the average population of each of these estate groups to be in the order of 20 to 50 people.

These family estate are the social and cultural focus of the *Pama Malngkana*. They contain the critical myth sites or 'story places', as they are known today in Aboriginal English, from which the group sees itself descended through patrifiliation.[14] This family country is what the anthropologist W. E. H. Stanner referred to as one's 'heartland'.[15] Beyond the estate, people of a small region sometimes saw themselves as distinctive in terms of particularly close social association. Examples are those estates clustered around a major river mouth or other geographic feature. An example of this among the Uutaalnganu are the members of two estates clustered around Cape Direction, among the Kuuku Ya'u those making up the estates bordering on the Pascoe River, and among the Umpila those around the Nesbit River mouth region.

Another feature of these particular dialect groups is the recognition of a named patrilineal moiety system.[16] Along this coast the names of the moieties are *kuyan* and *kaapay*, and Pelletier reports these (reasonably accurately) in Merland's rendering as *cayen* and *caapei*. Inherited by individuals from their fathers and, ideally, from the major myth centres of their estates, membership in the moieties both prescribes marriage partners (different moieties) and proscribes others from sexual relations, seeing them as incestuous (same moiety). Such incestuous relationships, even in modern times, have brought severe penalties.

Marriage, as Pelletier reports in his own case, is ideally arranged with a neighbouring group if someone in the right relationship exists, and if the cementing of closer desired relationships is possible. Brother–sister exchange of marriageable children is therefore a good way to do this, and in the 1970s at Lockhart community there were several pairs of families in very close alliance through this arrangement. Marriage here is ideally with a classificatory cross-cousin (e.g. child of a classificatory father's sister, or of a classificatory mother's brother) and this ensures that the moieties of spouses are opposite as required.

Kinship, or a presumed genealogical connection among people, is an all-important organisational and classifying principle among people in these societies. In Euro-Australian society we are of course familiar with a limited kinship system in terms of naming and obligatory recognition, but the classificatory kinship system of the *Pama Malngkana*, like those of many other kin-based societies, extends far wider than anything we experience in non-indigenous society. Thomson gives 27 terms for the various kin relationships among the Umpila[17] and the same is true for the Uutaalnganu and Kuuku Ya'u. For each pair of relationships (e.g. father/son or father's younger sister/older brother's child) there are prescribed behaviours to accompany the particular terms. The intensity of these behaviours can vary in terms of age, genealogical closeness or distance and whether there are subsequent connections through marriage.[18] They can extend from total avoidance, of the kind Pelletier touches upon, through to obligatory and ritualised joking.[19]

To be recognised as a fellow social human being in the pre-contact past required acceptance within this system through the application of a kinship term by a focal person placing a stranger into a suitable kin position. Pelletier's adoption by Maademan provides us with an example of this from his own experience. Even today it is not unusual for outsiders who have spent much time with Aboriginal people who still use these systems to be put into the kinship network, or 'adopted' as it is called, by one local taking the outsider on in a particular relationship. It can be appreciated that once this is done the individual is enmeshed in a kin network that applies throughout the community and that provides continuity in the quotidian activities of its members, and indeed beyond it through kin links to other communities. It is this system that provides the social mechanisms for people of one area to visit other groups, to move across the landscape from one area to another (though always after obeying the courtesies of asking permission from the other land owners) and to attend the occasional major ceremonies held in other territories along the coast. In short, it authorises the acceptance of the adoptees as known and recognisable human beings in an Aboriginal social system.

The spiritual life

Behind what is called the traditional law and custom of Australian Aboriginal people lies a complex set of cosmological beliefs about particular groups, particular tracts of land and sea, and particular creator spirits who gave form to the known world in the long-past creation time. Particular mythic charters (the 'dreaming') provide accounts of this time and give what Maddock and Stanner have called a 'plan of life'. It is this plan that articulates the rules for human action and that stipulates the sanctions that apply when those rules are broken. The anthropologist Kenneth Maddock has provided a good summary of this spiritual dimension of Aboriginal life:

> The Dreaming is viewed as a period during which enduring shapes were made, enduring connections established and repetitive cycles initiated, the material thus moulded having hitherto been inert, amorphous or in flux. These mythologically recorded events, which occurred in a past that no living man has experienced, gave Aborigines their 'plan of life', as Stanner [20] calls it.
>
> The cosmology, then, posits a metaphysical discontinuity, a duality, between men and powers, the latter having shaped the landscape in which the former dwell, formed the species with which they coexist and off which they live, and instituted the plan of life to which they conform. [21]

For the Aboriginal people with whom Pelletier lived, this creation time is known as *yiilamu*, and it is in this period that the various creator spirits created the mythic sites (*puula waya* or 'story places' in Aboriginal English) that provide spiritual focus within the geographic landscape. These are places where the creator spirits paused in their travels to carry out acts of creation of current species and human technologies (including a specific language), creating landscape features like rivers, creeks and other topographical features during their passage across the land and generally giving form to what had been formless beforehand.

There are particularly potent places where these creator beings came to rest, disappearing into the land or sea, or became metamorphosed into observable features today like rock formations or holes in the ground. Here their power remains, to be harnessed by elders with the special knowledge, or to be awakened into calamitous destruction by unauthorised approaches or behaviours. Older people will 'introduce' strangers and young people to these areas by rubbing them with underarm sweat, or at water sites by blowing water onto their heads. This is accompanied by calling out to the appropriate spirit to see the newcomers as being properly guided in the etiquettes required at the site.

In this way the terrestrial and marine environments of these coastal people came into existence by the potent action of creators long ago, and their spiritual essence remains, permeating all the landscape in general, as well as in particular places. The same spiritual essence is contained within the people who 'own' the land according to the mythic charter. Their spiritual being came from their lands, and on their death returns to it to be recycled again through living people. As one Aboriginal man explained it to me once with masterly economy when showing me a water spring that contained his major 'dreaming': 'When I was *piiwu* (wallaby) before time, this is where I finished up. I went down here.'

Spiritual beliefs need rituals to be observed in order for the mythic charter of 'law' to continue across generations, and for this section of Aboriginal Australia there were important rituals to be observed that were connected with birth, coming of age, marriage and death. This system has changed across the generations since Pelletier was with his Aboriginal families, but they still exist among these groups in modified forms.[22]

The male initiation ceremonies of the *Pama Malngkana* were extremely important, both for providing a passage to adulthood for young males, as well as for providing the occasions for major social gatherings that extended across all the dialectal groups of this coastal region. They took place late in the year at the end of the dry season when a number of fruiting trees and plants could provide large quantities of vegetable foods and when the clear coastal waters before the monsoonal influence allowed the easy hunting of mating green turtle, dugong and fish. The ceremonies consist(ed) of secret performances in special areas prohibited (*kincha*) to women, children and uninitiated youths because of the potent spiritual essence (*kuntha*) that could cause great sickness if offended. There are also related public performances where creator spirits were summoned to appear before the assembled community. This gathering of people in the pre-contact times also provided opportunity for sorcery accusations and other grievances to be aired, and these matters needed to be settled before the ceremonies could commence.

This often involved spear fighting and ritual punishment by controlled retaliation through spearing in the leg as Pelletier describes. The ceremonies have continued into modern times and are now the last remaining initiation ceremonies on the east coast of Australia to continue until today. Much of their detail remains secret and the Uutaalnganu and their neighbours continue to resist any publication of their details.

In summary, these coastal people were similar to other recorded Aboriginal people in the way the sacred and secular worlds enmeshed. The relationship between people, the natural environment and the ancestral spirits is complex, deeply significant, and provides the foundation for the operation of systems of 'law' and social order that are of course fundamental to the operations of all societies across time and space.

The coastal regime: land and sea resources

In the earlier section on the Peninsula's environment and climate I suggested that Pelletier had arrived in what could be described as a hunter-gatherer's 'land of plenty', and I now explore this statement further.

Both Ottley's and Merland's accounts make mention of the sea-going canoes used by these 'sandbeach people', which gave them great mobility in ranging over large marine habitats as well as their use of the coastal lands and waterways. The canoes in the Uutaalnganu area where we assume Pelletier lived could hold three or four adults; they had double outriggers for seaworthiness and stability, and were propelled by paddles. They featured a short platform on the bow, from which the harpooner could launch himself and the harpoon at a turtle or dugong. They were quite capable of travel over considerable distances at sea as, for example, when the outer Barrier Reef was visited, but they were particularly useful for travel and hunting in the closer inshore waters.

Dugong and turtles were (and are) available across much of the year when the water is clear, but especially in the months of November and December when the turtles float on the surface coupled in mating, and when dugong can be tracked in the clear water around the many sandbanks where their seagrass food grows. The south-east trade winds start to falter at this time and the seas remain calm, even glassy in the early morning. These conditions are ideal for marine hunting with the harpoon; the prey can be seen at a considerable distance, and canoe pursuit was swift and effective (even more so today with modern craft and outboard motors). A dugong or turtle provides a large amount of succulent meat, and a skilled and successful hunter becomes a man of renown (*pama watayichi,* or 'dugong man') who has command over the necessary hunting magic, as well as possessing outstanding hunting skills. The detachable-head harpoon used here is remarkably effective at capturing these large marine animals.

Thomson saw these groups as fearless sea-goers who took great pride in their ability to take large marine animals with their harpoons. But the offshore marine environment, while being extremely important to them, provided only part of their range in the seasonal round of hunting and gathering. The coastline, with its sand beaches, rocky headlands, mangrove flats, and creek and river mouths, provided a rich and varied diet of fish and shellfish. Women fished with lines, while men hunted with multi-pronged fish spears used with a spear-thrower (as we see described by Pelletier).

Immediately behind the beach are the low vegetated dunes that provided camping sites sheltered from the sun and a veritable garden of edible fruit trees and native yam species.[23] Here also are found many large mounds of sweepings made by the scrub turkey and the scrub hen. These mound-builders lay their large eggs in the pile of humus when the first thunder signals the oncoming storm season and, knowing this, the coast dwellers had another source of rich food at their disposal. At this time also the green turtles come ashore to lay their eggs above the high-water mark, and again the nests provided a plentiful food supply easily gathered.

We have seen how the annual seasonal calendar of the coastal peoples is marked by dramatic changes in rainfall and by accompanying pulses in the availability of many food sources.[24] Much of their living was finely attuned to these shifts in climate and resource base. The *Pama Malngkana* recognise various stages of the annual cycle, using the cyclic variation in wind direction, and other features like the dramatic thunder and lightning that accompany the onset of the wet season, to name the seasons. I recorded the following annual cycle with the Umpila people:

Ngurkitha ('wind from northwest')
— Main monsoonal period, February to April
Kuutulu ('wind from southwest')
— End of monsoon rains, April to June
Kaawulu ('wind from southeast')
— Early dry season, June to August
Kayimun ('dry time')
— Middle-late dry season, August to November
Matpi paa'inyan ('clouds building up')
— Build up for storms, November to December
Malantachi ('stormy weather time')
— December to February.

The wet season floods the landscape and brings forth a strong burst of growth in the grasses and plants along the coastal plain. As well, the swiftly flowing rivers and overflowing swamps and lagoons cause a large outflow of fresh water into the inshore sea waters, bringing to the coast plumes of sediment that prevent any meaningful hunting on the underwater sandbars and reefs for dugong or turtle. The flooded landscape also makes travel inland or along the coast difficult. This was the time when people gathered and settled in traditional wet season camping places, using 'beehive' huts made of bent saplings and covered with ti-tree bark to escape the rains. And it was also a time when the normally scattered people found the communal congregation difficult and the wet-season diet limited in variety.

This plentiful environment always has a potentially good food supply, but in the wet season the variety was limited, and there was a need to put physical labour into processing the various roots, tubers and fruits (for example, mangrove pods) in order to render them either edible or palatable. It was a time, old people maintained, when fights broke out. For these people, 'hard times' in the resources sense did not mean a lack of available edible species, but rather a shift to less pleasant foods plus the need to apply some physical labour to the food preparation. Bitter and/or poisonous substances had to be leached from certain pods, tubers, seeds and nuts by pounding and repeated soaking and washing.

From what old people who had lived in the bush have said, this was also a time when movement was limited through flooding and tempers frayed from the constant deluges. Clouds of mosquitoes in the sodden environment and enforced camping together in larger numbers than these hunter-gatherers preferred proved very stressful. The clearing of the skies and the return of the south-east winds allowed these wet-season camps to disperse, with people spreading out again along the coast into more congenial situations of small and independent family camps.

But as Thomson has also observed, the annual movement of camps in this region was not great. Such is the wealth of the resource base that these people might spend the greater part of the year at the shoreline, moving perhaps only a few kilometres north and south along the coast in the normal round of existence, with short excursions and stays inland to seek a known and liked resource base (for example, in the inland pools, eels, freshwater fishes and tortoises) or to attend the major initiation ceremonies that were held every few years along this coast. We can assume that Pelletier did not move a great deal from the Night Island area for much of his stay in the region, and indeed he makes scant mention of travelling any distance from his family home. This, as far as we can reconstruct (and also supported by some evidence from Pelletier), was how the Uutaalnganu and their neighbours existed for many centuries prior to European arrival. From around the time of Pelletier's departure this lifestyle for the *Pama Malngkana* was to be severely disrupted.

The contact experience: European incursions and their aftermath

The first contacts along this stretch of coastline came from the sea. William Bligh of *Bounty* fame arrived just south of Cape Direction (which he named and which was very close to Pelletier's later landing point) in 1789 after having been cast off the *Bounty* by mutineers in a longboat. He spent one night ashore in Uutaalnganu country fearful of attacks by "Indians". He noted the presence of fireplaces, but saw no people, and he continued his northward sea journey to Batavia. Philip Parker King carried out a survey of the inner reef waters along this coast between 1819 and 1820, but did not land. Occasional shipping was starting to use the inner reef passage, but there are no other recorded landings in the Night Island area until the 1840s.

In 1843 the survey ship *Fly* bartered with Aborigines in dugout canoes near Night Island. A surveying party from the ship climbed

Direction Hill at Cape Direction to take sightings, and they were ambushed on their descent by a party of Aborigines,[25] presumably Uutaalnganu people, and possibly by the very people Pelletier was to know well some few years after this incident. One sailor was speared through the chest and he died at sea shortly afterwards. The Night Island area was beginning to gain a reputation for having hostile inhabitants.

Until this time, there had been no land-based travel or exploration into this coastal area. Bowen and Bowen[26] state that Barrier Reef charts from the marine surveys were mostly completed by 1846 and that by 1859 the inner reef passage had become a 'marine highway'. This of course does not necessarily mean that these highway travellers attempted to land on the Peninsula shores — on the contrary, the inner reef waters were so studded with fringing reefs that larger boats would have made sure they stayed on the marked channel. It is also an exposed coast without any significant anchorages offering shelter from the south-east winds. Despite the increasing frequency of marine traffic in the area from about the time of Pelletier's arrival, the need for boats to keep a strict course threading the reefs along this area probably made it easier for the group to keep Pelletier hidden from view, as he reports his family group doing.

The ill-fated land expedition led by Edmund Kennedy left Rockingham Bay (where the town of Cardwell now stands) and started their journey up the eastern side of the Peninsula with the intention of reaching Somerset at Cape York. The expedition was beset by difficulties by the time it reached the Lockhart River area in 1848. Kennedy and his men swung inland a few kilometres at the Nesbit River, following the Lockhart River northwards, and then swung further inland into Kaanju country to follow the upper tributaries of the Pascoe River. They were initially travelling just 15 or so kilometres inland from the beach while following the Lockhart, but a range of hills lay between them and the Night

Island coast. Nevertheless, they were on the western margins of Uutaalnganu country, but they reported no contact with Aborigines. Kennedy and his men later emerged at the coast by following the Pascoe River to its mouth, and entered a period of successive disasters that saw Kennedy killed and only three others left alive.

Following Kennedy's passage along the Lockhart River, there was no further European land intrusion until the explorations of Robert Logan Jack, the Queensland government geologist. His job was to find payable mineral deposits in the northern Peninsula so that the settlement of northern Queensland could be boosted by mining influxes. At the time of his expeditions, the Palmer River goldfield was failing, and the mining population was starting to desert the area. Jack set out from Cooktown in 1879 with two Europeans and two Aboriginal assistants. He reached the short-lived, and by then deserted, goldfield at Coen and then set off to the northeast, following the upper waters of the Archer River. He mapped these drainage systems and returned to Cooktown.

In December 1879 he set out on a more ambitious journey, this time aiming to work his way much further north on the eastern Peninsula (where the mineral-bearing rocks are found) as far as Somerset at Cape York. In January 1880 Jack crossed the Macrossan Range east of the present town of Coen and entered the grasslands of the upper Nesbit River. Here he encountered what he described as 'warlike' Aborigines and he opened fire, killing at least one of them. We assume these people were Kaanju or perhaps Umpila. He then swung inland again, following roughly in Kennedy's tracks. He also reached the coast at the Pascoe mouth and further north at Temple Bay encountered a camp of Aboriginal men.

Jack was astounded at their ability to use 'broken English', and noted that one of them was a 'Captain Billy' who spoke 'very fair English'. Jack remarked that 'their conversation implied a familiarity with bêche-de-mer fishers'. [27] He also mentions the manned Piper Island lightship, which by then was one of several marking the inner reef channel. It is clear that while the eastern Peninsula inland from the shoreline was almost untouched by European land-based incursions (though not for very much longer), the northerly coastal strip was by 1880 well-visited by a variety of fishing craft seeking bêche-de-mer and pearl shell. We turn now to the seaborne incursions into the territories of the *Pama Malngkana*.

The major marine extractive industries in Queensland waters up to World War 1 were those taking bêche-de-mer, pearl shell and trochus shell. Bêche-de-mer fishing seems to have been the initial marine industry in the Torres Strait region, though it was very soon followed by pearl shell fishing. The trochus industry was the last of these to develop, starting about 1912. The literature suggests that bêche-de-mer fishers were operating in the early part of the 19th century in the Melanesian area, and there is even a report of the first bêche-de-mer station in Queensland at Lady Elliot Island (at the southmost point of the Great Barrier Reef not far north of Fraser Island) in 1804[28]. It seems that the bêche-de-mer industry started with small boats, and at locations relatively close to European settlement. We can note, too, that from the 1890s onward individuals began to cut sandalwood, which had been found on the Peninsula and which was a valuable export to China. One of these cutters later became highly influential among the *Pama Malngkana*, as we see below.

The literature suggests that in the Torres Strait a Captain Banner was a pioneer of the industry, establishing an island station on Erub (Darnley) Island in 1868. However, there appears to have been desultory small-boat gathering of the sea slug for some years before this. The arrival of Captain Joseph Frazer in the *John Bell* at Night Island in 1875 must have been at the very vanguard of the exploration and development of bêche-de-mer fishing in the remoter areas of the northern Peninsula. As best as can be made out from the scanty information on Frazer, his visit to Night Island when he took Pelletier was most likely a brief exploratory one and not apparently connected to an established processing base or 'station' there.

In 1857 a bêche-de-mer station was established at Green Island offshore from Cairns by a Captain Mein, and by 1868 Lizard Island off Cooktown was similarly being used as a processing base. However from about 1870 onward the industry moved into lesser known areas as the closer reefs were over-exploited. We can assume that this is about the time boats started to stay in the Night Island area, assessing the resource stock and exploring the possibility of setting up a shore base on the island. Unlike pearling, the bêche-de-mer fishing required a land base where the sea slugs could be gutted, boiled, then smoke-dried over fires. This processing required a large supply of firewood and space for the building of smoking and drying racks. Given the rapidly growing need to find new reefs to exploit, Pelletier's discovery was more or less guaranteed once the European boat masters took an interest in the area.

Frazer's arrival and removal of Pelletier occurred some 30 years after the visit by the *Fly*. The next mention of Night Island comes in a report that Captain Robert Watson, a bêche-de-mer fisher with a base on Lizard Island far to the south,[29] arrived to fish there accompanied by a man called Fuller.[30] By the 1870s the Lizard Island area was becoming depleted, and he moved operations to Night Island in September 1881. But by this time Pelletier had been back in France for six years. He had enjoyed an existence at the coast largely free of any European interference as best we know, and had departed just as the first marine contacts were being established.

From the mid-1870s onward the *Pama Malngkana* and their coastal territories came under ever-increasing pressure from more frequent European visitation. One small advantage for them was that their country was quite unsuitable for any pastoral activity.

This meant that any European arrivals on their lands were generally transitory ones — recurring seasonal visits to exploit marine resources like bêche-de-mer or pearl shell, or else to obtain land-based resources like sandalwood and minerals. In all of these cases there was no *permanent* occupation of the type seen elsewhere. In the pastoral belts of Australia, occupying Aborigines were seen as a danger to stock and station, and therefore requiring permanent 'dispersal', a convenient term that, at best, can be translated as removal to far-off government encampments or 'settlements' and, at worst, as murder.

There was value for these seasonal European visitors in having Aborigines present from year to year and in forming reciprocal partnerships with them in order to provide cheap labour as well as local guides for use both on land and at sea. But this did not prevent some unscrupulous boat operators in these remote areas behaving lawlessly in their treatment of the local populations. It was also a period that saw the arrival of European-borne sickness, and increasing dependence upon European products like flour, sugar, tobacco, opium and alcohol, with their subsequent effects on indigenous systems of authority and on health.

By the early 1870s the marine industries and the number of vessels plying the reef waters had grown to such an extent that the government needed to establish legal control in order to curb the excesses and abuses of Aboriginal people, which were starting to become known. To do this the Queensland Government in 1877 moved its administrative centre in the far north from Somerset at Cape York to Thursday Island. There was already a northern Resident appointed, and the government now added a resident Fisheries Commissioner, William Saville-Kent. From the start of this marine expansion conflict had erupted between some boat masters and local Aboriginal groups, often through the abduction of Aboriginal girls and women or the kidnapping of able-bodied men as labour. This in turn brought reprisals by Aborigines upon visiting boats.

By the 1880s this conflict had grown to the point where it was paralysing the fledgling industry, and the government could no longer ignore it. The Government Resident, John Douglas, catalogued examples of abuses and retaliations at, among other locations, Cape Grenville, Weymouth Bay, Lloyd Bay and the Night Island area on the north-eastern coast. At Night Island, a man named Kane, together with his crew, was killed by 'Night Island Aborigines'.[31] We can only speculate about how Pelletier would have survived had he not been removed in 1875. He would very soon have been exposed to more and more European contacts. Had he been allowed to stay with the Uutaalnganu he might well have been able to lessen some of the more destructive contacts by acting as a 'gatekeeper' and guardian for his particular group when faced by some of the more lawless boat crews. As we shall see shortly, another European in this area appeared to be successful in this role in the early years of the 20th century.

In 1896 Archibald Meston was appointed as a special Commissioner to investigate the abuses of Aboriginal people in the Peninsula. He recommended the establishment of special reserves from which Europeans would be totally excluded and the creation of boat patrols to enforce a ban on Aboriginal boat labour. In the same year the Police Commissioner for the area, William Parry-Okeden, investigated the killing of a European storekeeper named Poulsen on the Chester River, south of Cape Sidmouth, and a little beyond the Nesbit River. His report concluded that the Aborigines of this coastline were 'neither wild nor dangerous' and that he could find no 'wild blacks' left on the coast because of the extensive contact. Coastal Aborigines spoke 'a very good pigeon English' and were all 'more or less clothed'.[32]

As a result of these reports, the Queensland Government enacted *The Aboriginals Protection and Restriction of the Sale of Opium Act 1897*, which created the positions of Northern and Southern Protectors of Aborigines. This ushered in the period of missions and official settlements in the Peninsula and Torres Strait, though the earlier of these were created on the western Peninsula coast, through the Torres Strait Islands, and close to European settlement at Cairns and Cooktown at the Peninsula's base. No mission was established along the north-eastern coastline until Lockhart River Mission in 1924.

We can note also that the period from about 1880 onwards saw the sudden discovery of minerals in this area. From 1879 roving prospectors started to comb the waterways for alluvial deposits of gold, wolfram and tin. In 1879 a gold rush started at Ebagoolah, inland near Coen, and in 1892 another discovery brought a rush to the Batavia (now Wenlock) River inland from Lockhart. Mining similarly brought conflict with the spearing of two Europeans near the Stewart River and another near the Rocky River. The 1890s saw a rush to an alluvial goldfield on the Rocky River in Umpila country and another at Hayes Creek in the Night Island area. Cattle stations were spreading in the interior of the Peninsula, following the newly erected telegraph line, and mounted police began to operate in the region, often making savage reprisals in places where Europeans had been killed. By the turn of the century, coastal groups like the Uutaalnganu were caught in a pincer-like pressure of increasing European influence from both inland and sea.[33]

We are now some distance in time from Pelletier's departure from the Peninsula. But there is one further relatively early reference to Pelletier, that of Archibald Meston, which I mentioned at the beginning. In 1923 Meston wrote an article concerning a visit that he made in 1909 to the Night Island area. In it he reports on enquiries he made regarding Pelletier to elders including 'King Fred' of Hayes Creek (in the Night Island vicinity):

> Recently there has been a revival of the discussion on a Frenchman named Narcisse Pelletier, who was alleged to have lived with the blacks for many years on various parts of the Cape York Peninsula, and was finally picked up on Night Island. It is a bogus story from

start to finish. Narcisse Pelletier was a cabin boy on the ship St Paul, of Bordeaux, and she had 800 Chinamen on board when wrecked among the cannibals of the Louisiade Archipelago. What really happened was never known, the only consistent story being that all who got ashore were killed and eaten by Louisiade cannibals, only the cabin boy escaping.

The man found on Night Island had apparently been for some time with a Polynesian race, who had tattooed him, but the marks were not those of a Queensland aboriginal. Night Island is well known to me. It lies south of Cape Direction, and is a low, flat island, with coral beaches and belts of dense red mangroves.

To the blacks the island was known as 'Oang-gooboo.' None lived there permanently, but all the blacks of the adjoining mainland were known as Night Islanders, and their reputation was not the best. The whole story of Pelletier was sifted by me down to the bedrock among the old men of the wild tribes, and they knew nothing of any white man ever being among the blacks of the Peninsula.[34]

There is no doubt that Meston did visit the Night Island area and that he did make enquiries about Pelletier. King Fred is remembered in Lockhart history, being the possessor of a king-plate (which I have seen) inscribed as follows: *King Fred King of Night Island and Ashes River* (Hayes Creek). This was still in the possession of his (then elderly) sons in the 1970s. What is of more interest is that, as early as 1909, about thirty years after Pelletier's departure, older Aboriginal men in the Night Island area were denying any knowledge of Narcisse Pelletier. There are a number of reasons why this might have been so.

First, we can assume that Meston and Night Island people could converse in a basic manner by means of the 'Pidgin' Aboriginal English then in use. But what would Meston have asked about? A 'Frenchman'? Someone called 'Pelletier'? Someone who had landed in a boat? These terms would have meant little to Aboriginal people of the area. Meston would have apparently had no knowledge of Pelletier's Aboriginal name to use that for more precise enquiry. Second, we can assume that after approximately thirty years any particular memory of a European living among them (particularly if he had left no children) may well have become lost against the background of a growing stream of Europeans coming and going in the area through the expanding marine industries, mining and sandalwooding activities over the intervening period. Third, it is possible that all those who had known Pelletier intimately had disappeared in the maelstrom of intensive contact, reprisal killings and increased mortality through introduced disease.

In the 1970s, when I did mapping work along this coast, old men whose knowledge stretched back to the very early 1900s could remember no-one directly associated with the *Wanthaala* estate group (though they knew its precise boundaries), and there was much discussion about which neighbour should take over Aboriginal ownership of it. I found this to be a unique situation for the entire Uutaalnganu and Umpila coast and it perhaps signals a rapid decline in members of this group somewhere around the turn of the twentieth century.

From about 1905 onwards, this coastal region came under the influence of a remarkable entrepreneur, Hugh Giblett. He was a sandalwood cutter and occasional bêche-de-mer fisherman who set up a base in Lloyd Bay. He had decided on a novel way of transporting his cut sandalwood — by boat to Thursday Island, rather than by the then orthodox use of packhorse teams all the way south to Cooktown. Giblett became the 'Sandalwood King of Lloyd Bay' in the words of popular author Ion Idriess,[35] and he set up a close and symbiotic relationship with the Kuuku Ya'u and the Uutaalnganu in particular. Giblett used their labour, and in return provided them with money and the tobacco, food and alcohol they desired. He prevented other outsiders from interfering with his workforce, and he managed to convince various visiting authorities that he was doing as good a job as any missionary.[36]

After Giblett's death in 1923, the Anglican Church moved in swiftly, forming a mission at Giblett's old camp in Lloyd Bay. The following year superintendent Harry Rowan moved the small settlement around Cape Direction to Bare Hill, close to where Pelletier had originally landed. When the Lockhart River Mission was relocated, it meant that the mission population was located squarely in the centre of Uutaalnganu territory. This residence at Bare Hill, which continued from 1924 until the late 1960s, provided the opportunity, through oral education, for people to retain much traditional knowledge about the landscape and the locations of particular significance, the 'stories' and their local history that could otherwise have been lost. Nothing about Pelletier was included in this oral education. Despite periods of administration by sometimes unsympathetic but often ignorant superintendents,[37] the community managed to retain their initiation ceremonies, and to move about regularly along the coast for periods in the extended wet season 'holidays' and when they were not working. This was a period of reliance on bush foods and it was also useful for the mission as it removed the pressure of supplying rations in the settlement.

The Anglican Church handed over control of Lockhart to the State Government (without consultation with the inhabitants) in the late 1960s, and this ushered in a period of harsh administration by government officials who had to answer to a central bureaucracy in Brisbane. It also saw the forced removal of the population from the old mission site to a new one close to the Iron Range airstrip in Lloyd Bay. For the Lockhart River community, this period was dominated by the repressive and discriminatory regime imposed on Queensland Aboriginal communities by the National Party Government of Sir Joh Bjelke-Petersen who was Premier of Queensland from 1968 until his resignation in 1987. The Bjelke-Petersen Government tried to repress any resurgence in traditional Aboriginal cultural beliefs and practices and any Aboriginal interest in reclaiming access to, and ownership of, their traditional homelands.

'Land rights' was, in the Queensland Government's opinion, a dangerously misguided idea and one that could not be allowed to take root in Queensland Aboriginal populations in the wake of land rights activity in the Northern Territory. Anthropologists and other reformists working with Aboriginal people in the 1970s were seen to be dangerous advocates of these ideas and were labelled as the agents of more malevolent forces.[38]

In 1991, with a new Labor Government in Queensland, an Aboriginal Land Rights Act was passed, and this was followed in the next year by the landmark High Court Mabo decision on indigenous native title. This in turn quickly resulted in a national Native Title Act in 1993. Today Uutaalnganu people possess all their coastal territory as Aboriginal Freehold, and their Kuuku Ya'u and Umpila neighbours are at various stages of gaining similar title to significant areas of their traditional territory.

Where did Pelletier live in Cape York Peninsula?

Information regarding the actual location about where Pelletier arrived and where he spent his time is limited. Some information from Merland is clearly wrong: for example, as mentioned by Stephanie Anderson, he stated that Pelletier arrived at Cape Flattery, which is a very long way from the Night Island locality where Pelletier was later picked up in 1875. The linguistic evidence in Merland's book places Pelletier firmly among the *Pama Malngkana* of the east Peninsula coast somewhere between Temple Bay and the area around Cape Sidmouth. As we have seen, this area includes the territories of three major language groups, the Kuuku Ya'u, the Uutaalnganu and the Umpila peoples.

We can narrow the search somewhat from other evidence, and be fairly confident that his central living area during his seventeen years was somewhere in the Uutaalnganu people's territory, a strip of coast and adjoining sea extending from Lloyd Bay and Cape Direction in the north, down to Friendly Point in the south.

Merland states that the small 'tribe' of some thirty people that had adopted Pelletier into their families was called the 'Ohantaala'. This provides us with a pointer towards some factual information in support of this conclusion. There is a well-recorded site named *Wanthaala* located just a few sea miles south of Cape Direction, and on the southern side of the mouth of Dinner Creek.

This location is not too far north of the old Lockhart River Mission, and just 13 kilometres or so north of the coastal site where Pelletier was later removed under protest to the *John Bell*,[39] opposite Night Island. It is not unusual for family estates to take a group name from key sites in their small coastal territories with a few kilometres of sea frontage, and my recordings from the 1970s show the family estate that encompasses *Wanthaala* extending from Dinner Creek southward to a point at the northern margin of the old Lockhart River Mission site. In other words, the Wanthaala estate came right down almost to where Pelletier first arrived.

More useful evidence comes from Sir John Ottley, who travelled with Pelletier on the steamer that took him back to Sydney, following Pelletier's carriage on the *John Bell* from Night Island to Somerset. Ottley, a British lieutenant on leave in Australia, had the advantage of speaking French fluently, and was thus able to converse at length with Pelletier (once Pelletier's ability in French began to return) about his experiences living with Aboriginal people. There was one other great advantage for Ottley here: the steamer travelled the inner reef passage, which took them close along the coast from Cape Direction south to Princess Charlotte Bay, indeed just a few kilometres offshore.

Ottley was therefore able to talk with Pelletier from the deck, having landmarks familiar to Pelletier pointed out to him and, as well, places from which he had only recently been removed. Ottley feared that had canoes with Pelletier's friends appeared close by, Pelletier would have jumped overboard to rejoin them.

Ottley reports one key piece of information. As they passed along this coast, Pelletier identified the place where he had first landed, and where he had first encountered Aboriginal people. Ottley had the ship's officers confirm the location as First Red Rocky Point. This is located immediately to the south of the old mission site at Bare Hill, and just a few kilometres north of where Pelletier was picked up seventeen years later. Ottley made pencil sketches of the locations he discussed with Pelletier, but unfortunately these appear to be lost. Despite this, we can start to have some confidence in our conclusion that the *Wanthaala* estate territory was the 'home' of the group who found Pelletier and took him into their care. Pelletier reports in Chapter 2 that after being discovered by Maademan, his brother-in-law and their wives close to where Pelletier had landed, they rested for two days to allow Pelletier to regain his strength. While this was happening, Maademan went off 'to inform his tribe, which at the time was camped two or three leagues away, of the adoption that he had just made'.

A league is about five kilometres in length, and this means that the tribe would have been some ten to 15 kilometres from where Pelletier had been discovered. The account does not tell us whether the direction of Maademan's 'tribe' was north or south; nevertheless, the *Wanthaala* site is just some kilometres to the north of First Red Rocky Point.

These four pieces of information — the place where Pelletier first landed in 1858, the location of *Wanthaala* by modern researchers, the location of Maademan's group in relation to Pelletier's landing place and his discovery by Aborigines, and the Night Island coastal location where he was picked up in 1875 (most likely at an important site called *Chinchanyaku* opposite the island) — all provide us with a clear focal area of interest centering upon the northern Uutaalnganu coastal lands, in the general vicinity of Night Island. The locations are all within a distance of some

20 kilometres or so. His seasonal movements most likely ranged around this area in the normal seasonal cycle and he may even have extended his travels on rare occasions northward through Lloyd Bay, and southward to Umpila territory around Friendly Point and Cape Sidmouth. Canoes made occasional visits like these quite feasible when important ceremonies were being held.

Night Island (*Wuungkuku* in the Uutaalnganu dialect) has always been a focal island for Uutaalnganu people. It is just a few kilometres off shore, it was a major resource base, and it gives its name today, 'Nightisland tribe' in Aboriginal English, to the Uutaalnganu people at Lockhart township, as mentioned earlier.

Ottley further reports the puzzling information that Pelletier belonged to the 'Muckuddumah' tribe located some '40 or 50 miles' south of Cape Direction, which is a very long way from Wanthaala. This would put them approximately in the Friendly Point/Cape Sidmouth region, at the extreme south of the Uutaalnganu territories or at the extreme north of the Umpila lands, and some 25 or 30 kilometres south of the location where Pelletier was later taken aboard the *John Bell*. Friendly Point itself is right at the border of two family estates, one being the most southerly associated with the Uutaalnganu dialectal territory and the other the most northerly in the Umpila dialectal territory. It has the name 'Mukuychi', which could possibly be related to the word Ottley recorded, but this seems rather doubtful.

The source of Ottley's reference to this location for the 'Muckuddumah' is not clear but we assume he is reporting information taken from Pelletier on board the steamer. There seems to be no clear resolution of this problem, apart from the likely situation that the copy of Ottley's notes we are now working from is a later typed version of his original handwritten letter. It is not beyond possibility that the typed copy contains either a misreading or a simple mistranscription of Ottley's handwriting, and that '40 or 50 miles' was 'four or five miles' in the original document.

Wanthaala is certainly about that distance from Cape Direction. Alternatively, Ottley may simply have misunderstood Pelletier about this, or have been mistaken so long after the event since he was writing from memory almost fifty years after their meeting.

Ottley also recorded from Pelletier the name of a neighbouring 'tribe' as 'Ehchahns', which may possibly be a rendering by Ottley of 'Kaanju', the neighbouring large inland language group that occupies the uplands to the west of Uutaalnganu people as well as west of the Umpila and Kuuku Ya'u, or possibly of the term *iichul*, for people 'from the west' (*iichul(a)* = 'west'), which is an alternative referent for the Kaanju people.

The term 'Muckuddumah', first recorded from Pelletier by Frazer or Aplin as 'Macadama', has only one likely reference in these languages that I am aware of, namely the word *makuthuma* recorded by the linguist Geoff O'Grady around 1960 from Umpila informants he met with in Sydney. He lists *makuthuma* as meaning 'truly' or 'verily'.[40] In all these Sandbeach languages the word *maku* is found, and it glosses as 'true'. It continues to be used today at Lockhart River in the local Aboriginal English. O'Grady's *makuthuma* may be the fuller version, and *maku* an abbreviated form, according to linguist David Thompson. It is very likely that Frazer's or Aplin's initial conversations with Pelletier (when Narcisse's French abilities were severely diminished, according to Aplin) were sometimes at cross-purposes, with resultant linguistic misunderstandings. In the case of 'Macadama', Pelletier may well have been answering '*makuthuma*', the equivalent of 'that's correct' or 'truly' to something that he believed Frazer (or Aplin) was asking.

All we can say is that since linguistic misunderstandings are known to occur when anthropologists and linguists work with their informants, we can imagine what might happen when an English-speaking stranger attempts to communicate with a culture-shocked Frenchman for whom Uutaalnganu has become his major language, and who has lost much of his French linguistic ability! Nevertheless, Ottley at least clears up the matter of Pelletier's original landing place.

Final considerations

What are we to make of this account from the anthropological perspective? Without doubt the evidence Pelletier provided to his questioners about his participation in Aboriginal life has a high correlation with what research has later discovered about these coastal people. Sometimes the evidence reported by Merland is initially confusing, but recognisable after some scrutiny. An example of this can be found in the drawings of hook-shaped spears [see Appendix IV], which, after reflection, are seen as straight spears curled to fit a page. Other initially puzzling elements that have later been deciphered are recorded in commentaries within the text.

There is much of course that is immediately recognisable as true. The account of retaliatory punishment by throwing spears at the offender and finally spearing him in the thigh accords almost word for word with accounts that were recorded in the 1970s. The list of words that Pelletier gave Merland, together with their meanings in French, is again immediately recognisable in the overall sense. Some words that initially could not be recognised became clear to me and others familiar with Sandbeach languages once allowances had been made for French pronunciation. After all, Pelletier was reporting to a Frenchman, who used his own orthography drawing upon French pronunciation. Nearly all of Merland's language list has now been placed within the currently known lexicon; it is indeed a list of words and meanings from the *Pama Malngkana*'s dialects.

But there is another dimension to this account apart from an anthropological one, and that is the very human story which lies partly submerged in the reports of Merland and Ottley. We must consider the traumatic events that had befallen the boy Pelletier in his short life. As we have seen, he had been a cabin boy on ships from the age of eight, and in 1857, while serving on the *Reine des mers*, he had been physically attacked and injured by the first mate. He had left that ship and signed up the same year on the *Saint-Paul* which, after being loaded with Chinese, had become shipwrecked near Rossel Island in the Louisade Archipelago.

Narcisse had then endured subsequent hardships, including another injury in the attacks from the inhabitants of the island, a subsequent narrow escape with the captain and most of his crew, and then a difficult twelve-day sea voyage in an open boat under conditions of utmost privation until reaching the Cape York Peninsula coastline. His final ordeal was his abandonment on the Peninsula coast by the captain and his surviving men. It is clear that these latter experiences had burned deep in Pelletier's memory. A significant part of Merland's second chapter is spent in describing Pelletier's abandonment on shore, his terrible thirst, his feelings of despair, his fear of being eaten by the 'savages', and his final plea for God to save his soul in the likely event of his death.

And then, miraculously, he is discovered by two Aboriginal men and their three wives, and Pelletier makes a present of his tin cup and a handkerchief. At this point Merland's account conveys the feeling that a spontaneous bond has been created between the lost boy and his saviours, for that is what they turned out to be. Pelletier is treated by them with the utmost solicitude; water is obtained, fruits are gathered, all to give him immediate relief. He is treated as an invalid, and Maademan adopts him and gives him the name 'Amglo'. When he awakes the following day after the small group had made a camp, he finds himself apparently abandoned by Maademan and his brother-in-law. He is again cast into shock and despair, certain that he has once again been abandoned. But he is mistaken — Maademan and his group had been getting more food, and when they meet up again 'both he and the two men eagerly rushed to greet each other'. Pelletier then takes 'his new family' to a place where the boat crew had left blankets, and the friendship deepens. When, soon after, he is introduced to Maademan's tribe, he is rapidly assimilated into the group. As Merland puts it 'all fear was banished from his heart', he is now 'in the primitive state', and he is now 'Amglo, citizen of the tribe of Ohantaala'. I detect no sense of irony here in Merland's words. Merland is obviously affected by Pelletier's account of his rescue by the supposed savages.

It is not hard to see why Merland has so carefully given this account such feeling. Pelletier must have been passionate in recounting these dramatic times and the affection and trust he had quickly developed for his new friends. After the trials of his earlier shipboard life and his abandonment at the coast, he must have thought that he had arrived among truly civilised and considerate people. And of course, we must remember that all of this is happening to a boy of fourteen years of age.

Merland's Chapter 3 starts to deal with the ethnographic information that he apparently has elicited from Pelletier. Indeed, throughout this and successive chapters we encounter particular accounts that make sense in terms of what we have since learned about the society and culture of the *Pama Malngkana*. Merland's account of the moiety system, the rules for marriage and the role of women among the 'Ohantaala' all fall within this category. But we also encounter some sweeping generalisations regarding the lack of any social differentiation within the tribe: 'Never in its wildest dreams has the most radical socialism pursued such an ideal'.

We can see how Merland can jump to very broad generalisations like this in attempting to understand the hunter-gatherer way of life from very little information, but we get the feeling that he is joining up the dots, providing some Merland-inspired linkage across the small pieces of information from Pelletier so that he can present a continuous narrative. What he does not fully understand he seems willing to generalise about, and we are left with that feeling in the other chapters as well. The little nuggets of information, however, are there for those who can read them.

There is also another dimension in the narrative that reveals itself in both Merland's and Ottley's accounts; that is, the clear impression that when Pelletier was questioned closely on details of the 'savage life' he is a very reluctant informant. There is very little of his actual personal experiences compared with those he provided about the events leading up to his adoption among the 'Ohantaalas'. Questions about cannibalism, a topic that had morbid allure for 19th century Europe, caused him to close up immediately, even later, in his life back in France. Was this because he had engaged in some kind of ritual cannibalism where a small part of a deceased body is eaten ritually? There is no record of cannibalism in later anthropological research. Or was it because he found the European mode of categorising the 'savages' in the Hobbesian mould as primitive, brutish and animal-like extremely distasteful, given his deep knowledge of the very human qualities of his adopted families? We shall of course never know, but it is not beyond possibility that Pelletier thought that the culture of the humanitarians who had rescued him and then provided him with a complete social existence for seventeen years was beyond any understanding of ignorant outsiders. I am of course drawing a long bow here, and Stephanie Anderson has commented on the reluctance also of other 'white savages' to go into much detail on their lives. But we have a distinct image of a very sensitive boy and, later, man, who became deeply depressed, even traumatised, after he had been forcibly removed from his Uutaalnganu society. He may never have got over this, and the later accounts of his life suggest he never fully acclimatised to his rediscovered French life.

The whole Pelletier account goes far beyond just anthropological interest. Here are raised the recurring questions of who the 'savages' really are, what constitutes a so-called 'civilisation', and what indeed constitutes humanity. And there is a further question we might ask now, in the modern Australian political climate, as we ponder the issue of an indigenous 'stolen generation'. Might the Frenchman Narcisse Pelletier be considered a forerunner of these Aboriginal people taken from their families and homelands? Living as an Uutaalganu man for seventeen years, from boyhood to mature adulthood, might Pelletier now be considered to be as indigenous as his Aboriginal adopters? If so, might he, too, now be considered to have been stolen from his family? To my mind that is one of the regrettable dimensions of the Pelletier account.

PART TWO

DIX-SEPT ANS CHEZ LES SAUVAGES

NARCISSE PELLETIER

NOTICE

PAR

C. MERLAND

Avec portrait, Fac-simile, Musique et Dessin d'armes

SE VEND AU PROFIT DE N. PELLETIER

PRIX : 2 FRANCS

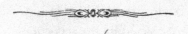

PARIS

E. DENTU, LIBRAIRE-ÉDITEUR,

Palais-Royal, 15-17-19, Galerie d'Orléans.

1876

PUBLIC LIBRARY
11 MAR 1913
OF VICTORIA

Seventeen Years with the Savages.
The Adventures of Narcisse Pelletier

Constant Merland

Introduction

'Attention all novelists, playwrights and public speakers': so concluded an article which appeared, a few months ago, in a widely circulated publication, about the imminent return to France of Narcisse Pelletier.[1] The *Univers illustré* will forgive me for not responding to its appeal. In the present circumstances I believe that the simple truth offers more interest than flights of fancy or dramatic scenes, no matter how moving. Up until now I alone have had the opportunity to read the notes taken by Pelletier himself[2] and to have long conversations with him about the seventeen years that he passed in a land inhabited by savages, but I make no other claim than that of lending him the assistance of my pen. I shall not deviate at all from the information that he has given to me; I shall take pains to retain the simplicity of his tale, without letting myself become too distracted by the reflections to which it might give rise, and without adding a great deal to it. For the most part I shall limit myself to putting a little order into muddled notes and disjointed conversations.

There is no doubt that the subject would lend itself to literary embellishment; no doubt there would be a place in it for science. But in trying to add some gloss to the picture might I not run the risk of falsifying its true colours? In discussing questions of geology and natural history, or in endeavouring to present the fauna and flora of an unknown country, should I not be afraid of relying on imprecise and uncertain data? My sole ambition is therefore limited to that of remaining a faithful narrator or, better still, a simple stenographer and modest scribe, a very humble task certainly, but one which presents the uncommon advantage of offering serious minds truth free of all the embroidery that too often distorts it.

'But are you quite sure,' some will ask, 'that what you have heard from Pelletier's lips is indeed the truth? Might your good faith not have been deceived? Were the tales you have been told not mixed with fallacy and fable? Are you sure that you have not been dealing simply with a storyteller, as those who come from afar so often are?'

In response, I believe that I can give complete reassurance to those who might have concerns of this kind. Pelletier kept his eyes open, he was a keen observer; his memory seems reliable and accurate; he is by no means seeking to draw attention to himself; he has firmly refused to take to the stage and put himself on show, even though he has been assured that it would be greatly to his financial advantage. Blessed with a simple nature and a shy manner, he speaks with a candour that comes close to naïveté. It is enough to have seen him and heard him to be convinced that lies do not flow from his pen or fall from his lips.

Seventeen years of a life passed in satisfying material and animal wants have not extinguished the finer feelings of his soul whose wellspring, as a child, had been his home and family; they may have slumbered for some little time in the midst of savage peoples, but as soon as he came into contact with civilised men they were reawakened with new vigour. We can see that as well as the interest that Pelletier's story presents there is, too, the interest attaching to the man himself.

CHAPTER 1

*Narcisse Pelletier's first year as a sailor. In 1858 he embarks
on the* Saint-Paul *for a two-year voyage. Arrival at Bombay, at
Hong Kong. Departure for Sydney. Shipwreck on Rossel Island.*

Narcisse Pelletier was born in Saint-Gilles-sur-Vie, in the department of the Vendée, on 2 January 1844.[1] His parents, honest artisans of that little town, cared for him devotedly in his early childhood and imbued him with the sound principles which guided them. As he grew older they wanted to ensure that his mind did not remain uncultivated; his time was spent at home, where he was given a family upbringing, and at the local school, where he received instruction at primary level. When he could read, write and do arithmetic, and possessed some grounding in history and geography, they thought about finding him a station in life.

Pelletier grew up looking out to sea, in the midst of a population of sailors, and listened with keen interest to the tales of their voyages to far-off places. He resolved that he too would sail the vast seas and see for himself whether the marvels they had told him about were true.

He had not yet reached his thirteenth birthday when, on 12 May 1856, he embarked at Les Sables[2] as a cabin boy, on the sloop *Eugénie*. His first voyage lasted five months. On 15 October that same year he disembarked at Luçon. Two months later he boarded the *Reine des mers*, anchored in the port of Bordeaux. On 24 May the ship left for Trieste and returned to France having visited the coast of Illyria;[3] it entered the port of Marseilles on 29 July 1857.

Not everything was rosy for a child who had passed from the gentle nurturing that he experienced in his maternal home to the harshness of life at sea. His health in the early days was keenly sensitive to the effects of a new environment; then he had to submit to a strict, sometimes brutal, discipline, devote himself to a completely new form of work during the day, and keep watch a part of the night, while making sure not to give in to sleep, for fear of the punishments that would sometimes leave their mark afterwards.

Narcisse Pelletier, more than any of the others, bore the brunt of these. The first mate on the *Reine des mers* was not content to administer the ordinary rebukes and punishments and gave him a nasty stab wound.

After such an act of brutality it was not possible for Pelletier to remain on board a ship where these methods of punishment were used. As soon as the *Reine des mers* had touched land he left the ship to embark on the *Saint-Paul*, under the command of Captain Pinard.

This time it was not a matter of a voyage of only a few months. This one was to be considerably longer; but no one could have imagined that Pelletier would be away for seventeen years. The *Saint-Paul* left for Bombay with a cargo of wine; from there it set sail for Hong Kong where it was to undertake a mission of a different nature. The gold mines of Sydney[4] were a source of great wealth to the English, but lacking the manpower to exploit them, they looked to China to fill this need. Captain Pinard appealed to the interests of the inhabitants of Hong Kong, presented to them all the advantages that they could gain from work for which the English paid generously, and ended up recruiting 317 coolies, who let themselves be seduced by the lure of soon making their fortune. It took a month to accomplish this operation, during which time Pelletier stayed on board without ever setting foot on land.

The Chinese were piled in on top of each other, and the *Saint-Paul* departed, the crew giving voice to the most joyful songs. Up until this time everything had gone well; it had been the happiest of voyages, with no bad omens to cause disquiet. Unfortunately, however, the *Saint-Paul* was slowed and almost stalled by a dead calm. As the provisions were not sufficient to feed all those on board it was necessary to reduce the rations, to the great discontent of the coolies.

When the *Saint-Paul* was in sight of the Solomon Islands the savages[5] of the country threw themselves into their canoes in great numbers and came up to the ship. In spite of the friendly signs that they were making, our sailors, who were familiar with their tricks and treachery, were uneasy and kept on their guard. These apprehensions were unfounded, except that, instead of the more solid provisions that the French would have liked to obtain, the blacks only brought them shellfish, which they paid for with handkerchiefs and other kinds of objects.

This meagre resource was very quickly exhausted, and as the *Saint-Paul* was still far from the end of its voyage it was necessary to reduce the food rations further and further. The Chinese were therefore put on half rations. Such a measure, which the circumstances made all too necessary, was taken very badly by the Chinese. They cried out in fury and threatened the French with mutiny. What could a crew of only twenty do against more than three hundred madmen? The captain resolved on a course of action. He was to have sailed around the Solomons: in order to shorten his route, he decided instead, even though it was less safe, to sail between the Islands and the Louisiade Archipelago.

The weather had changed; after the calm, big waves had risen; thick fog enveloped the *Saint-Paul*, blocking out the sun and preventing the men from taking their bearings. Three days passed in this way without the captain being able to get a clear sense of whether he was near or far from land.

He believed, however, that he had gone beyond the Louisiades and was cramming on sail when the *Saint-Paul* struck a coral reef situated in sight of Rossel Island, which is one of the islands in the archipelago. The account of this shipwreck can be found in the

Tour du Monde, 1861, 2nd half, page 81.[6] But as it is not entirely in agreement with that which Pelletier has given me, as it was in some fashion written as dictated by Captain Pinard, and as I have complete trust in Pelletier, I may be permitted to take up the story relying solely on the version given by the young sailor.

It was one o'clock in the morning. Pelletier was on watch with the first mate; the captain was in a deep sleep. They were heading into a mountain — but they mistook it for a squall. The captain, having been alerted, thought the same. He ordered the sails to be furled, the topgallants and the royals, in anticipation of imminent rain. At that moment they saw the rock against which the swell was breaking. The captain tried to tack: it was too late, his ship had struck against the crag. At the sound of the shock all the passengers woke up and went up on deck, making a great racket. In their fright they lost their heads and impeded the manoeuvres, which soon became impossible. A whale boat put into the water by the captain was carried off and broke against the rock. All they could do was to wait, amidst the greatest anxiety. At daybreak, with the *Saint-Paul* lying aslant, the ship's boats, a longboat and two dinghies, could be launched.

With the help of these craft, it was now possible to take all the coolies to a small island nearby. The crew did not take refuge there until after the last passenger had landed.

The island lay facing Rossel Island, and the natives could be seen quite clearly, a group of only ten who had gathered and were making friendly signs to the shipwrecked seamen. These men had a most distinctive appearance. They were black, and completely naked, their ears were pierced by cylindrical wooden plugs, their nasal septum, too, was pierced by a shell. One of their front teeth was missing, while their other teeth, like their lips, were blackened by the use of betel — a mixture of areca nut and leaves of the pepper plant — which they chew for a long time before adding to its effect by applying a thick paste of lime to their gums. They looked much more like fiendish creatures than human beings. The cries of the Chinese had frightened them at first, but they were soon reassured when they saw that these were cries of distress and not threatening shouts.

All the attempts to refloat the *Saint-Paul* had come to nothing; more damage occurred every minute and it was no longer possible to stay on board without risking grave danger. The following night the ship had broken up completely.

Although they were by no means reassured by the friendly displays that were being made to them, since they now realised that what lay before them was a Melanesian island — that is, they found themselves in the presence of the most inhospitable tribes in the world — the captain and the crew went on land. Necessity forced them to do so. All that could be grabbed from the debris of the wreck was a few barrels of flour, now reduced to a paste by sea water, a little salted meat and a very small quantity of tinned food. Moreover, they were completely lacking fresh water. To defend themselves in case of attack they were equipped with gunpowder and rifles, but they had no caps.

The captain disembarked with his crew not far from a stream and set up camp; from there he was able to see the Chinese left on the little island. While there remained only a small number of them, the savages, far from showing any hostile inclinations, brought coconuts and some other food to the shipwrecked men. But that night, having made numerous recruits, they made up their minds to attack those to whom they had first of all extended a helping hand now that they could see that they were in a position of strength. They grasped their opportunity when the captain, with eight or nine of his men, was taking water to the Chinese. Armed with stones of basalt, which are their only weapons, they rushed upon the unlucky few who had stayed on land. The battle was not long, or rather, it did not amount to a battle. Surrounded on all sides, the men were killed or taken prisoner. The only ones to escape their blows were Pelletier and an apprentice. Seeing that defence of any kind was impossible, they rushed into the water and, being unable to swim, they waded towards the little island, waist-deep in the water. The savages saw them and threw rocks at them, one of these rocks hitting Pelletier on the head. At the same time canoes were trying to cut off their retreat. They were about to fall victim to the ferocity of the savages when the captain picked them up in one of the boats and took them to the little island. They arrived there unaccompanied by the other sailors from the camp, to the great amazement of the Chinese who did not know the sad fate that had befallen the other men.

Emboldened by this first success, the savages, devouring with their eyes those whom they hoped to devour in reality, and believing that the sailors had no means of defence, advanced against the island, some swimming, others in pirogues. So numerous were they that the sea was quite black with them.

Their hopes were disappointed. At the approach of the enemy, the sailors, quite determined not to sell their lives cheaply, removed the nipples from the barrels of their guns and, while one shouldered his weapon to take aim at the man who was approaching, another, a brand in his hand, ignited the powder. The fusillade, in these conditions, cannot have been either intense or deadly; but it was enough to put to flight men who were quite terrified when a firearm exploded.

If the danger had been staved off, it was far from being averted altogether. Almost without resources on a small island where the sailors and the coolies were at risk of dying of hunger, and not having enough men to attack the savages who formed a strong guard, Captain Pinard had only one course of action: he would have to leave the Chinese on the little island, make for the nearest English possessions, beg for their help and return in haste to recover the poor souls who were going to be left there in direst need. In the *Tour du Monde* it was reported that once this decision was taken it was only executed with the consent of the Chinese. Pelletier affirms the opposite, insisting that it was without the knowledge of the Chinese and while they were asleep that what remained of the crew boarded the longboat. He himself had been told nothing; but seeing what was happening, he jumped on board and left with his companions.

Captain Pinard had left the Chinese most of the spoiled provisions that were able to be salvaged from the wreck, as well as the guns and the little ammunition that had been taken from it. Whatever privations they imposed upon themselves, these scant resources could not ward off death from starvation for more than a week at the most, nor did they allow them to attempt a landing on the shore and forcibly obtain the food they needed.

What became of these wretched souls? Did the Chinese succumb to their mortal fate or did they escape their sad lot? This time the *Tour du Monde* provides a faithful account of what happened to them. I shall give a brief summary of this here and wait until the following chapter to return to the cabin boy whom I abandon only briefly.

On 11 October [1858] the *Prince of Danemark*[7] took on board the six men who remained of the crew of the *Saint-Paul* [after their escape from Rossel Island]. This is what had happened to them. Six days before, believing that a small island where they had just landed was uninhabited, the men had hauled their boat up on to the beach and had gone ashore to spend the night. How great was their surprise and fright on awaking next day to see that their boat had gone! They quickly realised, when they noticed that the painter which secured it to the shore had been cut, that its disappearance was not due to a heavy swell or some other accident, but that unknown hands alone were responsible. Soon some natives came towards them and took them prisoner. They stripped them of their clothes and took them with them to the mainland. The crew felt far from easy, being kept under watch at an encampment and only receiving the most frugal and inadequate sustenance, when the *Prince of Danemark* came into sight.

Captain MacFarlane,[8] who was in command of the ship, saw the signals that the men were making, understood that they were being held prisoner by the savages and rushed to respond to their appeals. He negotiated their release and, for the payment demanded, even succeeded in getting their boat back.

Due to circumstances that there is no point in relating, the *Prince of Danemark* did not arrive at Fort-de-France[9] until 25 December 1858.

Two days later a ship with Captain Pinard on board left from there to retrieve the wretched castaways. But more than three months had passed since they had been abandoned, and all those taking part in the expedition were greatly concerned. Their fears were only too well founded. On 5 January 1859 the French neared Rossel Island and saw, on the reef where the *Saint-Paul* had been shipwrecked, its bowsprit and stern. On the island there reigned the silence of death.

Searches soon revealed the remains of two bodies covered over by pebbles and the littered shells from the shellfish that the Chinese had lived on.

The next day the commander came across a navigable river in which he anchored. Then, arming several boats for war, he gave orders to those in command to establish communication with the natives, to act with great caution, to gather any information they could and, finally, to try to save those who had managed to escape the terrible disaster of the *Saint-Paul*.

In spite of the signs of friendship which the French made to them, the natives, at their approach, fled in fear, even leaving behind their pirogues, which the French were very careful not to destroy.

As they were still travelling upriver, our sailors caught sight of a young man who was naked and standing waist-high in the water. Without uttering so much as a word, he made rallying signs and signalled his distress. This behaviour, so different from that of the natives they had met up until then, led them to think that they had come upon one of the castaways from the *Saint-Paul*.

It was indeed a poor coolie who, as soon as he had been picked up by our sailors, conveyed in a word the dreadful denouement of the tragedy from which he had escaped: '*All dead!*' he cried out [in English]. Then, with the help of signs and some words that he uttered in English, he made it understood that he and four of his companions — one of whom, he thought, was the master carpenter from the *Saint-Paul* — were the sole survivors of the massacre of the white men.

Knowing all the treacherousness, deceitfulness and cruelty of the savages, the shipwreck victims had remained on their little island for as long as they had been able to find some foods to live on. Using ingenious methods, they had managed to get themselves drinkable water by collecting what fell as rain and storing it in improvised containers. They had also obtained food from the shellfish beds adjoining the island. But there came a day when they ran out of everything at once. Two of these poor wretches having died of hunger (no doubt those whose bodies had been found) and the others now being threatened with the same fate, they were obliged to respond to the advances being made to them, but only with the deepest reservations.

The savages introduced themselves as friends when they came over to the island. They only took three or four coolies with them at a time and having put them in a place where their companions could not see them and where their cries could not be heard they massacred them with a dreadful and refined cruelty. To make their flesh tender and more succulent, they killed them by beating them with sticks, massaging every part of their bodies as they did so.[10]

It was in this way, successively and as they needed them, that they sacrificed so many victims. Only five men, who had been adopted by chiefs, escaped death.

Whatever indignation they felt at this savage ferocity, the French did not let their anger show: they were too intent on saving the poor souls whose existence they had just been told about not to conceal their feelings until the end.

Their boat was travelling down the river to rejoin the ship, which was anchored at its mouth, when suddenly they were attacked by a hail of rocks accompanied by frightful shouting. Fearing that the islanders would try boarding, the men rushed for their knives, their guns and their pistols. After several gunshots, the savages, who had hidden behind trees to avoid being hit by projectiles, fled, screaming even louder. Our men were keen to pursue them. But as they came nearer the bank the river was no longer navigable and, since the commander's order not to venture into a blind alley was categorical, they had to put off their desire for vengeance until the next day. Repeated shouting, interspersed with the sounds that the savages made by blowing into a conch shell they had made into a horn, could be heard throughout the night. It was clear that this was a call to arms and that the cannibals wanted to assemble all their forces for the next day's attack.

In anticipation of this our sailors again went back up the river, quite determined this time to exact terrible reprisals if the savages dared to take the offensive.

One of the boats moored not far from a village where, the day before, attempts to come to an understanding had not borne fruit. Coming under attack when they were getting ready to renew these efforts, the men who had gone on land regained their boat and, rejoining the other craft, made for the opposite side. The greeting they received there was far from friendly, but did not immediately take on a hostile character. Whatever means they tried to get the savages to hand over the prisoners from the *Saint-Paul*, it was impossible to get them to come to an arrangement.

Seeing that any new moves would remain fruitless, the captain's only thought now was to wreak bloody vengeance on the culprits for the massacre they had committed.

As the boats made towards a village that could be seen ahead, the enemy, from the bank where its forces were positioned, hurled stones at them but without causing much harm to those in the boats. During this time other savages, armed with pikes, made challenging gestures, while their enraged wives, threshing the water with long staves and uttering cries that were not even human, seemed to be saying to the men that they must give no quarter.

The French then armed themselves with their rifles and, uncovering a piece of artillery, opened fire on their attackers.

At the sound of the blast the savages took fright and fled, a cry of distress replacing the cries of provocation which they were proffering a few moments before; then they disappeared into the woods and not one of them was to be seen thereafter.

A group of twenty of the French disembarked and vainly went in pursuit of them, but they could not catch up with them. They then carried out their search in every dwelling in the village. The sight of a cross painted on a rod which went through the end of a pole fixed in the ground made them think that this village could have served as a prison to the castaways and that perhaps they were still there. Their search was fruitless; but they found, piled up in storehouses, all the clothing of the massacred Chinese, which they seized. Not being able to take their revenge in any other way, they then set fire to all the huts in the village, which were devoured by the flames in a few seconds.

The expedition seemed to be finished without achieving the desired result. However, before leaving, the sailors went over to the other side of the river with little hope of having any more luck. They saw no one. Distant moaning was the only sound that they could hear. The boats then regained the ship, which headed for the open sea and set sail for Sydney.

What became of the four wretched men whom the mission had tried in vain to rescue?[11] No one can say, but there is certainly reason to fear that the efforts made to save them may have had quite the opposite result. It would be a miracle indeed if, given their vindictive and cruel nature, the savages, in their rage, had not made those they had spared up until then submit to some dreadful torture.

Let us now turn back to Narcisse Pelletier and take up his story again from the time he boards the longboat of the *Saint-Paul*.

CHAPTER 2

Arrival at [Cape] Flattery. Pelletier abandoned in this land. His
despair. Meeting with a native who adopts him as his son.

The longboat left with the rest of the crew of the *Saint-Paul*, which comprised only nine men.[1] Although reduced by more than half its personnel, the provisions it carried on board were quite insufficient for a crossing of nearly three hundred leagues. They consisted of a dozen cans of food, a few kilograms of flour and a small supply of water contained in three pairs of seamen's boots. The rest of the provisions and the two whale boats were left for the Chinese.

During the day the boat was in a strait within sight of an island where a landing was made. There the crew managed to procure for themselves a supply of shellfish. At three o'clock in the afternoon they set off again and sailed somewhat aimlessly southwards, without seeing any other ships.

After two or three days the small quantity of provisions the sailors had brought with them was almost exhausted. There remained only a little flour from which they made a paste with salt water, drying it in the sun before eating it. Soon the ill effects caused by hunger began to be felt. To appease this vital need the sky came to their assistance. Exhausted birds came to rest on board and could be taken by hand; but as the sailors had no fire it was again to the star that gives us our light that the task of roasting them was entrusted. This required, however, much more time than it usually takes when the cooking of game is entrusted to an oven or the spit over a hearth. After plucking the birds, our poor famished men laid them out to dry in the burning rays of the sun for thirty hours, and it was when they were well dried rather than cooked that they ingested them. With no fishing tackle, they were unable to procure for themselves any of the fish nursed by the sea.

Nevertheless, they would have kept themselves alive without making a landing if they had not completely run out of fresh water. Reduced to drinking seawater and even urine to quench their thirst, they resolved to land on the first shores they came to, at the risk of falling among man-eaters, and of escaping the cannibals of Melanesia only to encounter monsters who were just as horrible and just as fierce. As two of the men, one succumbing a few days later, were close to death, there was no room for hesitation. It was better to brave whatever dangers awaited them than to remain in such a pitiful position any longer.

After twelve days of the cruellest waiting, finally, by the light of the moon, a mountain covered with tall trees was sighted. It was Cape Flattery in Endeavour Land[2] situated in the north-east of Australia. The men landed at night and went immediately in search of the food and water that they needed so badly. Only a small amount was found, which the crew shared between themselves.

At daybreak the presence of the sailors was betrayed by a dog which came towards them with terrifying howls. They killed it with a blow, but they left it where it was since they had no fire and it could not be cooked by the sun; and since they were revolted, too, by the idea of eating an unclean animal and their thirst was even greater than their hunger. They were only able to find themselves some fruit that was still green and some shellfish. They lived like that for three or four days but, with fresh water again lacking, the decision was taken to return to the first place where water had been found. Before they reached there a large number of savages, armed with arrows, appeared before them. Although they made signs to them to approach, our men were afraid of them and hastened to embark. The savages then fired several arrows at them but they did not find their mark.

When night had fallen, and as they were feeling their thirst more keenly than ever, the captain ordered the men to return to land and again to make for the place where they had first found a small amount of water. They set down about a league away from the spot where the first landing had been made. All their searching was in vain and the sailors returned without bringing back a single drop.

The captain sent some of the men back again, ordering them to follow the shore and to find their way back to the spring from which they had previously drawn water. They set off. Long hours passed and they had still not returned. Night began spreading her veil over the earth. The waiting continued. The anxiety became intense when finally, at about eight o'clock in the evening, the party reappeared, bringing only some muddy, brackish water.

This is what had happened to them.

They had indeed made their way following the captain's instructions. But, after an hour's walking, they had been stopped by a little river which, now swollen by the rising tide, had prevented them going any further. It was from this river that they had drawn the water which they had brought back with them.

For all of them the night was filled with sadness. The future, and a future which was very near, appeared to them in the gloomiest light. The death rattle could be heard coming from one of the sailors; the others were filled with terrible anxiety.

When daylight came the captain declared to his crew that it was necessary to do some exploring on land, that they would perhaps encounter some European settlements, and that this course of action was almost their only remaining hope of salvation. Consequently the sailors set off, leaving in the boat only two men, who were completely incapable of moving from it: one was the wretched soul whose pangs of death were continuing on, the other a poor devil with no strength left in him.

They made their way along the shore, always heading in the same direction. No doubt they hoped that it would be easy to cross the obstacle they had encountered the previous day as the tide was low.

Pelletier could only follow along far behind his travelling companions. He pushed on, barefooted, under a blazing sun, and the injuries that he had sustained when he had been pursued by the savages of Rossel Island caused him such terrible pain that he was forced to exercise great caution and slow his pace. Tormented by thirst, he did not want to lose track of the men, hoping to meet up with them at the place where the water was. They did find water eventually, but so little that there was scarcely enough for them to quench their thirst.

When Pelletier got there the men were pressed so tightly around a hole not wider than three metres in circumference that it was impossible for him to find a space for himself. Water was seeping out at the bottom of the hole but so little that, when the sailors surrounding the hole had moved away, there was none left. 'Stay here,' they said to Pelletier, 'the well has been drained but it hasn't dried up. Before long the water will begin to seep out again and you will be able to quench your thirst in comfort. In the meantime we are going to look for some fruit. We'll pick you up again when we return.'

Pelletier followed the advice that had just been given to him. But the water did not well up again and the sailors did not reappear. As nothing else was happening there, he turned on his tracks and made off in the direction of where the longboat should be; the sea had risen and the little river that he had crossed at low tide was no longer fordable. While waiting to be able to cross it, he returned to the waterhole, which still remained dry.

Exhausted, tormented by hunger and thirst, he lay down to sleep, despair filling his heart. But drowsiness overcame him and he was not long in falling asleep. When he awoke the tide was low and he could cross the river without difficulty. Hope then returned, and for a moment he thought he was saved. He would certainly meet up again with his companions, from whom he had been separated all night, share with them the fruits that they had gathered, drink the water that they had obtained and find safety and refuge aboard the longboat.

With this thought in mind, he hastened his steps and soon came to the place where the longboat had been moored. But it was not to be seen, nor could he make out any sign of a boat in the distance when he looked out to sea.

While he had been harbouring these illusions the longboat had left, abandoning him alone in an unknown land. What was to become of him now? We can understand the anguish he must have felt when we reflect on the scenario he had before him. To die of hunger and thirst, to become the prey of fierce beasts or to be eaten by the savages, such were the dreadful alternatives that seemed to be in store for the poor child. Even the strongest of souls would have been profoundly downcast at the prospect. Narcisse Pelletier was only fifteen years old.[3] He found resignation and courage in his faith. He threw himself on his knees, pleading for help from on high, asking God, if he had to die, to save his soul. Then, getting up again after a fervent prayer, he walked on, at random, with no real goal. He did not even know the name of the land that he trod and he followed the footprints that the natives had left in the sand.

The first living being that he set eyes upon belonged to the canine race. Dogs are very common in Endeavour Land. Most of them are in their wild state, but some are domesticated. The one coming towards Pelletier and sniffing him was of the latter kind.

But the young cabin boy, who subsequently became acquainted with the dog, did not know at that moment that the animal he saw before him was harmless. Fearing its approach, he went on the defensive and threatened it with the stick he had in his hand.

The frightened dog took flight and Pelletier, seeing that he had got rid of it, went on his way. He kept his eyes pinned on all the trees in the hope of finding some fruit to appease his hunger. Finally he caught sight of one covered with red berries, which the natives call *mongals*.[4] The berries were not yet ripe, and to get an ample supply of them it would have been necessary to climb the tree that bore them, which Pelletier was unable to do in the extremely debilitated state in which he found himself. It was with great difficulty that he succeeded in picking some of them. Despite their unpleasant taste and their bitterness, he ate them greedily and his strength was a little restored as a result.

He had left the beach to strike inland. Not far from the shore there was a mountain where some beaten paths could be seen. On he went in that direction, but the thorns scattered along the paths lacerated his feet so that he could only proceed with the greatest difficulty. When darkness had fallen, obscuring the path he was travelling along, he renewed his prayers to God and propped himself up against a tree to pass the night. At that moment heavy rain started falling. His clothes, which only consisted of trousers and a shirt, were soon soaked. The next day he started off again, but he was in such a state of exhaustion that, for all his courage, he was by now unable to continue much further. It was then that he saw three women, who were entirely naked. The women, in turn having caught sight of him, were very frightened. They took flight and rushed off to rejoin their husbands who were in the woods, and told them of the strange encounter that they had just made.

While not greatly reassured by the sight of them, Pelletier did not know if he ought to rejoice or despair about their disappearance, since he was set to die of fatigue and starvation if nobody came to his rescue. But then, half an hour later, he heard slow steps coming towards the sandy hollow where he found himself. It was two men, armed with arrows,[5] who were walking with the utmost caution. When they were within reach, they addressed Pelletier, who, naturally, could not understand them. These two men were of middle age. One of them was horrible to behold and, in any other circumstance, Pelletier would have tried to hide from his sight. But this was the moment of reckoning, and besides, flight was now impossible. He therefore made signs to them to approach. Seeing clearly that they had nothing to fear if they did so, as he could barely stand, they responded to his overtures. When they were close to him Pelletier tried to make them understand that he was abandoned and that he was dying of hunger and thirst. The two savages were brothers-in-law. The man who was soon to become his adoptive father was not moved by feelings of compassion alone; he also placed certain conditions on his assistance. Pelletier was holding a small tin cup. He asked him for it and, having received it, he passed it to his brother-in-law. Understanding that this was a powerful means of winning them over, Pelletier also offered them his white handkerchief.

From this moment the alliance was made: it was never to be broken. In exchange for the presents that they had received, they gave him water, held out their hands to him to help him walk and tried to make him understand that they were going to give him something to eat. They took him to the spot where their wives were hidden. Maademan, one of the brothers-in-law, had two wives, one old and the other young, both abducted from a neighbouring tribe. He had not yet had children by them. When they found themselves in the presence of the new arrival, they were terrified. Nothing could make them overcome the fear that such a strange figure instilled in them. They wondered what kind of a man it could be and what purpose brought him to these parts. Without the assurances made to them by their husbands that the individual whom they saw would do them no harm and that there was no danger in approaching him, they would have taken flight again and hidden in the woods.

The two savages hurried to bring Pelletier fruit, including

coconuts that the sea had thrown up on the shore with other debris. The cabin boy's stomach was so weakened that he was not able to tolerate the coconuts and, as the other fruits were not of sufficient quantity, Maademan and his wives went off to get an ample supply of them. The women soon returned, bringing fruit that Pelletier was able to digest. Maademan did not return until evening: he had been on the beach to make sure that Pelletier was indeed alone and that no trap was being laid for him. Although he had not seen anyone, he was ill at ease. So, for fear of an attack by night, he moved Pelletier away from the shore to pass the night in the middle of the woods.

They left together and lay down near a big fire which they had lit, as they are accustomed to doing, less to keep from getting cold than to ward off the mosquitoes.

At daybreak, while Pelletier was still sleeping, Maademan and his brother-in-law got up without making a sound and left him deep in sleep.

Finding himself alone when he awoke, Pelletier had the most gloomy thoughts. Why had those who had received him so well the day before abandoned him the next day? Were the signs of friendship that he had received from them a ruse to hide their intentions? Had they left with the intention of enlisting their friends, killing him, sharing the spoils and perhaps using his body to make a great feast? With such thoughts crossing his mind he burst into tears and again called on divine protection.

The cabin boy was mistaken: the two savages were on the contrary filled with the best intentions. They only had gone away for a few moments in order to go and get his breakfast, which was to consist of fruit that they had put in the earth to hurry its ripening.

Pelletier arrived in Uutaalnganu territory well into the dry season and this comment about force-ripening ties in with information Chase provides about the Wongai plum:

'Most favoured of these late dry fruitings is the *muungkal*, the Wongai plum (*Manilkara kauki*) [*muungkala*]. It is found only along the beaches and river estuaries, and it provides huge crops of fruit. It was the appearance of this major food which allowed population concentrations of over 100 people at the one site in order to carry out ceremonies. The scheduling of such important events was not totally at the mercy of the ripening: turtles were gathered and kept alive by tethering on the beach and by being turned over and placed in shady places. The *muungkal* could be force-ripened by burying in wrappings of leaves of certain trees (e.g. *Euroschinus falcatus*)[6] or else preserved by drying the ripe fruit in bundles in treeforks.'[7]

Chase adds: 'the bundle is buried in the ground (sand, usually). It takes about 4 days to ripen them (so I was informed).' As well as the species named above, plants whose leaves are used to wrap the unripe fruit for burying are *yaanchan* (*Premna corymbosa*), *uuthi* (*Exocarpus latifolius*), *ancha* (*Pittosporum venulosum*), and *mathan* (*Celtis philippinensus*).[8]

Pelletier had in turn arisen, and ran along the shore without seeing anyone. His two night-time companions had seen him and were indeed making signs of friendship to him, but he did not see them. When he had recognised them, he responded to them as best he could, and both he and the two men eagerly rushed to greet each other. Once they had met up with him again the savages gave Pelletier as much fruit as he needed, and Maademan, who had no children, adopted him as his son and gave him the name of Amglo.[9] The three women then came up and Pelletier, wishing to pay his debt of gratitude to his new family, took them to the place where the crew had gone to quench their thirst, and where they had left several blankets. The savages seized them, shouting out with joy and again making the most vigorous displays of friendship to Pelletier. On seeing these declarations of affection, whose sincerity he could no longer doubt, all fear was banished from his heart.

As Pelletier was still very weak, Maademan wanted him to stay and rest for two days. He entrusted him to the care of his wives and went to inform his tribe, which at the time was camped two or three leagues away, of the adoption that he had just made. Pelletier having regained his strength, on Maademan's return they all set off for the place on the shore where the tribe had gathered. When they arrived, the women and children, who had never seen a white man before, were very frightened and hid themselves. Little by little, however, they gained confidence and, curiosity getting the better of their fear, the women came forward. At the sight of a young and beardless face they were convinced that the person they had before them was one of their own sex and two of them, who for a moment found themselves alone with the new arrival, wanted to make certain of this. On seeing their mistake, they burst into laughter and took themselves off very quickly.

While going on their way, Maademan and his brother-in-law had obtained an abundant supply of fish using their arrows. They gave some of them to Pelletier and they did not disagree with him too badly. However it took him quite a long time to become accustomed to the diet of the savages. He got used to it in the end and, little by little, he completely regained his health and strength; and little by little, too, he took on all the ways of the people with whom he was living. After a certain time all that distinguished him from them was the colour of his skin and the shirt and trousers which covered his body. It was not long before this last feature disappeared. One day while he was bathing, the savages tore up his clothes and shared out the shreds of material to use as a decoration for their foreheads.

So there he was, he, too, in the primitive state. It is no longer the cabin boy Narcisse Pelletier who will be the subject of our discussion but Amglo, citizen of the tribe of Ohantaala. His personality will often recede into the background as we turn to the description of the customs, habits and beliefs of tribes among whom civilisation has not yet penetrated. A curious study, then, whose elements had been lacking until today and which certainly deserves to gain the attention of the public.

CHAPTER 3

Endeavour land.[1] *Natives of the country, their ways and customs.*

The land where Pelletier was to spend long years is by no means uniform in appearance over its whole extent. I shall only be able to give a very succinct description of it as his tribe, although nomadic, barely travelled over an area of more than twenty square leagues and Pelletier, from whose dictation I am writing these lines, never penetrated very far into the interior of the country.

This reflects a pattern of movement recorded by anthropologists. Chase describes how in the dry season 'countrymen' lived together in 'main camps', possibly of 80 people, at sites with a good water supply. From there they could disperse periodically in smaller groups to exploit the resources of their estates. The wet season saw the congregation of even larger numbers of people in the few wet season camps when movement was restricted to a quite limited area.[2]

Thomson had earlier described the very limited range of movement of people at Port Stewart on Princess Charlotte Bay throughout the time of his fieldwork there in 1928 and 1929. Despite the intermittent and brief excursions of small groups their 'headquarters' remained at the Stewart River estuary.[3] Chase and Sutton note that Thomson's observations about 'the remarkable sedentism of the coastal groups from this area of coastal Cape York … is confirmed by present-day informants who spent their younger days in traditional camps. Specific camping sites for a group over an annual period had a total range of only several kilometres of beachfront and immediate hinterland.'[4]

The coast is very flat so that a large expanse of sand and rocks is left exposed when the tide is out. It is edged by magnificent trees whose luxuriant vegetation suggests that the soil in which they are growing is very rich and would provide vast potential for cultivation. The roots of these trees partly protrude from the earth and afford shelter against the rain.

The mountains, which are only a short distance away, are even more wooded. There are fir trees, but only a small number of them, as well as palm trees and many other trees whose family I could not even begin to identify.

Effective exploitation of the coastal environment required thorough knowledge of its resources. Chase notes that such knowledge is 'extremely detailed amongst older people' and that he, together with other researchers, 'has collected detailed ethnoclassificatory information on 400 plants, and as well, birds, fish and reptiles which occur in the region.'[5]

Some being of a heavy, hard wood, others of a wood that is soft and light, they could be used for very different purposes. Their leaves fall during the period of extreme heat. A lot of dead branches fall from them as well, which means that the natives do not have to cut wood to make fire. If there are fires in summer, there is no snow and ice in winter. The year can be divided into two seasons that are little different in temperature but have completely different meteorological conditions. In the first rain is rare, in the second it falls very heavily.

The dry season lasts approximately from July to November, the wet season from December to June, although coastal peoples in fact divide the year into six named seasons.

The quadrupeds and the birds are mostly to be found in the mountains, which are therefore inhabited by tribes of hunters. The vegetation, generally very pleasing, is not however uniform. There are areas where only bracken grows; others are swampy and inhabited by crocodiles. The wild beasts against which man, in some regions of our globe, wages a sometimes dangerous battle are not to be found here.

In fact the coastal region of Cape York is home to some very dangerous animals. Chase records the attitude to the land and its dangers of Uutaalnganu people when they made return visits to their homelands:

'The land, long unoccupied throughout much of the area, was seen as having "come wild". Old tracks and camping grounds were overgrown and the neglect of occupation sites and graves was thought to make the country dangerous. It was threatening, though familiar, land. Returns were often marked by emotional events. Graves were cried over, apologies made to the spirits of dead relations, and the country was fired in order to clean it up and to place again a living Aboriginal signature on it. People moved carefully in long-deserted areas. Forces which might have been angered by the desertion were likely to strike back in revenge through such natural agents as crocodiles, snakes and other dangerous species.'[6]

The domesticated animals that help us to till the soil, serve as mounts and pull our carts, give us their milk or their flesh for our sustenance, or offer us their fleece so that we may make garments from them are not met with either.

Snakes are very common there and of a wide range of species. There are huge snakes as well as very small ones. It is only the latter which are venomous and their bite is sometimes fatal.

Kellaway and Thomson make the following observations about indigenous attitudes to the King Brown Snake Pseudechis australis[7] and to the taipan Oxyuranus scutellatus:

'Pseudechis australis, next to Demansia olivacea, is probably the commonest large venomous snake on Cape York Peninsula. … It is aggressive and when molested will fight savagely, rarely attempting to escape.

'It is well known to the aborigines on the east coast as "Ngumai."[8] Although they fear it as they do all snakes, venomous or otherwise, they do not regard it as being nearly as dangerous as another snake, "tai-pan," [*thaypan*][9] which shares its habitat.'[10]

Thomson notes that: 'The natives hold the taipan in great dread, and it appears to have been responsible for many deaths among them. It is a dangerous and aggressive reptile, having a very long curved fang, and yielding a large quantity of venom.'[11] Thomson promoted the word 'taipan' as 'an excellent vernacular name for the species',[12] and the Kuuku Ya'u term *thay'pan*, as he transcribed it, is now in common usage. He notes that this species is 'undoubtedly the largest, and probably the most dangerous, venomous snake found in Australia',[13] so Merland's statement that it is only the small snakes that are venomous is incorrect, unless he is comparing such snakes to the pythons (see Chapter 9).[14]

An insect whose bite is no less unbearable, even though it is not as dangerous, is the mosquito because, if precautions were not taken to ward them off, one would not be able to sleep at night. They are present in countless numbers.

Hale and Tindale[15] describe the considerable nuisance posed by mosquitoes:

'Wings of large birds provide fans with which flies and mosquitoes are warded off … Smoke fires provide more efficient protection against the hordes of mosquitoes and sand flies, and on a still night many natives were seen carrying a smouldering root or stick with which to repel the little pests. These insects worry the natives far more than flies, and at times prevent them from sleeping; their abundance may be appreciated when it is stated that in some of the riverine jungle areas the writers experienced difficulty in aiming their guns owing to the obscuring of the sights by the hovering clouds of mosquitoes, which were also attacking all exposed parts of the body.'[16]

Further details about animals will be kept until the chapter about hunting and fishing.

Endeavour Land is called '*Pantiaquina*' by the savages.[17] It numbers many tribes, but these tribes are very small. There were barely more than thirty men in Pelletier's tribe. Its name was '*Ohantaala*'.[18]

The patrilineal estate, the locus of what Merland here refers to as the 'tribe', in fact the patrilineal estate group, was the core territorial division for daily living, material and spiritual, as Chase explains:

'These estates contained the myth and totem sites which linked an individual to land as territory, to the life forces of people and the environment, and to the remote past and as well as a score or so of named feature sites (resource, geographic feature). At the level of estate, individuals had primary rights over particular resource concentration sites e.g. yam scrubs, fruit-tree groves, bird nesting sites and shell beds.'[19]

Each tribe has its own name; but those who belong to them only have two names collectively: 'Cayen' and 'Caapei', which alternate from tribe to tribe. Thus, according to whether they are adjacent, if the inhabitants of the first tribe are called *Cayen*, those of the second will be *Caapei*, those of the third *Cayen*, those of the fourth *Caapei*, and so on for the rest. Pelletier was a *Cayen*.

These are the equivalents of the exogamous moiety names *kuyan* and *kaapay*.[20] The situation described above by Pelletier can be visualised from Rigsby and Chase's description of the landscape and seascape as 'a checkerboard of estates of the moieties'[21] and Chase's mapping, and maps, of the alternating blocks of *kuyan* and *kaapay* territories down the coastal strip make this even more apparent.[22] The moiety system, which has continuing relevance to Lockhart River people, is regarded as 'a fact of nature'.[23] It is given symbolic expression in myths involving trickery, which oppose *kuyan* and *kaapay* in the form of Cassowary and Emu or Dugong and Wallaby. Chase notes: 'A person's moiety is said to be manifested in a variety of physical traits: hair shape, physiognomy, and lines of the palm of the hand. The geographic landscape likewise exhibits distinctive moiety features: the contrasts between light and shade, the angularity of branches on certain tree species, the shape of hills, and so on.'[24]

This difference in group names could suggest a difference in races, but that is certainly not the case. Their anthropology is absolutely the same: an average height similar to our own; poorly developed muscles; protruding abdomen; black skin with a slightly yellowish tinge; eyes that are frequently bloodshot; flattened nose; lips that are broad rather than thick; large mouth; prominent cheekbones; hair that is not frizzy and is generally cut short, but is worn full-length by some of them, and similarly for the beard; receding forehead; head covered in lice; every part of the body and every feature adding up to a whole that is horribly ugly and revoltingly dirty. Such is the very unflattering but faithful portrait which we have before us;[25] but it does not prevent both sexes from seeking to please and being inclined to vanity.

By contrast with what we see among savages of other countries, there are no castes to be found here, no social stratification, and no chiefs; everyone is on a footing of complete and utter equality. If the tribe possesses a common territory, individual property is unknown.

This statement conveys no idea of the strict sense of ownership in relation to estate lands, including adjoining areas of sea, and rights to the use of the products derived from them. Even the information Sir John Ottley gleaned from Pelletier stressed the importance of ownership of land. He writes, 'We gathered that the various tribes of blacks inhabiting this part of the world hold very little intercourse with each other. Each tribe occupies its own tract of country and any intrusion on this is promptly resented, quarrels being apparently very frequent.'[26]

Rigsby and Chase discuss in detail the relationship of Sandbeach People to land (and sea) and the property rights, rights *in rem*, that flow from this. This relationship derives from the spiritual connection to a specific country of origin that is linked to beliefs about the original creative acts of the Stories as they are known, or spirit people, in the landscape, their continuing presence there together with the spirits of ancestors, and to the concept of a spiritual alter ego that comes from a specific place after conception and returns there after death. They write:

'People's rights *in rem* to country derive from their spiritual relationship to it *in animam* and depend upon it. This provides the root of their traditional title to land.

. . .

'...specific groups of people have specific rights in specific tracts of land 'as against the world'. These include rights to live on the land, to use and enjoy it in various ways, to speak of and present themselves as its owners and to exclude others in various ways from exercising the same rights.'[27]

Chase shows how recognition of estate membership — 'belonging to country' — still operates today as 'a strong ideological force' at Lockhart River even though countryman groups no longer live on their estates and may visit them very infrequently.[28] He writes:

'Territories form the basis of social identity, and this can be expressed in a variety of actual living arrangements. Aboriginal people conceive of a system of absentee landlordism just as we do, and "ownership/custodianship" on the one hand, and "occupancy" on the other, are entirely different dimensions. Indeed, estates can be visited nightly in dreams, just as realistically as physically visiting an area. Thus, to see a population no longer actually living in the bush in small groups, does not mean "detribalisation" or "non-traditionalism". Accordingly, one can make little understanding of the social processes of Cape York Aboriginal communities unless this territorial basis for social organisation is understood.'[29]

Anyone who comes along can cut and hew and take whatever pleases him, without any fear of being prevented from doing so. The products of the land are for everyone; no-one can appropriate whatever it might be by claiming any special rights.

This is a misconception either on the part of Pelletier, which seems unlikely given his long residence, or Merland. Rigsby and Chase, in their discussion of Sandbeach People's property and usufruct rights in their land and sea country, write:

'In past times, the sense of property was also well developed [as it still is], and owners regularly monitored their land and sea country to see who was on it or had been on it. Outsiders were expected to present themselves to the resident owners and to make themselves and their intentions known. If they did not, the residents assumed that they were up to no good, that they were there to use resources without permission or to bring harm to someone. If owners discovered the tracks or signs of outsiders where they did not belong, they might then send a messagestick to the offenders and invite them to come give an account of themselves. Such a meeting could result in a spearfight. Failure to account for their actions could lead to a well-aimed spear without warning. If owners caught outsiders in the act of trespass and unsanctioned use of resources, they would throw spears at them both to drive them away and to punish them.

'People also speak of fish and game as property even when it is free ranging and not under anyone's control or possession. Owners expect to be given a share of fish and game taken from their land or sea country, and the same pattern obtained in the classic situation.'[30]

No-one plants and no-one sows. The riches of the soil are not exploited by human hand; what man takes from it for his own use grows by itself. There is not a house, a cottage, a cabin or even a hut in which to shelter from bad weather or to serve, in case of illness, as a comforting abode. There is the earth on which to rest one's head, the vault of the sky for a roof: nothing more is needed. Animals have their dens, even reptiles hollow out a place to hide away; here it is only man who abandons himself completely to what nature provides. In the quite exceptional case of torrential rain, if he does not take his usual shelter under the roots of trees he will cover his body with large palm leaves or else bend and bind together some bushy branches over his forehead. These are the only measures which his skills and intelligence suggest to him.

This is a curious observation of Pelletier's, and one *The Times* also reports him as making,[31] as various types of shelters have been well-recorded for the area, the type varying with the season.[32] These could be 'simple windbreaks and platform roofs to more solid structures of bark and leaf thatched huts which were used for protection in the wet season from the rain and the clouds of mosquitoes'.[33] In their article, Hale and Tindale include two photographs of shelters at Port Stewart noting that the people there 'erect dome-shaped huts ten to twelve feet in diameter, covered with bark and shaded with boughs'.[34]

Never in its wildest dreams has the most radical socialism pursued such an ideal.

The absence of land ownership is not exclusive of any portable personal property. Every man has his own little set of tools which belongs to him personally. The canoes are not in this category: they belong to those who made them, rarely to one individual.

Rigsby was told by one informant that canoes were owned by their maker-owners: 'A borrower had to ask and get permission to use a canoe and its gear, and the person who took another's canoe without asking could expect to have a spear thrown at them with no warning. The borrower also had to give a substantial share [of their catch] to the owner'.[35] Personal property included items such as spears, firesticks, axes and dillybags, which individuals made for their own use. Husbands and wives could and did share each other's possessions (subject to gender restrictions).[36]

Private property of the kind that I have just described, or that which comes from hunting, fishing or the gathering of fruit, is by no means always respected. It is not hard to find thieves in Endeavour Land, and they will often take for themselves the fruits of other people's labour. Lazy people, beggars, the old and the infirm — those who do not seek to provide for their own needs and those who are quite unable to do so — are found there as they are everywhere. And as everywhere, too, you will meet with compassionate souls, helping hands, as well as hearts that are hard and unfeeling. Many stand out because of their highly intemperate speech or their mocking attitude. The truth is therefore by no means to be found on everyone's lips.

Although moral qualities are not treated with disdain, it is physical prowess that is most highly prized. Expertise in making canoes and arrows, and the skill shown in hunting, fishing and physical exercise, especially dancing, are the most powerful claims to esteem. But this esteem does not confer either rights or authority.

Chase writes of the high status of dugong hunters, and other forms of acquired status in Uutaalnganu society:

'In this region certain older men acquired great prestige for expertise in tracking and capturing dugong. This potentially dangerous hunting activity required not just a keen eye and physical skill, but as well a considerable knowledge of dugong behaviour and the various bush medicines (*upari*) and small rituals needed to make a capture. These men were *pama watayichi* ("man for dugong") and were accorded the honour after death of having their graves marked with arranged piles of dugong bones. A man might also be *wulmpamu*, a "boss" for ceremonial performance. In addition to having deep ceremonial knowledge, such men were credited with healing powers. During initiation ceremonies, they acted as singers, drum players and performance managers.

'Both of these categories belong to the wider classification of *pama mukana* ("big men", "men of importance"), whose words are listened to, and who can be influential in general day-to-day decisions. Some men, in addition to acquiring these prestigious titles, were also *pama yikan* or people with great skill at using the long hardwood spears which are made for both fighting and hunting. When associated with a quick temper, a "big man" could be seen as extremely dangerous and to be avoided. Older women could accumulate status through becoming "boss" for songs and dances associated with the *wuungka* widowhood ceremonies, and the supportive *chaawul* ceremonies which accompany initiation ceremonies. Individual women could be recognised for high personal qualities in everyday life, but they could not be formally classified as *mukana*, or "big".'[37]

Kylie Tennant reports the words of Billy Daniels, an Uutaalnganu man who showed her the beach graves of 'the great hunters' of 'the old time' at Cape Direction.[38]

"'These feller," Billy said, "rich men. Not rich in money. They strong — good spears. Rich by wallaby, turtle, dugong. This thing I tell." He meditated, trying to find the right words. "These rich men, strong hunters, they say — 'Do not forget our law. Do not forget.' I tell the young men. We need a thousand pound for our co-operative.[39] But if we have a thousand pounds we not as rich as these men were rich.'"[40]

Merland also refers to dancing as a way of earning respect, and dancing is still today, now in the introduced form of 'Island-style dance', a way of gaining status.[41]

I have just mentioned the notion of moral qualities; among savage peoples there is a sentiment which no one, I imagine, would ever have suspected. Seeing them in a state of nature, living a completely animal existence, who would not have thought to find sexual promiscuity and a complete absence of modesty? In fact quite the opposite is true; the feeling of modesty happens to be even more pronounced than in civilised societies.

Men and women, except for spouses, barely go near each other. The distance separating them is almost always at least eight metres. Several times throughout the day they will move far enough away not to be seen, and the women will disappear at the slightest indisposition, not returning until any sign of their condition has ceased. There are never any improper conversations, never the slightest indecency of behaviour or tone of voice. It is quite true that this extreme reserve is also imposed by another sentiment, that of fear.

Chase describes the category of closest kin who are referred to as *kuunchi ngathama puuya*, 'relations of my own heart/life force'. Those who fall into this category are one's parents and siblings, parents' siblings and their children, and grandparents and their siblings. 'Behaviour with these kin is marked by a lack of joking, and by marked respect in food-sharing, positioning of camps, eating, talking and other social behaviours'. Verbal and physical intimacy among adults of this closest kin category is forbidden.[42]

The husband has the most absolute rights over his wife, or rather his wives. He can use them as he sees fit. He can give one, or several of them, to his brothers. He even has the right of life or death over them. When he exercises the latter, however, it is not always with impunity since the relatives of the sacrificed woman will seek to avenge her.

Chase notes that it was the husband's duty to punish his wife physically for bad behaviour. But serious injury or killing was another matter: 'If she was permanently crippled or killed, her family could rightfully come to demand retribution, either by a spearing, by gifts or by the "loan" of a girl to grow up in their camp for future marriage into the wife's group'.[43]

The men are extremely jealous, the women perhaps even more so. Since polygamy is very liable to arouse this feeling in women, those who seem to be preferred by the husband are continually spied upon by their rivals, who would be only too happy to see them lose favour in his estimation. To achieve this, they will use any means at their disposal. They will present the most innocent behaviour in a bad light and show no hesitation in spreading malicious gossip and slander. Being naturally extremely talkative, the women find it very difficult to keep quiet. They can be asked to obey in any other respect, but it is impossible to get them to remain silent. Because of this, there arise continual quarrels between them, often involving fisticuffs. When this happens, the husband has only one way of restoring peace to his household. Since his rebukes are almost always futile, he separates the brawling women by giving them a good hiding.

Although the women are not allowed to defend themselves, not all of them tamely submit to the law that is imposed on them: there are some who will return blow for blow.

Chase notes: 'A woman could dominate her husband if she was strong enough, and I was given several examples of women who had indeed regularly beaten their husbands with yamsticks and refused to take any physical abuse'.[44]

Pelletier can even remember a case where a woman murdered her own husband. As soon as she had committed the crime she fled, disappearing so far into the interior that it was impossible to lay a hand on her.

Pelletier was often witness to the summary punishments carried out by his adoptive father. Maademan made no bones about it, and more than once blood flowed under his blows. At such times Pelletier folded his arms and did not say a word, as his intervention might have left him open to the same kind of unpleasant consequences. These beatings only came to an end with the death of the older of the two wives. This poor woman having been killed by a savage whose canoe she refused to clean, the younger wife now remained in sole possession of her husband's heart. The arrival of two daughters strengthened the sweet bonds of matrimony, and after that there was nothing but perfect harmony in the family. For the rest, Maademan was not a wicked man. He was always devoted to his adoptive son and, a very rare thing in the tribe, he only once inflicted physical punishment upon him.

As slander spreads so quickly, prudence demanded of both sexes that their conduct be all the more restrained. And since, at the least suspicion, enduring feelings of resentment would grow up between the husband who believed himself to be wronged and the perpetrator of the wrong, feelings which could have the most serious consequences, a strong sense of restraint was imposed upon those who would not have been held back by finer feelings.

If the women are far from perfect, it must be acknowledged that their fate is not an enviable one. Married by their father from a very tender age, as soon as they are three or four years old, they are not allowed to break their conjugal ties. No ceremony takes place on this occasion, the father's will clearly expressed is sufficient to give the necessary consecration to the marriage. It is well understood that these very premature unions are only an engagement for the future, but from the moment the marriage is contracted there is no going back on it. It is wholly in the father's interests that it should be so, as his son-in-law, from the first day, must come to his aid whenever he asks for it. In the early days of the marriage the spouses see each other often so that they may get to know each other. But when the little girl reaches the age of seven all relations cease, not to be taken up again in a definitive way until she reaches puberty. Except that from this age until the day she is handed over to him the husband is obliged to provide her with food. Not only is marriage not permitted up to the fourth degree of consanguinity, but a girl cannot be married to a man belonging to her own tribe either. It is even required that the collective name of the members of her tribe be different from that

PELLETIER

of the individuals comprising her husband's tribe. A *Cayen* can therefore only marry a *Caapei*.

Chase notes that moiety affiliation is inherited patrilineally. This means that the preferred cross-cousin marriage system dictates a spouse of the other moiety. To have sexual relations with a person of your own moiety is seen as incestuous.[45]

There is generally a large age difference between husband and wife since, on the wedding day, the father is hoping to find a son-in-law who can come to his assistance and feed him if needs be.

In the course of discussing how camp fires were an index of living arrangements and social relations, Thomson describes the way in which an Umpila marriage came to pass and was recognised:

'The simple act of sharing a common fire in the presence of the camp constitutes the marriage ceremony in the Ompela tribe. When the time for marriage arrives the mother of the girl tells her to go and light a fire. At this she sits with her grass baskets used for food collecting, and her other domestic utensils, while her betrothed sits on the opposite side of the fire with his spears and spear-throwers. As my informant said simply, "Next day they go hunting," i.e., they are married.'[46]

While the man, except for when he is hunting or fishing, is often idle, the woman, as soon as she is strong enough, works ceaselessly. To her alone has fallen the responsibility for digging the produce from the soil and gathering the fruits which her family cannot do without. Her hands and a stick, which has one pointed end lightly blackened by fire so that it will wear out less quickly [*kachin*, yamstick], are what she uses to dig in the earth. From an early age she devotes herself to this hard work, which is not interrupted either by pregnancy or nursing the newborn babies.

Elizabeth Giblet, an Umpila elder, describes the hard life in 'the old time' when her people lived at the Old Site near Cape Direction where the Anglican Mission had been set up in 1924:

'Before we gotta walk to go out camping. We had to carry our swags and go from place to place. Everything easier this new way, everything closer. I explain this to this new generation, like my granddaughter, it was a very hard time before. In our place, our outstation, we used to make little humpy. We used to make fire in the night to chase mosquitoes, very hard — you had to look for firewood. We used to put the fish in the coal fire. We used to eat damper with sugar bag (puntu — native honey), like syrup. We used to bury the yam in the sand. In the old time.'[47]

When her labour pains are beginning to be felt, the woman in question retires to the woods, helped by a woman friend. This friend, with the consent of the father and mother, names the newborn child.

Chase provides more information about childbirth and naming:

'An expectant mother returned to her own country, or to her F's [father's] people, wherever they were camped, for the birth. Ideally this was in the estate cluster precinct, and each community camp had a 'main place' close-by which was a maternity site. Here the midwives supervised the birth and provided post-natal care for mother and child. People acquired an interest in estates which contained their birthplaces (*ngaatyi nguturu*: "place of the navel") [*ngaachi nyuchuru*], for it is here that the afterbirth (*muulngka*) is buried. The actual site of its

burial is *kinytya* ("sacred and forbidden") [*kincha*] to both
mother and child for the rest of their lives.

'At birth, a series of special relationships was created
between the baby and particular kin. As the umbilical cord
was being severed, names of close, but not actual, FF-s
[father's fathers] were called out. The name which coincided
with the actual separation of the cord provided the *manthala
nguturu* ("name of the navel") [*manthala nyuchuru*] for the
child, and this "FF" entered into a strict avoidance and
respect relationship with both the mother and child. The
cord was encased in beeswax, bound with orchid stem and
given to a [classificatory] "MB" [mother's brother] to wear
for the duration of his life. This particular kinsman was
determined by calling out names of "MB-s" when the baby
first started to hiccough in the weeks after the birth. The
man whose name coincided with the end of this hiccoughing
became *kaala ka'unta* ("MB-hiccough"), and again a strict
avoidance relationship was created between the child and
its mother on one hand, and this man on the other. These
"forbidden relations" (*kuunytyi kinytya*) [*kuunchi kincha*]
were expected to provide unqualified support during the
child's life, and there were frequent exchanges of gifts. The
"MB-s" who formed the pool of names called during the
hiccoughing were all in the *tali* [distant kin] category of kin,
and the one who became *kaala ka'unta* was moved into the
category of *thuypi* or "close". His daughters were prohibited
from becoming wives of the child. In this manner, birth
established cross-linking relationships between patrilineal
and matrilineal kin, and as well, it established particular
relationships between individuals and the estates of their
mother's fathers.'[48]

With the pleasures of motherhood adding to her pains and
labours, she is as much a female feeding her offspring as a mother
raising her children. For the first six months she takes them to the
fields with her in a basket, which serves as a cradle.

Says Chase: 'This basket or *ulku* would usually have been made from the tough leaf sheath of a Livistona palm (also *ulku*), which was soaked until pliable, then pleat-folded at each end and "sewn" or pegged into a permanent fold. The basket thus created was lined with soft paperbark to make a baby crib.'[49] Hale and Tindale provide photographs of a baby in one of these baskets.[50] These vessels could also be used to carry water. An *ulku* is shown in the photographic section.

When they get to this age, she props them on her neck, where they sit with their feet hanging over her chest and their little hands clinging on to her hair. When she gets to the place where she will look for food she puts them down on the ground and only goes over to them to give them the breast. She nurses them like this for five years. Such a prolonged period of breastfeeding explains the low fertility of the women who, even though they do not submit to Malthus's laws, never have more than three or four children.

Although mothers show their children some other signs of affection, there is one such sign, seemingly the most natural of all, which is completely unknown to them. A mother never kisses her child and a child never throws itself around the neck of its mother to kiss her. Moreover, this expression of friendship, gratitude, respect and love which is so common in our society has not spread to the savages. A husband will not plant a kiss on the lips of his wife any more than a mother will do so on the lips of her child.

However, maternal love does not disappear as it does in animals when youth succeeds childhood. On the contrary, this feeling remains deeply rooted in the woman's heart and is lifelong. When her son, now come to manhood, is away from home and she awaits his return, the mother spends her nights singing, in a tearful voice, '*Kayo papa, kayo papa!*', 'I am your mother, I am your mother!' [In Kuuku Ya'u '*ngayu paapa*', 'I, (your) mother'.[51]]

Another kind of affection is felt between all the members of the family. Brothers and sisters, whether or not they have the same mother, or even though they are linked by adoption, and even relatives at one step removed, never regard each other as strangers. It must be said, however, that sons are sometimes regrettably hot-tempered towards their parents and that their fathers will often give them a good thrashing.

As for the woman, she is almost always a slave for her whole life. If her husband or, more accurately, her master, precedes her to the grave, his death does not signal that her deliverance has come. She is part of the inheritance and passes to the man's brother whose personal property she becomes.[52] If she is a burden to him he is entitled to give her to another man.

Women do not remain in a state of widowhood and are only properly independent when they no longer have either a husband or brother-in-law. Almost always in these cases they are old and can no longer work. Then their sons, or other charitable souls, see to their needs.

Chase describes the strict delimitation of men's and women's spheres of work and power in the traditional setting. Women were regarded as inferior to men, subservient to their husbands and subject to their chastisement. Their subsistence work was arduous and constant. They had their own ceremonial dances but no ceremonies of their own. They were subject to strict prohibitions in relation to men's secret sacred knowledge and activities, and to some permanent food prohibitions. They were not allowed to be present at the hunting of the big game animals. Nevertheless, the old women whom he met in the 1970s were nostalgic for their bush life and accepted its rules. Individual women might come to dominate their husbands while some husbands were much kinder to their wives than a description of the gender status quo suggests.[53]

Children have barely left their mother's breast when they take up exercises ideally suited to developing their strength. They have no games strictly speaking; their amusements consist of races and hand-to-hand combat. These contests are not always harmless. Started in fun, they often end up in fits of anger accompanied by vigorously delivered punches. It is also at an early age that fathers get their children to practise throwing their arrows. They make weapons that are suitable for their age and set up a target for the young marksmen. The winner is always acclaimed by his companions who strive to outdo each other in competitiveness and skill. As boys grow and gain in strength, the length and weight of their arrows is increased and, by the time they are adults, they all know how to use them with skill, and are ready for hunting, fishing and warfare. There is another form of exercise which they take up of their own accord and at which, quite untutored, they very quickly become first-rate.[54] From the age of seven they swim like fish. Among the savages the childhood years are thus divided between wrestling, arrow-throwing and swimming.

Writing of childhood activities he observed at Stewart River, Thomson notes that 'Model spears, canoes, weapons and implements are often made for children. Boys are given small play spears, the tips neatly padded with paper-bark. Spinning tops are made from a variety of seed capsules and fruits and make-believe babies are made, sometimes of mud, to serve as dolls'.[55]

Transported at the age of fifteen to a milieu so different from that in which he had lived up until then, Pelletier gradually took on its customs and ways. There are some influences that are like contagious illnesses: they exert their control by proximity and contact without it being possible to avoid them. Once he had learned the language of the savages, which did not take him very long, Pelletier talked with them constantly, and it could not be otherwise as he shared their way of life. In his tribe and in the neighbouring tribes he found some who liked him very much; but it was quite the reverse with others whose feelings of repulsion towards him were obvious. The children especially often made fun of him because of his colour.

One of the things which left him open to continual taunting is too odd for me not to mention it. The savages of both sexes exhibit uncleanliness to an unbelievable degree. When the ground is soaked, their bodies are covered in mud; when it is hot, they are coated in a thick dust which adheres by sweat. None of them pays any attention to the dirt or seeks to remove it by washing himself.

Such a coating may have served as a protection against mosquitoes, which were numerous, as mentioned at the beginning of this chapter. A contradictory comment about cleanliness is made in the *Times* article: 'He [Pelletier] is clean in his person, and says that the blacks among whom he has lived are so also'. [56] And Bruce Rigsby observes that there is no reason to think that the personal cleanliness of Sandbeach People, whose preference is for at least one daily 'swim', is not traditional.[57]

Pelletier had maintained the habits of cleanliness that he had acquired as a child. In such circumstances he would bathe or perform his ablutions. He went so far as to wash his hands every day. While this habit did not make him any enemies, it had left him open to teasing by all and sundry, who would laugh heartily and point at him. He also attracted the jealousy of those who could not easily forgive the superior skills that he had developed in the art of making arrows.

If this skill seems insufficient reason for such envy, Thomson's remarks about valued spears as objects that might be endowed with *kunta*, a highly charged supernatural power similar to the Melanesian *mana*, are enlightening. European objects, he says, 'possessed none of the intangible force called k*u*nta. But I have seen more than one finely made spear that was considered too valuable to be thrown, and I have been hunting with a native whom I knew to be hungry, when he would not throw a spear for this reason. I was able to purchase more spears than I wanted for a trifling quantity of tobacco, but when I saw a magnificent spear, carrying a crown of about thirty-five stingray spines, in camp, and endeavoured to purchase it, I was met with a curt refusal. The spear was removed as soon as I had gone, and although I later offered fabulous quantities of tobacco for it, repeated over a period of months, all sorts of inconsistent excuses were made, and I was never allowed even to see it again. I believe that this spear was handed down from one man to another; the bearer would never have thought of using it, for it would certainly have broken to pieces if it had been thrown. But it was an object of extraordinary value.'[58]

But there was compensation in the true and faithful friend he had made of one young man, the bonds of kinship having brought them together.

Sassy,[59] the son of Maademan's brother, was almost the same age as Pelletier. He had to help his father, just as Pelletier did, and they had to use the same methods to this common end. The two cousins met up often and soon they went about their activities together. There was one serious occasion on which Pelletier may have owed his survival to Sassy's powerful intervention.

Pelletier had to watch over a huge piece of turtle meat which was not meant for him. One of the savages thought that he had taken the lion's share and, as he claimed to have rights in it himself, he threw himself upon the defenceless Pelletier. The man was even making ready to drive his arrow into him when Sassy ran up and, threatening him with his own weapon, forced him to let go. Pelletier, who did not have his weapons with him, luckily found an arrow to hand with which he was able to defend himself. Their friends ran up at the sound of the fighting and separated the combatants, who had only wounded each other superficially. After some brief explaining they made up their differences. Besides, among the savages feelings of rancour are almost unheard of. They are like big children who, after giving each other some hearty clouts on the head, think no more about it and return to being the best of friends.

All that remained with Pelletier of this incident was its memory. But another one has left a mark on his lower right leg, which he will have all his life. There is a fish of exquisite flavour that is reserved solely for the old men. To eat it before one has white hair is to leave oneself liable to the most severe punishments.

Chase notes that the 'fish' in question was most likely dugong. In earlier times the infringement of food prohibitions incurred severe consequences. The meat of the dugong was forbidden to all but initiated men and was subject to the most severe prohibition.[60] Foods are divided into *minya mukana* or 'big meat' — game that can attain a large size (over three kilograms in weight) and only a few select vegetables, *mayi mukana* ('big vegetable food') — and all other foods, *minya* (or *mayi*) *chu'achu*, 'small meat (or vegetable) food'. Chase notes: 'All *minya mukana* were prohibited in pre-contact and early mission times to children, young married women, uninitiated men, widows, and others of both sexes who were under the temporary prohibition of birth, initiation ceremonies and death.'[61] Thomson provides a long list of *minya* subject to *kincha* during the initiation process. He notes that dugongs were subject to a different taboo: 'No young man is permitted to eat dugong until long after he has been initiated.'[62]

One day when he was feeling hunger pangs, and no doubt being spurred on by gluttony as well, Pelletier dared to make a meal of this particular fish.

Unfortunately he was noticed and there was knowledge of his act in his tribe. Far from being proportional to the offence, the punishment was excessive. However, it was not immediate, and before it was inflicted upon him the glutton had time to digest his repast. Pelletier maintains that, without his knowledge, on the ninth night following his meal, a person whose identity he never discovered placed a pillow made from narcotic plants under his head. These plants made him sleep so deeply that some hours later the same person, using a quill of bone dipped in poison, came and made a deep wound above the outer malleolus[63] without him feeling any pain. He did not wake until morning.

In Chase's opinion this suggests an account of sorcery practice stated *post facto* following an ulcer or other such sore or wound.[64] Sorcery was practised in the traditional setting and a technique corresponding to what is reported here was that of 'visiting the victim at night in spirit form to cut open his body and insert a poisonous object. The wound was then magically closed and the victim left unaware of the operation.'[65] Chase points out that sorcery was invoked as the explanation for all deaths apart from those of the very old or the very young, and for sickness.[66]

The wound caused him acute suffering and the surrounding tissue became inflamed over a wide area. Then came abscesses, ulcers and a large sore that spread over all of the lower part of the leg. Those who looked after him evinced no doubts about what it was that had caused the injury. It was not the first time that they had seen such a thing. Many others before Pelletier had been unable to resist the temptation to which he had succumbed and all of them had been cruelly punished. But as there is no preferred place to make the injection and all parts of the body are equally exposed, it is not the legs in particular which bear the brunt. There have been unfortunate souls who, pricked near their eyes, have lost their sight as a result. As for Pelletier, it was a long time ago now that the injection was made and the wound that has resulted from it is not yet completely healed over. I was in a position to look at the wound and I observed that the scar tissue is still red and swollen. In the middle there is an ulcer of rounded shape almost two centimetres in diameter.

I wonder, though, if the treatment applied to the wound has not contributed to prolonging it. The savages, with their herbal ointments, have a rather sorry array of treatments, and their medication has perhaps quite aggravated the injury that they purported to cure.

Although their tribe is continually on the move, the life of the savages is generally uniform and monotonous. Aside from their frequent wars and private quarrels, which often end in injury, aside from the punishments they incur, and aside, too, from some festive occasions, their life is rarely marked by incident.

In Pelletier's tribe, where one day's fishing generally provides food for 48 hours, the following day was given over to rest, repairing canoes, making arrows or visits to the tribes of hunters. As these tribes live in the mountains, Pelletier barely ventured there.

Pelletier may well have been talking here about the neighbouring inland groups belonging to the Kaanju language territory. They are known as *pama kanichi*, 'on top' or 'mountain people'.[67] Thomson comments on 'a mutual fear between tribes' of eastern Cape York and notes that 'All Mälkänidji [*pama malngkanichi*, 'beach people'] speak of the Kanidji (bushmen) [*kanichi*] as if the latter were constantly descending in *wäppä* (avenging) [*wapa*][68] excursions upon them whenever they ventured inland'.[69]

The little tracks that he would have had to follow were studded with thorns and he could not travel over them with impunity as the savages do because his feet had not acquired the thickness and toughness of theirs.

He spent his leisure time with his family, gradually becoming accustomed to their ways, sharing their tastes, becoming, in a word, a true savage. Although recollections of his country of birth were not entirely wiped from his memory, the days of his childhood appeared to him to belong to such a distant past that he was sometimes inclined to wonder if Saint-Gilles really did exist, if its church, its harbour and its ships were not just a figment of his imagination. He had completely forgotten the language of his country and would not have been able to form a single letter with a pen, not even the words 'father' and 'mother'.

With the intention of making him even more fully a member of the tribe, Maademan, in the last years that Pelletier spent with him, thought about finding him a female companion. He married him to a very young girl belonging to a neighbouring tribe.

Thomson says that a Kuuku Ya'u girl would be married before puberty and that the reason informants gave him for this was that she would not be afraid of her husband, having grown up with him.[70]

The story of their romance affords no real interest, and novelists would have difficulty finding in it any touching episodes or taking from it any moving passages.

The bride seemed to feel more antipathy towards her husband than liking. Most of all she was unable to forgive him for the whiteness of his skin. And in terms of their ages the union was not particularly well matched either, as Pelletier could have been the father of the girl who was being given to him as his wife. When they parted, Pelletier was in his thirty-second year, while she appeared to be in her seventh. It is unnecessary to add that the union was still one in name only. Pelletier will therefore be able to contract a marriage in France without fear of being pursued for bigamy. His fiancée will be able to marry him without being apprehensive that, on the day he dies, children from the north of Australia will come and fight with hers over the inheritance he has left.

CHAPTER 4

How thought is expressed. Language and gestures.
Maademan's narrative.

There has been much discussion about the origins and formation of language and agreement is still far from being reached about this interesting question. While some claim that linguistics is a natural science, others say that it is an historical science; there are others again, and they seem to me to have the correct interpretation, for whom language is the province of both nature and history.[1] But one point on which most people agree is that the degree of civilisation of different peoples can be gauged from the degree to which their language has evolved. Here there is always accord. In a word, among savage and primitive peoples where no civilising influence has penetrated, it is held that language, far from being developed, has remained in a rudimentary state. It is made up of a limited number of monosyllabic words, almost wholly of tones that are given particular meanings by different intonations of the voice. Thus in seeking to understand the way thought is expressed, we should, in such cases, look to the musical scale rather than to the composition of the word, the same word having a different meaning according to whether its pronunciation is drawn out or rapid, according to its musical key.

Man's first words were necessarily imitative words, onomatopoeic words, as grammarians call them, which, as far as possible, showed the thing that he wished to express by means of the sound of his voice. This was, as Monsieur Letellier[2] says, the *practical word*, that which preceded all others. But when he turned to intonation it could only offer him very inadequate means of making himself understood. This is because the vocal cords do not produce the same intonations in all men, far from it, as their functioning is governed by particular anatomical dispositions; because age, sex and illness have a significant effect upon the larynx; and because, finally, there are many other factors that can distort its tonality as well, meaning that thought may not be given accurate expression.

A powerful auxiliary that we have retained to give more force to speech resides in gesture. It had to suffice in many cases and to make up for a lack of vocal power. Nowadays a thorough study has been made of sign language; on the stage it has become an art; in the schools of the deaf and mute a veritable science. It is so much a part of our nature that several of our gestures are the same as those of the savages of Cape Flattery. Like us, for example, they nod their heads as a sign of affirmation and agreement; like us, they move their heads from side to side as a sign of denial and refusal.

But, in certain circumstances, when the speakers were separated by a barrier which prevented them from seeing each other, or when the dark of night spread over the earth, all communication by this means became impossible for them.

Even to this day there are, in Africa, men belonging to the same tribe who, in the depth of the night, cannot carry on extended conversations.

Among some peoples there was indeed a means of communication apart from the voice, gestures and facial expressions, one which left its mark after the person who had made it had departed. This was the tracing of emblematic signs in the sand, on wood or on stone, and the beginnings of hieroglyphic science, which was to give birth to symbols and writing.

It is a long road from the first instinctive cry and the imitative word to the formation of language. Progress could only be made step by step, with the help of reason and in the conditions which I shall describe.

The imitative word had been the primordial word; it changed over time and, but for a few exceptions which are met with more often among savage than civilised peoples, it finally disappeared almost completely.

The *practical* word evolved; instead of simply expressing feelings, it came to express thought. Thanks to particular intonations that everyone was able to use, those rendered by the vowels, it could be extended and generalised among the same group of people, to be spoken and understood by all. This progress was of capital importance. Although he had only a very small number of words, man could henceforth express facts that barely changed in the early period of humanity.

With the help of the *practical* word, the representation of life and fact was certainly available, but it did not convey the mode of action, or the personality. Here the *theoretical* word came to its aid. In order to form this kind of word, synthesis and analysis were needed. Its gestation necessarily took many years and, even more than the *practical* word, it could not come into being without a great effort of reason. At the same time two of man's senses, hearing and sight, came together to facilitate the achievement of this marvel. While the *practical* word made fact known, images of different forms, and composed of different elements, served to complement it. When the voice lacked the power to make thought understood, images could transmit it in part. Ordinarily it was expressed by the *practical* word and the [graphic] symbol together.

The *theoretical* word, which replaced the symbol, arose from the articulation of the vowels and of the diphthongs, where two vowels are joined in a single vocal sound.

Composed of several syllables, the new word often expressed simultaneously the person, his mode of existence, his obligations and his prerogatives. The *theoretical* word did not depose the practical word; they proceeded together hand in hand.

The relations of nation to nation and of people to people made no small contribution to the richness of language. Mutual borrowings were made and, more than once, with two peoples merging into one, their languages, over time, formed a sort of alloy. So it was, through contact between the Romans and the Gauls, that the languages of the victors and the vanquished gave birth to the Gallo-Roman language and that, when later the Francs established their domination over the remnants of this part of the Roman Empire, their conquest bringing together three peoples of diverse origins through common needs, the French language was formed.

In order for a language to progress, for it to become more highly developed, it must necessarily be in the state that I have just described. Savage tribes, those which have remained in a primitive state and have never made contact with peoples of different origins, have retained their language almost as it was spoken in the first days of their existence.

We are told that in distant and little explored regions one may still meet with tribes whose entire vocabulary is made up of less than two hundred words.

The theory about the formation of languages that I have just described would be an idle digression if I were not to compare it with the language to which I shall now turn. I have borrowed this theory from the learned master whose name I have already mentioned.

Although it appears to me quite reasonable, the very superficial study I have made of the language whose elements Pelletier has provided me with does not provide any confirmation of the theory of the eminent philologist.

And yet the savage tribes of Endeavour Land have, more than any other, retained the characteristics of primitive peoples. Centuries have passed them by while nothing has changed in their customs, their tastes or their habits. Having never been in any relationship with civilised nations, they are virtually as they must have been when fashioned by the hand of the Creator. How is it that their language, although not a fully developed language, has, as we shall see, shaken off the vestiges of early infancy?

First of all, far from only comprising a few hundred words, the vocabulary of these tribes is truly a rich one.[3] The savages have certainly never thought of classifying genera and species, but they nonetheless have words to express both of these. The word *yomba*, 'tree', for example, is not applied indiscriminately to every ligneous plant [in Kuuku Ya'u *yumpa*, 'wood' or 'stick']. Each species has its own name. The same goes for the members of a family: *gatimenil* is 'grandfather' [in Kuuku Ya'u *ngachimu*, 'mother's father']; *mémerai* or *mémé*, 'grandmother' [in Kuuku Ya'u *miimi*, 'mother's mother', and *miimiray*, 'mother's mother-exclamatory']; *peperai*, 'father' [in Kuuku Ya'u *piipiray*, 'father-exclamatory', 'father' is *piipi*]; *pappei* or *papa*, 'mother' [in Kuuku Ya'u *paapay*, 'mother-exclamatory' and *paapa*, 'mother']; *iondela*, 'brother' [this may be another rendering of *yaaden*, which Merland gives further on as the term used by a sister for her younger brother. In Kuuku Ya'u 'younger sibling' is *ya'athu*]; *capoul*, 'eldest brother' [in Kuuku Ya'u 'older brother' is *yapu*]; *yaaie*, 'sister' [in Kuuku Ya'u *ya'a*, 'older sister']; *natchimen*, 'uncle' [in Kuuku Ya'u 'mother's father' is *ngachimu*, the gloss as 'uncle' is incorrect]; *namné*, 'cousin' [in Kuuku Ya'u *ngami'i*, 'father's older brother's child' or 'mother's older brother's child'].

And similarly for all the parts of the body:

hair	*jaunou* [In Kuuku Ya'u 'hair' is *yangan*.]
forehead	*pouha* [In Kuuku Ya'u 'forehead' is *pipul*. The transcription given by Merland is closer to the Kuuku Ya'u term for 'head', *pa'an*.]
eyebrows	*mesmeneuille* [*milmuy*]
eye	*bomtreuille* [In Kuuku Ya'u the term for 'eye' is *ku'un*. However Thomson gives the Umpila word *tuntoi* for 'eye'[4] and Hale and Tindale similarly give the Umpila word as *tuntui*.[5]]

ear	*malo* [No Kuuku Ya'u or Umpila equivalent is apparent for this word. The term for 'ear' is *yampa*.]
cheek	*campa* [The Kuuku Ya'u equivalent is more likely *kampa*, 'jaw'. The term for 'cheek' is *kulkul*.]
nose	*nisi* [The Kuuku Ya'u equivalent is *niiyi*.[6]]
beard	*bouhoutienne* [In Kuuku Ya'u 'beard' is *watum*. However, Thomson gives the word *potjän*, approximating to Merland's term for 'beard' in parallel usages, for example to describe the frayed end, or 'beard', of a cane or other stick used as a brush to paint the men's bodies for ceremonies.[7]]
lip	*cahaman* [The Kuuku Ya'u term for 'lip' is *thalnpuy*. The Kuuku Ya'u equivalent for this word is more likely *kaama*, 'mouth'.]
tooth	*camman* [*kaman*]
tongue	*tapicou* [*taapi*]
neck	*capou* [*kupun*]
back	*monté* [*muchi*]
arm	*comcoul* [The Kuuku Ya'u equivalent is *kangkul*, 'elbow'. The terms for 'arm' are *puntha*, 'lower arm', and *palnta*, 'upper arm'.]
hand	*mahiu* [*ma'a*]
shoulder	*tahoban* [*thiman*]
chest	*pidna* [*pina*]
breast	*tioutihen* [In Kuuku Ya'u 'female breast' is *nyuunyu*. However, Hale and Tindale gloss 'breast' as *tjotjo* or *nyuwanyu* and 'nipple' as *tjotjo* from their Umpila informant.[8]]
stomach	*tallée* [*thul'i*, 'stomach (internal)']
thigh	*caunelan* [*kanthan*]
knee	*poinco* [*pungku*]
leg	*brallé* [This could be a distant transcription of the word *tali*, 'calf of leg', where Merland has again substituted 'b' for the initial consonant 't'.]
foot	*atraba* [No equivalent is apparent for this word. The term for 'foot' is *ta'u*.[9]]

In running through this long word list we cannot fail to notice that none of the words that compose it resembles a mere guttural cry; that these words must therefore have undergone substantial transformations before this century; and that, finally, while there are still numerous monosyllabic words in our highly evolved language of French, these have completely disappeared from the language spoken by the savages of Endeavour Land.

Now how are these words combined with each other in order to express a complex action?

The savages are poor grammarians; they have no articles, no pronouns, no grammatical object. Verbs are not conjugated; they are always used in the infinitive. Singular and plural are one and the same.[10]

The substantive always precedes the verb, often the latter is omitted, the juxtaposition of two substantives or of a substantive and an adverb being sufficient to express what is meant.

Thus: 'we have to go fishing tomorrow' will be translated by the two words *agalluda alcoman: agalluda*, 'fishing', and *alcoman*, 'tomorrow'. [No equivalent is apparent for *agalluda*. The equivalent for *alcoman* is *ngulkuma*, 'tomorrow'.]

'To put a wooden keeper in the ear', *cacopa malo: cacopa*, 'wood', and *malo*, 'ear'. [No equivalent is apparent for this expression.]

As for the verb, as I have just said, it is placed last.

'We shall eat turtle tomorrow', *troucoullou alcoman incongabo: troucoullou*, 'turtle'; *alcoman*, 'tomorrow'; *incongabo*, 'to eat'. [In Kuuku Ya'u this would be *tukulu ngulkuma yankunyampu*, 'turtle tomorrow eat-we' (David Thomson).]

If there is no exact term, it is replaced by a circumlocution. The feeling of hunger, for example, is expressed by the words *oli menen*, 'flat stomach': *oli*, 'stomach' and *menen*, 'flat'. [The term for 'hungry' is *uuli* or *uulimana*.]

'These men are very hungry', *pamma oli menen*, *pamma* meaning 'man'. [The Kuuku Ya'u term is *pama*, 'human being',

'Aboriginal person'. Throughout the Sandbeach region Aboriginal people today commonly refer to themselves as 'Pama'.]

In a few albeit rare cases, a different word is used by the mother and father to express the same meaning. When the father calls his son, he says *Peaden*; the mother *Moupa*. [The Kuuku Ya'u terms are *pi'athu*, 'son' (or 'daughter'), father speaking, and reciprocal with *piipi*, 'father', 'father's younger brother' and *piima*, 'father's younger sister'; and *maampa*, 'son' (or 'daughter'), mother speaking, and reciprocal with *paapa*, 'mother', 'mother's younger sister' and *kaala*, 'mother's younger brother'.] An older sister calls her young brother *yaaden*; a younger sister calls him *yapaïe*. [The Kuuku Ya'u equivalents are *ya'athu*, 'younger sibling', and *yapu*, 'older brother'. The term *ya'athu* is reciprocal with *yapu*, 'older brother', and *ya'a*, 'older sister'.]

Although the nouns of number are limited to *niella*, 'one' and *paamo*, 'two', counting, thanks to addition, is not restricted because of that. [These terms are *nyii'ilama*, 'one', and *pa'aamu*, 'two'.] If one wishes to express the number three, one says *paamo niello*; the number four, *paamo paamo*; five, *paamo paamo niello*, and so on. When a very large number is involved it can be seen that it would take so long to express it that one would be breathless. Thus, to express the number one thousand, it would be necessary to repeat the word *paamo* five hundred times.

For counting, the savages use gestures much more often than speech. When they count up to ten the left hand clasps the last two fingers of the right hand for *one*; then the first two fingers for *two*; the thumb, *three*; the middle of the forearm, *four*; the elbow, *five*; the middle of the arm, *six*; the right shoulder joint, *seven*; the right clavicle, *eight*; the left clavicle, *nine*; and the left shoulder joint, *ten*. That is as far as they go. If they wish to express the number eleven, or twelve, they will return to the beginning again. Strangely enough, we can see that this method of counting contains the basic elements of the decimal system.

If I said earlier that the language of the savages, in the richness of its vocabulary and the number of syllables which make up its words, appeared to suggest some contradiction with the theory of the philologists, I am far from wishing to claim that it might be compared with that of civilised peoples. It is true that it is adequate for expressing thought when that thought only pertains to purely material acts; it is much less rich when it comes to abstract ideas, the labours of the mind and moral sentiments. This is because, for the savages, the satisfaction of bodily needs, as well as of the coarser appetites, is the most pressing requirement; and because the stirrings of the soul that they feel at unexpected events in their lives are shown, according to their nature, by joy or by tears, by the beating of the heart and not by the working of the brain.

Among the savages, thought never soars up towards the higher realms, it never embraces intellectual questions, it never debates accepted beliefs or seeks to pursue them further. Heedless of tomorrow beyond all imagining, their way of thinking pays no mind to the precautions that must be taken against troubles that may arise; it does not consider moderating consumption of the riches that nature offers in anticipation of future need; it has no understanding of progress; it does not know what it is to strive for improvement. The pleasures of life, a clear conscience, or the calm of the soul are not its objectives; in a word, it always remains down to earth: it proceeds as much from instinct as from reason.

But let us not be too categorical. Yes, undoubtedly, the language of the savages is very poor when it comes to expressing emotions, which they feel only in a very limited way, but as they are not completely lacking in these, they also have words that correspond to them.

Thus:

good	*menné* [*mini*]
bad	*oüo* [*wu'u*]
courage	*aillala* [*ayala* means 'hard working', 'keen']

cowardice	*yachioaho* [*yaaki wu'u* means 'lazy']
good-hearted	*ayalla* [no doubt an alternative transcription of the previous *aillala*]
passionate, amorous	*wolpillgobey* [a man known as a womaniser is *wulmpil kupi*, 'greedy for woman'][11]
handsome man	*pamman menné* [*pama mini*, 'man good']
beautiful woman	*yequihuman menné* [*wayimu mini* or *ukulngkumu mini* is 'woman good']

In the case of societies in which the transmission of thought leaves no trace, in which the only tools man has to express himself produce an effect that is as transitory as the flight of a bird and in which images are lacking and marks do not exist, we can well see how the story of the past resides wholly in memory and tradition.

Merland does not mention message sticks, an interesting communication device that Hale and Tindale observed at Princess Charlotte Bay:

'While trading for old bags and baskets at Stewart River numbers of message sticks were noted among the contents of some baskets which were being emptied for our inspection. This led to our being able to secure a series of these interesting objects; some of them were of recent date, others were old. In no case was there any attempt made to indicate a message by symbols on the stick; the communication passed verbally with the piece of wood.

'The makers of the various sticks were known by peculiarities in style of workmanship; thus these objects were evidences of good faith, giving authority to the verbal communication. They may also have had some slight mnemonic value.

...

'After messages have been delivered the sticks are usually retained for a long period, being either stowed in string bags or tucked away among the leafy coverings of the huts.

'When interest was expressed by us, more than a hundred old ones were produced for inspection within a few moments;

only in a proportion of the cases could the message be recalled. The verbal messages related to the sending of parcels of spears; arrangements regarding the cutting of canoe trees on the Normanby River in exchange for spears; promises to meet at specified places, either after the elapse of so many moons, at the time when some fruit was ripe, or when certain flowers of seasonal nature were blooming.'[12]

They add that 'an uncarved piece of hardwood … is frequently carried among a man's personal effects. It can be adapted either as the peg of a spear-thrower or as a message stick.'[13]

To learn, to be informed, one must refer to the memory of those who have seen, to the memory of the old people. But as this faculty is a long way way from perfect, becoming weaker with time and age, the teachings that it gives are very incomplete, when they are not filled with errors and fables. Moreover, they cannot reach very far back except in taking on the character of legend, that is to say of beliefs which, because they are not questioned, can offer little in the way of truth.

I shall therefore grant only a modicum of credence to the following story told to Pelletier by his adoptive father, a story all the more suspect because Maademan had not been a witness to the event he was relating and because it had happened a long time ago and at quite a distance from the tribe in which he lived.

'During my early childhood', he said, 'a man of a certain age, belonging to the white race, was abandoned by his crew at a place on the coast situated eight or nine days from where we live. This man was fearful and faint-hearted; he never wanted to venture into the woods for fear of being eaten by the wolves, even though there were none in this country. Three years spent with the savages had done nothing to cure his natural shyness. It turns out that he was not eaten by the wolves but by one of his own kind. This is how it happened. One day when he was being pursued by some boldly provocative young girls, his outraged innocence could stand their advances no longer and, in a moment of anger, he killed the girl who was drawing closest to him. Rapidly grasping the full seriousness of his crime and fearing the punishment that awaited him, he thought to avoid it by taking flight. Remaining in hiding during the day, he waited for night to fall to head out to sea in a canoe. Unfortunately he was careless enough to take fire with him. Perceiving its glow, the father of the murdered girl, who had just learnt of her death on his return from fishing, threw himself into a canoe, paddled vigorously and soon reached the fugitive. He killed him with a blow of his gaff, took him back to land and consoled himself for the loss he had just suffered by feasting on the man's flesh.'

What is true may sometimes not be credible.[14]

If it is true that his fellow castaway, as chaste as Joseph and much more easily provoked, did punish these improper advances by death, and if he was sentenced in turn to the same punishment, then Pelletier will not have been the first white man to have lived with the blacks of Endeavour Land.[15]

The savages, who scarcely have any knowledge of history, have even less of the calendar. They do not think about the division of time, do not measure it, only distinguish darkness from light, and take life as it comes without counting their days on earth. They cannot have words for expressing months and years as they have no conception of them. As well as that, Pelletier was not able to find out what their average life span was and does not know whether it is longer or shorter than ours.

Even without taking into account the complexity in the notion of time and the cultural specificity of different systems of time reckoning, this statement fails to convey that Sandbeach People of course divided the year into seasons, as we saw in the previous chapter, and seasons were associated with the availability of particular foods as well as social events and particular modes of living. More precise time reckoning is referred to by Hale and Tindale in the quotation above about the message to be conveyed by message sticks fixing a meeting 'after the elapse of so many moons', or by specific seasonal indicators.

Time on the grand scale was certainly imagined as divided into periods, extending from the mythical past to the present day. Donald Thomson describes how one of his Umpila informants summed up this sweep of time:

"*Wulmpamo* (the Big Men) *pontị̈nä* (finished) *koko-go* (talk-to) *yiạdji-go* (the middle people-went); *ṇäna* (we) *pạrrä ṇätjịnya* (find)."

'Freely rendered: "After the Big Men, the Middle People lived, last we come and we find the white man," i.e. the white man did not exist in myth or tradition, he has no antiquity, but has been "found" by the fathers of the present generation.'[16]

David Thompson has provided this transliteration and an alternative translation of the Umpila man's words: *Wulmpamu punthina, kuukuku yiachiku, ngana para ngachinya*: 'The time of the Old Ones is finished. Then came the time of the Middle People. Now we find the time of the White People.'[17]

The period preceding the arrival of Europeans is referred to as 'before time', and since Europeans came time has been cut up into shorter periods associated with a key element or figure. Chase describes how people at Lockhart River now conceptualise the past, both recent and distant:

'Lockhart people conceive of their past in terms of phases, categories of time which relate the present living period to the mythical past. The period of living memory is known as *kuma*, and the limits of this lie with the oldest remembered ancestor. This period can be referred to as *puula-kuma* ("father's father time") or *piinya-kuma* ("father's older brother time"). It covers all events which can be validated by eyewitness account. Furthermore, it can contain periods within it which are identified by the use of the name of a focal individual: thus "Giblet-kuma", "Warby-kuma",[18] and as one informant jokingly told me, "Chase-kuma". The present time is *nyi-kuma* ("now time").

'Before *puula-kuma* lies *anthanthama*, or "long time before": a period for which there are now no eye witness accounts, but which is believed to have consisted of men and women in their present form. This is the period of famous "big men" whose names are still perpetuated in territorial group names and in stories which old people heard from their senior relatives. This is the time of the earliest European contacts and key stories (for example, telling of the first coming of tobacco and flour) relate to this period. It is sometimes referred to as *antha yi'atyi* [*antha yi'achi*] ("middle ages").

'At the far limits of the past lies *yilamu*, the mythical past. This was the time of creation and of the formation of the various totemic sites in the landscape: a time when *pama* or "Aboriginal people" were first created. While people can argue over details or interpretations of *anthanthama* and *kuma*, *yilamu* is fixed: its only verification lies in the possession of myths or in the visual evidence of sites connected with the activities of the mythical ancestors.'[19]

Chapter 5

Beliefs. Superstitions. Treatment of illnesses.

R are indeed, in our world, are peoples who have no belief in the existence of higher beings. There are good fairies and bad, spirits kindly and comforting, wicked and diabolical. There are those who will charm and deceive, those who come to our rescue in times of gravest danger and those to whom idols are raised. And there are those who can be moved by prayer or who can only be persuaded by bloody — sometimes human — sacrifices. The parts of the globe where the truths of the Christian religion have not yet penetrated are their shared domain. They all have their believers, their worshippers and their cult.

Almost uniquely, the savages of Endeavour Land have no idea of the existence of God, nowhere perceive the celestial hand ruling over human destinies, have never thought about the immortality of the soul, and have never been concerned to know whether, after death, there is reward for the good and punishment for the evil. When Pelletier, once he had learned their language, came to speak to them of an eternal and omnipotent God, they understood nothing of such talk; in vain did he persevere in wanting to teach them his beliefs, they just turned their backs and laughed at him.

The question of whether Australian Aborigines, and other non-European peoples, had religious beliefs was a subject of much debate in 19th century anthropological circles and this is reflected in Merland's interpretation here. The dearth of information concerning such matters as totemic beliefs and initiation in Pelletier's account is discussed in the introductory essay and Chase's Commentary. An understanding of the spiritual beliefs and practices of the coastal peoples of the region can be gained from Thomson,[1] Laade,[2] Chase[3] and Thompson.[4]

'But who then,' he said to them, 'created the first man, the animals that you hunt, the trees that give you their fruits and the plants and the fish that nourish you? Do you believe, when it takes you so much effort to make a canoe, that the earth was formed by itself, that it did not require an all-powerful hand to preside over its creation?'

'Oh! as to that,' replied the savages, 'you have nothing to teach us, and we know as well as anyone else who created the earth. Look up above, can't you see the moon which is looking down at us? It is to the moon and to the moon alone that the earth owes its being. The earth is the moon's child, no other power can lay claim to its creation.'

If Pelletier replied, 'But who then made the moon?' they remained silent, not wanting to continue the discussion, or else they ridiculed him and treated him as a fool.

When there was no light from the moon, when it was not full or there was an eclipse, these phenomena had the simplest of explanations: it was one of the moon's inhabitants who, as he was dying, covered it with blood, in whole or in part.

As to the dear old fellow that, in our countryside, little children see in the moon, the savages are perfectly familiar with his story. In his lifetime he was called *Traouais* [*taway*, 'moon']. A strong and vigorous man, who took great pleasure in fishing, he had an infallible means of getting as much fish as he wanted. To this end he used a plant whose juices had the same properties as the Levant nut: it killed the creatures of the deep without making them unfit to be eaten.

The Levant nut is a South and Southeast Asian climbing plant, *Anamirta cocculus*. Poison from the dried plant was traditionally used to stun or kill fish. Plant poisons were frequently used in freshwater fishing in the Umpila dialect area.[5] Thomson describes these poisons as 'extremely potent'.[6] One fish poison used by Port Stewart people was *Derris trifoliata*, var. *macrocarpa*, known as the 'Dynamite Plant'.[7]

One day when Traouais had made a really extraordinary catch and had brought it back to land, it happened that an enormous fish which, it seems, had only partly succumbed to the effects of the juices of the plant, awoke from its torpor. It opened wide its enormous jaws and, instead of being eaten by the fisherman, it was the fish that swallowed this new Jonah. Traouais immediately went up into the moon. Since then, everyone can see the big man at the heart of his new abode. It is because of his presence in the star which, by night, sheds its light upon the earth that the natives have given it the name of the famous fisherman. The word 'moon' is expressed in their language by the word *traouais*.

No matter how good a fisherman Traouais was, it is possible to become his equal without having to go up into the moon. In order to do so it suffices to eat a man, a white man in preference to a black man. This is why one of the savages, who nonetheless had no taste for cannibalism, but who was consumed by his love of fishing and by his ambition, fully intended to eat Pelletier if he happened to die before him. He did not let him remain unaware of his intentions, at the same time assuring him that he was too good a friend to hasten his death.

If cannibalism was once practised among the peoples of this region, it was certainly not the straightforward matter of individual intention and decision that this description suggests. Pelletier's extreme reticence on the subject to Ottley, as mentioned in the introductory essay, is also reason to question Merland's way of presenting the subject. Chase, in his Commentary, notes that 'There is no record of cannibalism in later anthropological research.'

Among the savages, shooting stars, a topic about which there has been much discussion, receive a quite different explanation from that given by science. This explanation is not theirs exclusively: many peasants in the Vendée believe it as well. Shooting stars are produced by the passage of dead people who are leaving this earth to go and live in another place.

Thomson describes beliefs about shooting stars:
'When they see a "shooting star" the people know at once that somebody is dead. … If, as of course most frequently happens, the star merely passes across the heavens, they say that somebody from another ŋartji [ngaachi, "camp/place"] has died, but if, as once occurred while I was camped with the Yintjingga tribe on the Stewart River, a report is heard, the watchers cry "Mumpa!" [mumpa] They know that somebody is dead and that his mipi [mitpi, "spirit of a dead person"][8] has come to join his ŋorntäl [nguunthala, "fontanelle-'wind'"] in their own country.'[9]
Chase reports a slightly different version of the relationship between stars and spirits: 'a falling star (mil'a) is interpreted as the movement of the spirits to and from their estates searching for those who would threaten the survival of descendants.'[10]

The savages do not therefore believe absolutely that everything ends with death, as one might think when hearing them deny the existence of the hand of a creator. They believe in metempsychosis[11], though not as Pythagoras taught it. According to that philosopher, the human soul passed into the body of an unclean animal or into that of a man who was superior, according to whether the person had done good or evil during his lifetime, to return later in another form. They firmly believe that every black person, without exception, returns to life by changing colour and that, once they have become white, they go and live in a land situated to the west of theirs.

Pelletier was therefore to them merely a black person who had come back to life.

The same was believed of other Europeans such as William Buckley, James Morrill and Barbara Thompson who found themselves living with Aboriginal people. It was a widespread belief in traditional Aboriginal societies that spirits of the dead were white-skinned,[12] which in cases like Pelletier's facilitated their acceptance by their Aboriginal hosts. Chase notes that the Uutaalnganu word for 'white man', *para*, probably comes from the term for a dead person's ghost. Peter Sutton lists a number of languages for the western Cape York Peninsula region in which the term for European had the original meaning of 'ghost'.[13] And at the other end of the continent Tasmanian Aborigines used the word *Num.mer*, a term for 'ghost' or 'spirit', to refer to white people.[14]

Sutton, writing about early encounters between Aboriginal people and the Dutch on Cape York Peninsula, illuminates how the coming of Europeans was first perceived by indigenous Australians and incorporated into their world:

'First encounters with Europeans were arguably experienced by Aboriginal people in anything but territorial terms. They were most often, it seems, primarily an encounter with relatives who had gone to the spirit world and returned. One could flee from them, ignore them, get annoyed with them or attack them, without abandoning the view that they were the dead, and one's own dead. The dead were always a potentially malevolent and "tricky" group of social beings, as anyone who has camped with traditionally minded Aboriginal people will know. They were family who remained part of one's real world, even when long ago cremated or buried in body. One should bear in mind here the matter-of-factness with which Aboriginal people of traditional mind conduct life in an environment richly peopled by the spirits of the dead, by departed people to whom words are regularly said, and whose signs are often seen or heard, especially at night, in the fleshly world.'[15]

One thing they must do in order to obtain some quite desirable pleasures in their second life is to extract one of the incisors of the lower jaw.

In this region an incisor of the *upper*, not lower as Merland states here, jaw was knocked out.[16] Merland's account gives no idea of the complex of spiritual beliefs and social relationships underpinning this practice. Thomson has described the rite of tooth avulsion in detail.[17] The rite resulted in the subject being assigned a personal totem linked to his mother's moiety, and established a special relationship with particular members of his mother's moiety. A divinatory process beginning at birth culminated in the extraction of the tooth, usually around puberty, but it could occur later than that. In right-handed people the upper right incisor was avulsed, and the left in left-handed people.

The fact that Pelletier declined to undergo this operation suggests that he cannot have been fully incorporated into the social and cultural world of his adoptive relatives. While his adoptive father is mentioned a number of times in the book, there is no mention of an adoptive mother. The circumstances of his adoption may have rendered the full performance of this rite impossible given that the process culminating in tooth avulsion began at birth.

If they want to drink clean water in the other world, it is absolutely essential for them to undergo this little operation.

Thomson reports: 'If the tooth has not been removed the *mipi* (ghost) [*mitpi*, "spirit of dead person"] will be compelled to drink foul water — water containing maggots — after death. This is a well established and widely held belief, and curiously enough, several informants independently made the same statement both as to the foul water and the maggots.'[18]

Having no religious beliefs, the savages do not address prayers to Heaven to ask God for a change of weather when they need it. They have to hand a sure and infallible means of influencing the weather as they see fit. Is the soil utterly parched by the sun's rays? Will they run out of water and soon find it hard to quench their thirst? If so, they will make up a big bundle of certain plants and place the charm into ground that has retained a little moisture. After this they do not have to wait long for rain. But sometimes their success is greater than they had been expecting. Torrential and continuous rain will follow upon a desperate drought, they will be hit by hailstones even as they shelter under the trees and, finally, a deluge now threatens to inundate the earth where a few moments ago there was nothing but dust and yellow leaves. In order to avert this danger all they need to do is to take from the ground the grasses whose effect had been powerful enough to bring them rain; it will be no less powerful in bringing back the fine weather. They have only to set them alight and immediately the clouds will dissipate, the sun will light up the verdant countryside with its rays, the now cooler atmosphere will waft gentle breezes, joyous birdsong will be heard, and the country will become a delightful Eden.

Thomson's observation that 'Yintjingga' men were renowned for their rain and thunder magic — 'as far north as the Lockhart River I heard the Stewart River referred to as the home of rainmakers' — shows that rainmaking was not always the simple affair presented here.[19] The ceremony performed to make rain and thunder 'consisted of a rite, elaborately performed, accompanied by a spell of great length'.[20]

From rain and shine, let us pass to thunder and stormy weather, a quite natural transition.

Since God is a myth, thunderclaps are not, as the pagans believed, the noise made by the tiles that the master of Olympus in his anger rained down vengefully upon the heads of the pale humans. Rather it is the noise of the struggle fought in another region inhabited by white men. The outcome could be disastrous to the blacks if the wicked carried the day, and if they did not ready themselves to put up the most vigorous resistance to their enemies.

The sound of thunder is nothing but the sound made by the bad men of the white race rolling along blocks of iron, which they intend to use to crush the blacks. Happily, among the whites, there are some who are good and generous by nature. While some, armed with metallic levers, push the blocks of iron[21] one way, moving them closer to the abyss from where they can be hurled down upon the blacks, others stand up to them and exert their efforts in the opposite direction. Out of these clashes sparks fly and thunderclaps resound. Lightning and the sound of thunder have no other cause than this.

But as the good might not always be victorious, and as their defeat would be fatal to the blacks, the latter do not stand with their arms folded waiting for the conflict to be decided. On the contrary, they get ready for the fight. Assembled in large groups, they cry out with threatening shouts, as well making provocative gestures to the rascals who want to harm them. Now as the wicked men are almost always lacking in courage, the cowards withdraw, their blows becoming gradually weaker, and soon they can only be heard in the distance. Finally they cease altogether when the wretches fall back and take flight.

As we have just seen, all these beliefs have more to do with fables than with the supernatural. If the brain of the savages is barely touched by reason and their imagination is sometimes like the madwoman in the attic, it is still the case that spiritualist aberrations, which sometimes border on madness, are much less prevalent among them than among civilised peoples. We see nothing resembling mesmerism, spiritualism, illuminism or conversations with the dead or with imaginary beings. With the exception of certain important natural phenomena for which they find strange explanations, they are only concerned with things which are palpable and material.

In the treatment of illnesses, for example, where so often we see cultivated minds and intelligent men neglect science in favour of superstitious or ridiculous practices in the search for a cure for those who are dear to them, the savages only have recourse to the means they can obtain from nature. Do they make good use of them? Far be it from me to make such a claim. Do they have a sound knowledge of the properties of the topical remedies they use? I doubt it very much. Is the bloodletting they perform always appropriate? This can certainly be denied. But all the same their methods are aimed directly at the illnesses they have to treat, without having recourse to sorcerers and astrologists.

In just a few words I shall give an account of their therapeutics and medical materials in their entirety. This treatise will barely exceed a page. Let us begin with the types of diseases encountered, which are also very limited.

Most of the illnesses which, at home, decimate the human species are completely unknown in Endeavour Land. Although they may be exposed to rain when they are covered with sweat, and what they use to protect themselves is quite inadequate, respiratory infections are very rare and, for the most part, not serious. They are normally limited to mild cases of bronchitis that get better without any need for treatment. As to tuberculosis, I have reason to think that it is completely unknown, Pelletier having assured me that one never encountered those coughs which persist lifelong, are accompanied by a great weakening of the body and loss of weight, and whose end is always fatal. Nor had he ever been aware, either in his tribe or in the neighbouring ones, of any cases of eruptive fever. He had never seen any measles, scarlatina or pustules other than those produced by mosquito bites. He had never come across anyone who bore the traces of small pox. The only epidemic which had arisen in the tribe over a period of seventeen years was dysentery. He himself contracted it, but not very seriously.

Pelletier does not know if the women, during their confinement, are subject to serious mishaps in giving birth or if they are exposed to the puerperal fever which has such disastrous effects in our region because, when the time comes to give birth, the women withdraw into the woods, far from men's eyes. However, he is much inclined to think that everything goes well because, after about three weeks have passed, they reappear, carrying the newborn baby in a little cradle. He cannot recall ever having heard that any woman had died giving birth to her child or some time after the birth.

Neuroses are unknown there and no one has ever seen a person who was mentally disturbed. As far as I can judge from symptoms whose accuracy I cannot vouch for, the most common illnesses are sunstroke, sporadic fevers and rheumatism; as well as these, bites from venomous snakes always have serious consequences, even when they are not fatal.

The treatment of all the illnesses varies little and there is no need for a long course of study to learn how it is done. Except for the case of snake bite, treatment consists of a purely external medication. Therefore anyone is able to put it into practice and there are no specialists who practise medicine.

Merland's comments here about medicine, its practice and its practitioners as a domain of limited and purely secular dimensions avoid any mention of secret knowledge, perhaps showing Pelletier's reticence about discussing it with him and making it known. Chase reports that, as with material resources, 'knowledge, usually secret, concerning ceremony, sorcery, healing, sexual attraction and so on' is passed down following links of kinship and marriage:

'Secret knowledge … is usually given by a senior woman or man only to a junior relation when judged mature enough to accept it, and then only individually to a junior kinperson of the immediate family. Thus, actual father's father or father's older brother will pass on this knowledge in secret.'[22]

Thomson notes that his informants were very reluctant to impart magical knowledge, partly because they were aware that it was disapproved of by whites. The mission at Lockhart River had been established in 1924 and mission authorities strongly discouraged elements of traditional culture.[23] But as well as this awareness of official disapproval and fear of punishment, Thomson observes that 'it is regarded as impolitic to boast of the possession of magical knowledge.'[24]

For all illnesses that have a generalised effect on the organism, bleeding of the forehead is practised. The instrument used for this operation is a piece of broken bottle. Armed with his piece of glass, the person who attends the sick person makes several lengthwise incisions that cut right through the thickness of the skin. They must be vertical and must extend from the hairline to the space between the eyelids; once the incision has been made the surrounding tissue is tapped gently with a wooden switch to increase the blood flow. When the operation is over a herb endowed with particular properties, which has first been chewed and coated with saliva, is applied to the incision. The nature of this topical remedy varies according to the nature of the illness, but it is almost always supremely effective in curing it.

This procedure, as can be seen in his photograph, was carried out on Pelletier, who will always bear the scars it left on his forehead. He had been ill for a long time and subject to the most violent headaches every three days. The treatment was a complete success. After several days he made a complete return to health and regained the strength he had lost because of his illness.

The forehead is not the only part of the body on which this kind of bleeding is practised. Every localised pain calls for the same procedure to be applied to the part of the body where it occurs. Noticing scars on one of his elbows, I asked Pelletier where they had come from and I learnt that they were the result of incisions that had been made to cure the pains that he felt in that joint.

In some cases the women tie a herbaceous band around their husband's head without practising any bleeding. They press their lips to it, using a prolonged sucking action. These efforts and the bitterness of the plants they use draw blood to the gums and bring about a light haemorrhage in the woman's mouth, bleeding that she thinks is coming from her husband's head. It goes without saying that the husband, who holds exactly the same belief, invariably feels his pain lessening, if it does not go away altogether.

Hale and Tindale note that 'Fillets of string or other material are sometimes wound tightly on the head — not as an ornament, but to cure headache.'[25] Waist belts could have a similar use for stomach pain.[26]

The most serious and most common injuries are the result of personal attacks, private acts of revenge, wars between tribes and punishments inflicted on the guilty. Here again we find that herbaceous topics are used. But would these injuries not heal more quickly and more surely if it were left to nature to take care of them?

Finally, mosquito bites, which are always so painful and are sometimes followed by a rather extensive swelling, receive the same treatment: a localised bleeding and the application of chewed herbs.

I have just said that bites from venomous snakes were extremely serious. Among the general ill effects which are brought on as a result, there will be extreme dryness and constriction of the throat. Only in this case is an internal medicine used. The patient swallows a raw tuber which he has first chewed for a considerable time. According to Pelletier, this tuber is endowed with remarkable properties for curing snake bites.

Aside from venomous bites, the universal panacea, the remedy for all ills, is bloodletting with the subsequent application of a herb ground up by the teeth.

The model of death and illness held by Uutaalnganu people and their neighbours is not clear from Merland's account. 'All deaths,' writes Chase, 'other than those of very old people or very young babies were seen as the result of sorcery, and social life contained a series of such interpretations of death and sickness'.[27] Identification of the sorcerer and counter sorcery would be practised if the victim had died. For an affected man who had fallen ill, 'a "doctor" (*mapurungu*) could give him bush medicines, or remove the poisonous objects by sucking or by letting blood from the face and arms'.[28]

CHAPTER 6

Respect for the dead. Funeral ceremonies.

Among the savages feeling prevails over the work of reason to a great extent. We learnt earlier of the mothers' anguish when they were awaiting the return of their children; when their parents die the pain of their loss is revealed in even more moving displays. If, as in India, the women do not end their days by throwing themselves upon the pyre which consumes the body of their husband, their wish is likewise that bodily suffering should be added to the pain in their heart. So that they may never cease to be aware of the loss that they have experienced, they want its indelible imprint to be clearly visible to them for the rest of their lives. With this aim, they make deep incisions on the upper part of their thighs, leaving scars which will never disappear. As a sign of mourning, they blacken their faces and bodies with charcoal, bind ties torn from trees across their chests and cover their heads with a little cap of herbs that they make themselves.

A mourning cap collected by Thomson in 1929 was described as follows for an exhibition of mortuary objects from the Donald Thomson Collection:

'The cap smeared with mud (*pi-pi*) is worn for periods after the death of a close relation, the length of the period depending on the closeness of the relationship. The period ends with a ceremonial feast and until this ending, and the discarding of the cap, a widow mourning her husband will continue to rub her body with charcoal and she may not speak, though she may use the formalised gesture language.'[1]

Hale and Tindale describe, with photographs, the mourning cap and mourning strings referred to by Merland and a number of other mortuary objects:

'Some special objects are used at the burial and during mourning, and special customs are observed. Rectangular tablets, known as "opamaka",[2] painted with red ochre and white pipe-clay, are placed in branches of trees at the place of the ceremony. These are usually made by the men, and vary in number according to the importance of the deceased; in some cases they are fashioned from the spear-smoothers of a dead man. The hair of the corpse is cut off, and bound over with *Livistona* twine to form sausage-shaped or cylindrical bundles, which are hung around the necks of mourners as a sign of grief; often these pendants are covered with beeswax so as to wholly conceal the underlying hair and string. If available, a ceremonial net dress ("iyawur") and cap ("akwama"), made from fishing nets used by the deceased[3] are worn, the relatives taking turns in the wearing of this costume during the wailing, crying, and dancing. The dresses and caps appear to be rare, but we were able to secure two ancient examples. Painted wooden staves or "wailing-sticks," five to seven feet in length, and with a lump of gum at one end, are used at the ceremony and elsewhere, and afterwards are placed on the temporary grave of the departed, whose possessions are hung upon them; in some cases two such sticks are held, perpendicularly, one in each hand, by a relative during wailing. If a good hunter dies the young men sometimes cut out the ulna from both arms, and the bones are afterwards used for making the heads of turtle spears. During the mourning period following the burial a widow plasters herself with mud, both head and body, and may also wear a painted wooden pendant around the neck, plaited strings wound around the arms and sometimes round the neck also. When these strings are removed from the necks of women they are rewound and worn by male mourners; in the latter case the loop of the chain-strings is passed over the head and under one arm, so that it extends diagonally across the chest and back; generally two sets of strings are thus worn … Hair pendants are also worn by mourning relatives, who do not trim their hair for months, and, in the case of men, allow the beard to grow unchecked.'[4]

All the other members of the family wear similar mourning attire. If a child precedes his parents to the grave the mother will blacken both her face and body, while the father daubs himself with white from head to toe. Mourning is worn for one or two years and for all of that time no changes may be made to it.

The social significance of bereavement among the coastal peoples of northeastern Cape York is further reflected in the attribution of special status terms to relatives in mourning.[5]

On the day of the funeral ceremony the whole tribe is called together and no one fails to come. After the feast come the dances, which are quite different from those at joyful festivities. Only the women's voices can be heard. The songs are mournful, monotonous and always interspersed by sobbing.

The men dance a sort of *danse macabre*. They do not carry images representing death, but they embrace, pressing their bodies together, and after numerous embraces they allow themselves to fall, as if they themselves had ceased to live.

Chase notes that he has never encountered this men's dance, but the women's dance referred to above is most likely the *wuungka* ceremony. Only women sing and dance in this ceremony and it signals the lifting of various mortuary restrictions.[6]

The parents are not content with weeping over their dead; they do not want to be separated from them until the last possible moment and, for fifteen to eighteen months, will carry them everywhere with them. As they do not know about embalming, the following is the method which they use for the preservation of the corpses. The bodies are buried and exhumed three days later. After a corpse has been underground for seventy-two hours the skin will adhere less firmly to the underlying tissue. The mourners then equip themselves with wisps of straw and they rub the corpse so energetically with these that they are not long in removing the skin completely. Once this first procedure has been carried out they expose the body to the sun's burning rays, lighting a big fire right around to keep the flies off. After a week, the corpse, now completely dried, looks like a mummy.

Once the corpse is no longer liable to decomposition they make a wrapping for it using the bark of a tree which is easily detached from its ligneous part, then they secure this firmly around the body with lianas. They next fix in place two rods, one vertical extending the length of the body and preventing it from sagging, the other horizontal, and both of them being likewise attached with lianas. This arrangement allows the body to be carried by two people, with each end of the horizontal rod resting on the shoulder of the bearers. The holy relic accompanies them everywhere until the time comes for them to give it a burial place in the earth.

Chase provides this description of mortuary practices:

'In early times, the corpse was buried for a week or so, then gutted and the outer layer of the epidermis peeled off to make the body white. It was then wrapped in a coffin of stiff messmate bark (*Eucalyptus tetradonta*) which had a carrying stick inserted through the bundle. This coffin was then smoked over a fire and carried around with the group. During this time, the *mitpi* ["spirit of dead person"] remained with the corpse and the group, and relatives were required to carry out the correct behaviours of bereaved kin to keep the spirit in a benevolent mood. Spirits were most dangerous immediately following death when they were confused and violent. Constant wailing, laceration of the body and food prohibitions "settled it down" by demonstrating the affection with which the dead person was regarded. After some months, when the flesh had withered and the bones were heard rattling in the coffin, the container was opened, and the bones cleaned and painted. The remains were then repacked in a new coffin of ti-tree bark (*unytyi*) [*unchi*] to the accompaniment of a feast and a renewed demonstration of grief. All close relatives of the deceased were invited to the final disposal ceremonies when the bone bundle was buried.

...

Final disposal by burying was ideally carried out in the estate of the deceased ... It was essential that the corpse was buried within country of close relatives, where the grave and spirit could be cared for, and recognised by following generations.'[7]

They do not deposit these cherished remains at the foot of a tree, on a river bank or in the hollow of a rock; they have a particular place set aside for this purpose. Their burial ground bears the name *Manillecalgo*;[8] it is a place of veneration for all. Every dead person is covered over with shells, fishbones and animal and whale bones, and on top of these, by way of a tombstone, there is a turtle's head.

There is a photograph of a grave resembling this description in Thomson's 'The dugong hunters of Cape York'.[9] Chase notes that this shows the burial site of major elders who were skilled hunting men. The graves (on the coast) were covered with dugong rib bones and skulls of turtle and dugong. He has recorded the graves of *pama watayichi* ('dugong men') in

'Nightisland' and Kuuku Ya'u territory. Thomson notes that 'With the sandbeachmen the final burial takes places on the seashore. The grave is placed just above spring tide level, and the bones of dugong which have previously been removed from the water and accumulated ... are arranged upon it.'[10]

Only old people are buried immediately after their death, without their corpse first having accompanied the family in all their wanderings. It is not that their death inspires no more than passing regret, nor that they enjoy less regard than younger people, but it is thought that their body, weakened by age, would not be suitable for the drying procedure, and if this were incomplete it would prove impossible to carry it long distances without breaking it.

Respect for the dead, which is almost a cult for the family of the deceased, even exists for the dead of the enemy. Far from removing the scalp of the warrior who has just fallen on the battlefield and taking it as a trophy, as is done elsewhere, the victors here behave towards the body as if it were that of one of their close relatives. When it has dried two men take the corpse on their shoulders and take it back to the tribe to which the warrior belonged. They run no risk in fulfilling this sacred mission, the burden which they are bearing being a safe conduct that the enemy, no matter how fierce, always respects. It once fell to Pelletier to accomplish such a mission, a task more moving than dangerous.

Rigsby notes that returning the bodily remains to the deceased's home country is a regional Cape York Peninsula cultural pattern and that in this instance it provides evidence that, at least on this occasion, Pelletier travelled beyond his group's normal range.[11]

I should add in conclusion that the memory of those they have lost never fades completely from their minds; a sign, a word, will be enough to reawaken it. Therefore they take the most scrupulous precautions not to recall the dead. They refrain as far as possible from speaking to the living relative of the loss he has suffered, and when they are forced to do so by the demands of conversation they always use a circumlocution. If, for example, Maademan had happened to die before his wife, they would never have said his name in front of her. They would have said: Sassy's uncle or Pelletier's adoptive father.

Should we not be overcome with amazement at finding such feelings among savages, among peoples living in an almost bestial state? And when, looking around us, we see with what speed time puts grief to flight, should we not blush for our civilisation? It is true that among the tribes of Endeavour Land the children are not waiting on a large inheritance from their parents, and that the death of a father or mother, of a brother or sister, or of some others of their close relatives, will not realise for them what we call *great expectations*!

CHAPTER 7

Dress and adornments. Gatherings, feasts, dances and songs.

The costume of the savages! Nature alone has borne the cost, and yet the ladies there can hardly be paid the compliment which Zaïre received from Orosmane:[1]

Art is not made for you, you have no need of it.

On the contrary, men and women could well benefit from concealing their figures under some frills and flounces. It is only on important occasions that, taking some branches of greenery from the trees, they will make themselves a costume worthy of being celebrated in song by the pastoral poets.

In the *Times* article, however, Pelletier is reported as describing the garment worn by the women as 'a fringe of cords extending from the waist to half way down the thigh'.[2] One of these garments can be seen in a photograph by Thomson of an Umpila woman.[3]

As well as this garment, special objects were worn as part of mourning dress as described in Chapter 6. Hale and Tindale comment that such objects 'are not altogether to be considered ornamental, in fact, they have a rather depressing influence on the wearer, and he discards them after a time so that he will not continue to feel mournful'.[4]

And so, on dance days, they will put around their waists and heads the small branches which they have picked. The privileged few who have been able to obtain brightly-coloured ribbons from the whites with whom they have engaged in passing trade will decorate their forehead with one of these. This ribbon, cut to make a band, is usually a piece of red handkerchief torn into strips, which the *chic* of both sexes have shared between them. The belts and the green circlets are absolutely plain and are never studded with flowers. Everyone paints his body according to his own taste. But as the whims of fashion show little variation, the colours used are almost always the same.

Hale and Tindale provide more detail (and photographs) in describing armlets and belts:

'Pandanus armlets are quickly made. A strip of screw palm leaf, twenty inches or so in length and from one to two inches in width, is used; the method of manufacture is similar to that described by Roth for other tribes, namely, one end of the strip is split into tags, and a corresponding number of slits made near the other end. The leaf is first rolled to the desired diameter and the tags are passed through the slits and knotted inside the armlet.

...

'A single string may be used as a decorative waist belt (and is also used as a ligature to relieve abdominal pain). The natives obtain a certain amount of European cotton material, and in some cases this is adapted to form armlets, belts, etc. A flour-bag may be picked to pieces and the material made into twine for chain mourning-strings, waist-circlets, or armlets.'[5]

They also describe the weaving of a type of fine waist belt or circlet, then rare, crafted from a strip of yellow fibre and two lengths of *Livistona* string: 'the completed article is yellow with a longitudinal median blackish line of the fibre on each side.'[6]

That sums up the contribution of the milliner. That of the jeweller is not much greater. The necklaces, which are the most eye-catching of the adornments, come from abroad; they are given to the savages by the English in exchange for fish or other objects. Normally they are made of shells; sometimes they are made of shiny stones.

If it is correct that necklaces were obtained from the English in Pelletier's time, Sandbeach People did make their own necklaces. Hale and Tindale report that:

'Necklaces, particularly those made from *Nautilus* shell, are plentiful. Those seen in the Princess Charlotte Bay districts consisted of small rectangular pieces of the shell, each piece pierced with a single hole. The shell is strung on two strings of *Livistona* fibre, which are made to pass through the hole from opposite sides, so that the pieces of shell closely overlap. ... These necklaces are worn by women and children, occasionally also by men, but are apparently rarely used as fillets.

...

'Grass and reed necklaces, which consist of scores of short pieces of the stem strung on a string, are often made. They may be of considerable length, but are not so highly valued as the shell ones.'[7]

As well as these necklaces Hale and Tindale describe pendants made of *Nautilus* and pearl-oyster shell, oval or blade-shaped, worn on a string around the neck. [8]

The task of the hairdresser is simpler still.

Those who let their beard and hair grow do not arrange them in any particular way. [Hale and Tindale note that 'The hair (and in men the beard also) is generally kept close-cropped; during mourning periods it is allowed to grow unchecked.'[9]] Ostrich feathers, so common there[10] and so sought after by our ladies at home, are never seen on the heads of the female dancers.

There are other personal adornments that anyone who has even the slightest desire to look attractive, not just the men and women of elegance, cannot be without. Some of these can only be obtained at the cost of acute pain and suffering; but if one wishes to be held in some esteem, if one does not want to lay oneself open to gibes and jeers, it is absolutely necessary to submit to this discomfort and even to demand it.

The first of these, which only the sex wielding absolute power has the right to wear, is attached to the ear lobe. This is not the diamond of which our fine ladies are sometimes so proud. The jewel of the savages is of a quite different kind and of a quite different shape and is bigger in size. It is a cylinder of hollow wood, at least six centimetres in length and almost two centimetres in diameter. Moreover, the size of this cylinder varies: the bigger it is, the more highly it is valued. Here is the procedure used to set it in the ear lobe. One begins by piercing the lobe with a sharply pointed bone, as if it were merely a matter of fitting an earring, and a cylindrical object the size of a quill is inserted into the opening. The next day it is replaced by another which is slightly bigger and the day after by a third, which is bigger still. With increasing dilation the opening becomes large enough to accommodate a cylinder that is thicker and longer than a thumb.

The ear lobe is then pulled down by the weight it bears, and there are even cases in which it may get to the point where it is resting on the shoulder. This is the height of beauty, conferring great success on the happy soul who possesses such an advantage. Normally a plug is worn in each ear; Pelletier was content just to adorn his right ear in this way.

Chase notes that the ear plug was made of a short section of wild bamboo, and it was also used as a carry pouch, for example for tobacco. He observed older men with the slits for such plugs and the nose pins described below in the early 1970s.[11] Some sort of ear plug can be seen in the photograph of Narcisse

Pelletier taken in Nantes which appeared as the frontispiece to Merland's book, but not in the earlier photographs taken of him. The *Times* report describes the ear plug Pelletier was wearing when he was recovered and says that he gave it to one of the sailors of the ship that took him to Somerset (the *John Bell*).[12]

Wooden cylinders used as ear adornments are not exclusive to the savages of Endeavour Land. The fashion has spread to far-off places. It is even found in India, especially in the tribe of the Lenguas.[13]

Let us now pass from the ear to the nose. The nasal septum is pierced with the same instrument which was used to pierce the ear and an elongated shell is introduced into the newly-made hole. The shell has almost the same thickness as a piece of straw and barely extends beyond the wings of the nose.

The cylinder and the shell are removed at night and put back in place at daybreak.

Hale and Tindale report that most of the Port Stewart people had the septum of their nose pierced for nose-pegs. These were often of 'a smooth cylindrical piece of wood or bamboo' but several men 'were seen wearing curved nose-pins cut from the ribs of the whorls of the *Megalotractus* shell; some of these were large, seven or eight inches in length'.[14]

We have seen that the extraction of one of the incisors of the lower jaw guarantees that one will be able drink water of good quality in the next life.[15] It provides another advantage from which one draws immediate benefit: that of enhancing the attractiveness of the face. Pelletier was unmoved by this prospect. At the risk of being unable to quench his thirst except with foul-smelling and muddy water after his death, and at the risk of retaining an unsightly blemish, he wished to keep all of his teeth.

Hale and Tindale report that 'it is considered proper that all men and women should have parted with an upper incisor before marriage takes place'.[16] Pelletier's failure to do this may be another reason, aside from his white skin, why his bride-to-be did not look on him very favourably.

He could not escape a final operation from which he had initially recoiled, one whose fine scars he will carry with him always. The operation is certainly very painful, but as it confers the gift of attractiveness, and as those who refuse it are held up for ridicule, there was no room for hesitation. The operating procedure is quite simple. The instrument used is a piece of glass and in the same way as a surgical knife. Deep incisions are made with the shard on different parts of the body, beginning almost always with the abdominal region. These must be horizontal. Since the end in mind is to obtain quite obvious scars which are raised above the level of the skin, the incision should not merely leave a linear mark. To prevent this, every two days care is taken to pull back the edges of the wound and to apply pressure to each side of it, in order to push up the tissue underneath and to catch it up if it does not protrude sufficiently. Much care is taken not to suppress the fleshy buds which develop and, when a well-defined scar is produced, a second incision, above or below the first, is begun, which is made and treated in the same way. People do not limit themselves to two cicatrices; it is rare if less than five are made in the same area. From one part of the body they will then pass on to another. The person who bears the most scars and in whom they are the most obvious is without question the most handsome. Both sexes are equally keen to show off this rare distinction.

Chase notes that this accords with what he recorded in the early 1970s: the horizontal chest scars for men were to 'tighten' the chest and make it appear more attractive to women.[17] Some of the newspaper reports about Pelletier's recovery wrongly interpreted his scarring as having come about during his initiation. Billy Daniels, one of anthropologist Wolfgang Laade's main informants at the Lockhart River Mission in 1963, made this comment in Aboriginal English about scarification:

'Well, that thing he be not cut for the Bora [ceremonial complex centred on initiation]. Sometime he get cut before the Bora. They got certain time, got certain time [to do this] ... Got different kind law here before, — that's olden day. If you no got a mark there you [are] not man, you see. Might be spew pass on to you [= they spit on you], [then] you must feel sorry [= ashamed]. Bottle [a piece of bottle-glass] must come and cut you ... That thing we call him *matai*, that mark, that flash-thing on the chest. Some got two, some got three, some got four ... That been very, very long time [ago] too. As soon as white man came this country that been finish off.'[18]

Hale and Tindale report that 'both sexes commonly cut transverse scars on the lower part of the chest, as well as one or more rows of vertical cicatrices on the upper arms'.[19] The photographs of Pelletier show a number of cicatrices on his chest and upper right arm. The procedure described in *The Times* by which such scars were acquired echoes Merland's account. [20]

We can see what agonies must result. Skin is highly sensitive, and cutting it with an instrument whose blade is not well sharpened — as must be the case with the shard of glass — inevitably causes very sharp pain which becomes excruciating because of the nature of the dressings and through exposure to the burning sun. How is it that secondary infections — erythema,[21] erysipelas[22] and abscesses — do not develop from these different causes? But apart from the pain, it appears that everything goes as well as may be. Doubtless the victim has suffered and doubtless he has spent many sleepless nights; but what sweet recompense there is to come! How flowers can make us forget the thorns! He now possesses the delightful gift of being attractive. Is any price too high to pay for that?

It is during the big gatherings that all these embellishments make the biggest splash. On certain days of the year, which are not fixed in advance, each tribe gives a feast to which the neighbouring tribes are invited. Dancing is the main attraction.

Chase and Sutton note that 'Ceremonies (generally held towards the end of the dry season) were numerous, and rich in song, dance and accompanying mythology. Elaborate decorations and body paint designs accompanied these.'[23] Hale and Tindale provide descriptions of a number of men's and women's dances they observed at Princess Charlotte Bay. Although none of them were Uutaalnganu or Umpila dances, the details they provide corroborate and amplify Merland's description of dances in this chapter.[24]

Today at Lockhart River the tradition of dancing has continued, but in a different form. Formal and competitive dance performances by men, *thaypu* or 'Island-style dance', with major teams coming from three identity groups, are an important part of certain festive celebrations.[25] Chase writes that Night Island people, who form the *maathuy* or 'pelican' dance team, 'have a rich inheritance of songs and dances due to their early prominence in the lugger industry, and as well to a number of ancestors who were prolific composers of favourite songs and dances'.[26]

As with us there are several kinds of dances; as with us, too, the dance begins in the evening rather than during the day. Since the moon does not provide sufficient light, it is essential to come to its assistance. In the absence of lights and candelabras, the tribe uses torches made with the bark of a tree call *alquier* to provide light for the guests.

The word *ulku* corresponds to *alquier* and refers to a species of Livistona palm. Thompson gives his transcription *ulku* two meanings: 'water bag' and 'palm tree' (*Archontophoenix alexandrae*).[27] Thomson writes of the uses of the *ulku* as a vessel for water and vegetable food and to make ceremonial masks, when a discarded palm basket is often used.[28]

The orchestra is made up of four or five musicians who sit on the ground and start up the songs, which all the voices repeat after them. They have no instrument as accompaniment, not even the reed pipe. They keep time by beating together two sticks made of iron or wood.[29]

Hale and Tindale describe a dance on Flinders Island off Bathurst Head:

'The old men sat in a group and sang in high-pitched voices. Several of them accompanied the singing by beating pairs of tapping-sticks; the women sat together in a group at the opposite end of the cleared space, and also beat time by striking their cupped hands against the upper and inner parts of their thighs. From time to time one of them rose and placed branches of trees and bundles of grass upon the fire to provide added illumination to the scene.'[30]

The men and women do not mingle in the dance: they keep at a distance of seven or eight metres from each other. Standing in a line, they dance one after the other, or all together, according to the type of dance, never taking each other by the hand. They spread their legs widely, and their most remarkable steps are the wonderful leaps they make. Arm movements are also part of the performance: they raise their arms up to the sky as high as they can reach, and wave them about with great animation.

Again, Hale and Tindale describe a very similar dance from Flinders Island:

'No name was given to the following dance, in which the men stood in a line and stamped vigorously; their legs were wide apart, and they held leafy twigs in their hands, which they first displayed high above their heads, and then suddenly with a jerking movement withdrew behind their backs, only to raise again equally suddenly a few moments later. These alternating movements were kept up for nearly an hour, during which the women shuffled as before, in the background.'[31]

Chase notes that Merland's description resembles the *malkari* ('shake a leg') dances. 'These are essentially secular amusement dances which can tell a story. Dancers spread their legs, keeping on their toes, with knees bent. They rapidly "flutter" the knees with their arms raised. Dances can include mimicking animals or various comic human actions. They were a favourite vehicle for tales of contact which could show a European digging a posthole, losing his way, riding a buckjumper and so on.'[32]

The dancing of the women is rather like that of the men but it is a little less exaggerated.

It is in this pleasant exercise that the charms of the two sexes are particularly evident. The handsome dancers attract a great deal of attention and more than once the ladies, captivated by so many pleasing attributes, will throw them a sweet look on the sly, but without so much as speaking to them. Caution demands it. The merest word, the merest sign, if noticed, would arouse wild jealousy; the movements of the dance would soon give way to a fight.

While the young people dance, the old people indulge in conversation and the children play.

The songs vary according to the dance. Most of them are composed merely of a single phrase repeatedly continuously, a phrase whose words, with some rare exceptions, do not belong to the language of the country. Where do they come from? This is something that is very difficult to know. What is certain is that those who perform them do not know what they mean.

Thomson, in discussing the Kuuku Ya'u initiation ceremonies he had witnessed over several months, comments about this lack of knowledge of the words of the songs. While he had recorded many chants in phonetic script, he says that 'these provided no key to the meaning of the songs because the language was either archaic or had been brought into Cape York Peninsula with the cult and had no meaning for the drum men except as an accompaniment to the sound of the drum'.[33] Chase, too, notes that he found that the words of songs performed in ceremonies were not necessarily understood.

It has been my good fortune to have been able to have these songs set to music by a distinguished composer of my own town,[34] Monsieur Edouard Garnier. He has chosen to accompany the songs with a study which will be of great interest from an artistic point of view. It will certainly constitute the most curious part of this publication. I am very grateful to Monsieur Garnier for having allowed me to reproduce the songs. They can be found as an appendix to this book.[35]

The feast begins in the daytime. It is the tribe in whose territory the gathering takes place that bears all the costs. With this aim, and contrary to normal practice, it has stocked up on provisions. The menu for the meal is composed of yams, some other tubers, fruits, fish, shellfish, furred and feathered game. For the beverage there is honeyed water, but without the addition of certain aromatic plants which, in the form of mead, can impart intoxicating qualities to that drink through fermentation.

Hale and Tindale describe how a length of lawyer cane was used for collecting honey: 'One end of a long cane is frayed till it forms a brush; the brush-like end is inserted into the opening in a tree leading to a bees' nest, and is twisted about until a mass of honey and comb is collected on it.'[36]

Pelletier told Ottley that collecting honey [*puntu*, sugarbag (bees' nest)] was women's work.[37]

After the feast, which usually goes on for a long time, it is time for sleep and rest. The singing and dancing will begin again the following evening. The gatherings normally last two days, after which the tribes go their separate ways, lavishing on one another signs of the warmest friendship.

CHAPTER 8

Tribal wars. Fights between individuals. Punishments inflicted on the guilty.

Harmony does not always reign between the tribes, far from it. Often war will follow upon the friendliest relations. It is not ambition, the thirst for conquest, the desire to extend one's rights or the lure of riches and absolute power which give rise to them. They spring from purely individual causes, such as violence against individuals or, most often, the taking of women, with or without their consent. Tribes never have to defend their territory against the encroachments of a Cyrus or an Alexander. Rather it is when Paris takes Helen from Menelaus that the call to arms goes out.[1] Here is how things proceed in the normal course of events.

The structural significance for Cape York societies of the pattern of armed conflict which is described in this chapter is referred to by Sutton when he notes that:

'[Lloyd] Warner's words about north-east Arnhem Land, perhaps with the substitution of "armed conflict" for his "warfare", could have been written about pre-conquest Cape York Peninsula also: "Warfare is one of the most important social activities of the Murngin and surrounding tribes [of north-east Arnhem Land]. Without it, Murngin society as it is now constituted could not exist."'[2]

Where there is mutual consent, the woman, on the pretext of going to look for yams or fruits, draws as far away from her companions as she can and goes to the place of the rendez-vous which has been given to her in a secret discussion. The seducer and his accomplice have barely arrived there when they make haste to flee, fearing terrible vengeance.

In the case of a violent abduction, the guilty party almost never acts alone; most often a friend will accompany him. If the innocent victim he drags away against her will decides to resist, both of the men threaten her with their arrows. Fear of death then overcoming any other feelings, she will leave behind, but not without regret, her tribe and her family.

It has to be said, however, that surprise is normally rather difficult. In this region there is a bird which, as a forward sentry, never fails in its duty. In vain does the enemy take the greatest precautions, in vain does he go forward only on tiptoes: the bird cannot be taken by surprise. Even if he steps as lightly as Camilla, the blades of grass not bending beneath his feet,[3] a warning cry will signal his approach.

There is not enough information to identify which sentry bird Pelletier might be referring to here. In this region there are a number of bird species which will give warning cries when disturbed. Athol Chase notes that Friarbirds (genus *Philemon*) 'talk' language and will sometimes give warnings, as will the Blue-winged Kookaburra (*Dacelo leachii*), while the Mangrove Golden Whistler (*Pachycephala melanura*) signals tide change. Another possibility, suggested by David Clarke[4], is the Little (or Papuan) Cuckoo-Shrike (*Coracina papuensis*).[5]

The husband is not slow in learning to which tribe the abductor of his wife belongs. So that she will be returned to him, he gives voice to the most vociferous demands. If these have no effect, the whole tribe will take the side of the outraged spouse. All his kin spread out into the neighbouring and friendly tribes, shouting at the top of their voices: '*Caouis! Caouis!*' [In Kuuku Ya'u, *kuway.*[6]]

In response to this appeal the tribes rise up en masse and, at a general assembly, declare war on those who seem to be participants in the abduction by refusing to deliver up those responsible.

And so it is farewell to hunting, to fishing and to all the other activities. Wholly given over to a desire for vengeance, the warriors leave, followed by their fathers, their children and their wives, leaving to the latter the responsibility for obtaining the food they need.

The campaign is always a short one. Waged for the same reason, the Trojan War lasted ten years and, in bringing her back under the conjugal roof, Menelaus must have found Helen somewhat aged. Here things happen more rapidly and the *Iliad* of the savages would only have very short verses. If one sometimes finds an Andromache inconsolable at the death of Hector, or if Aeneas is more than ready to carry Anchises on his shoulders, the fiery Ajax, the wise Ulysses, Agamemnon, Pyrrhus and Nestor never make an appearance.

As ever the savages advance on the enemy having no man as their commander. They have no scouts and no outlying pickets. Their campaign plan is very simple and demands no strategic research. The two armies, which rarely number more than eighty men on either side, advance towards each other without seeking to surprise the other party, or to set them an ambush. The warriors entrust some of their arrows to the children who walk along behind them, and stand ready to fight. As soon as the two armies have come together, the war cry '*Coübedè! Coübedè!*' [no Kuuku Ya'u equivalent is apparent for this term] — an insulting term which corresponds to the coarse expression often used in France to refer to a woman of easy virtue — goes up from the assembled ranks.

But it is only when they are at a distance of thirty metres from one another that the fight begins. The combatants never fight each other hand to hand. Having neither lances, nor axes, nor clubs, it is their skill alone that decides the outcome of the battle.

Joining with the cry of '*Coübedè!*' repeated by both camps, there are indistinct shouts to which all the savages give voice as they hurl their arrows. In order to separate them, the old men, at the risk of being struck themselves, throw themselves between the two enemy armies, trying as hard as they can to stop the combatants and prevent them from reddening the soil with their blood.

Chase notes that these are usually the actions of people who have close kin relationships with people on both sides of the combat. At Lockhart River, in the 1970s, these actions could still be seen occurring in fights and the close kin who would interpose themselves were known as 'blockers'.[7]

The women do the same: they weep and they moan. Then before long, excited by the shouts of their husbands, they too start attacking each other. While the men continue to shoot at each other from a distance, the women approach each other, trading harsh blows as they set to.

The fight does not finish for lack of combatants. When a certain number of soldiers have been wounded and when some of them have bitten the dust, the army that has come off worse takes flight, leaving the field of battle to the victors. The latter are ruthless; they never take prisoners. They finish off the poor soul lying wounded on the ground, even if it means returning his body to his family or his tribe. The fugitives make off into the distance and pursuit is never zealous.

It is very rare for war to last for a long time. After the first engagement the old men, happier now than at the beginning of the action, resume their peace mission, and each tribe goes back to its own territory, without clinging to the hatreds which with us perpetuate wars between different nations. Peace is made without a ransom being paid, without lands being ceded, without needing to prepare the way by lengthy negotiations and without any other guarantee than the laying down of arms. Often peace is reached without the purpose for which war had been waged having been achieved, even though the tribe which began it remains victorious. If in fact it happens that the husband sometimes regains possession of the wife who had been taken from him, neither is it rare that she and her abductor make off into the interior and disappear without anyone knowing what has become of them.

No matter how sincere, peace rarely lasts for long. The same spark will reignite the fire, the same cause, once renewed, will yield the same results. During his time with the *Ohantaala* tribe Pelletier saw twelve wars break out. He did not restrict himself to the role of impassive witness but took a very active part in them. He was lucky enough to emerge safe and sound, without bringing back any injury from them.

Punishment of crimes is very limited: thefts, insults, even blows when they do not result in very serious wounds, all remain unpunished. Only killing and wounds made with arrows incur a severe punishment, but they only attract the death penalty in exceptional circumstances. If, for example, a man is guilty of murder or of causing serious injury, he must stand at about thirty metres from those whom the family of the deceased or of the wounded man has appointed to exact vengeance. Armed with arrows, they fire about thirty of them at the guilty man. These can deliver a fatal blow but it is very rare for this to happen. To prevent this, he is assisted by a friend who tries to ward off the arrows with a stick. [They used a *yuli*, or spear-thrower.[8]] If he has been lucky enough to avoid being struck, all is not yet over for him. He must then go to the relatives of the victim so that one of them can thrust an arrow into his thigh. Even if the arrow has passed right through his flesh, the ensuing wound will not be as painful as the operation required to extract it. As it is impossible to pull it out without causing dreadful pain, since its point has several hooked ends, and as any attempt at extraction would only result in more tearing of tissue, it is necessary to resort to another procedure. A large incision is therefore made with a glass blade and, when the tissue into which the hooks have penetrated is cleanly cut away, the arrow is pulled out with no difficulty. The arrow is always driven into the rear and upper part of the thigh.[9]

When it is a question of a simple wound the law of talion is applied to the guilty party! According to whether the arm, thigh or any other part of the body has been wounded, the arrow will be thrust into his arm, thigh or the corresponding part of his body.

In the case of murder the killer is obliged to blacken his face and body as a sign of mourning and is not able to wash himself until the day that the body of the victim is laid in its final resting place. He is forbidden to speak to his [the victim's] relatives other than by signs.

If the wound is not very serious the perpetrator still blackens his body for an indeterminate time. When the wounded man is better an assembly gathers to decide if he is permitted to put aside his mourning garb, the custom being to wear this for a wounded man as well as for a dead man.

Finally, where a death has occurred, in order for the guilty party's crime to be pardoned completely, so that after his punishment has been completed he is allowed to speak with the relatives of the man he has killed, he must, for a certain time, provide them with foods of the highest quality. This obligation is not limited to the relatives in a direct line; it extends to all the other members of the family. It is also imposed on the perpetrator of a simple wound, but in that case only the wounded man receives a food payment; his relatives do not have a share in it.

No court of law determines the penal sanctions. Custom has the force of law; no one seeks to escape its demands. One could not do so anyway without leaving oneself open to private acts of vengeance.

In Endeavour Land the arrow, as we have just seen, is therefore at once the instrument of murder and that of punishment. We shall find that it is the most powerful tool used by the savages to obtain the main foods of their diet: meat and fish.

CHAPTER 9

Hunting. Fishing. Culinary Arts.

It is from hunting and fishing that the savages seek their most appetising food, much preferring its products to those of the land. The country is rich enough in game, and the coast in fish, for them to be able to find there what they need to satisfy their gourmand's sensuality, or I should say their gluttony.

Chase and Sutton summarise how the Sandbeach People of Cape York seasonally exploit the rich resources of their land and sea environments:

'Constant camping on the immediate beachfront provides a strategic location at the centre of a complex environmental mosaic and allows rapid exploitation of general ocean and estuarine foods as opportunity arises. At the same time this location provides a central base for operating outward in either direction on land or on sea to harvest seasonally specific plants and animals.'[1]

Even snakes and crocodiles make a tasty dish for them. The large snakes, those which are much greater in size than the venomous snakes, are the only ones they eat.

The largest snake in Australia, the Amethyst or Scrub Python (*Morelia amethistina*), is found in this region. The python exceeds five metres in length with unconfirmed reports of specimens eight metres in length. It preys mainly on mammals and will even consume large wallabies and tree kangaroos.[2]

As for the crocodiles, this is how they hunt them. But, before going any further, I wonder if the huge lizards which Pelletier calls crocodiles are not caimans. D'Orbigny[3] affirms that there are no crocodiles in Australia. Whatever the case, I shall adopt Pelletier's terminology. Besides, the question is of no interest in relation to the hunt itself.

Pelletier, not the scientist, was correct. The area where he was living is a habitat for the Estuarine or Saltwater Crocodile (*Crocodylus porosus*), *ayntikanu* in Kuuku Ya'u, which can grow up to seven metres in length.[4]

The crocodile lays its eggs on marshy land and will barely leave them while waiting for them to hatch. The female even prepares some brushwood in advance, arranging it to serve as a bed for her young ones as soon as they are born. The eye of the hunter can easily detect the tracks left by the crocodiles and, well aware that they are not far off, he gets ready to make it his prey. To this end, he arms himself with a sort of pike made from a very hard and resistant wood. Throwing himself upon the animal as soon as he sees it, he will strike it on the head and attempt to gouge out its eyes. With every blow that it receives the poor crocodile cries out with a sound like a dog barking, until, mortally wounded, it lies motionless on the ground. Then the hunter drags it or carries it off on his shoulders, according to how large and heavy it is. He will not leave without looking for its eggs, which he usually finds quite easily. What he obtains from this hunt allows him to feed himself and his family and friends for several days.

Hale and Tindale report that men would kill crocodiles in the Stewart River 'at every opportunity', first using their spears to gouge out the eyes to put the animal at a disadvantage before they deliver the final blow.[5]

In the absence of crocodiles, the hunter is happy to turn to much smaller lizards. He is very fond of them as well as of hedgehogs,[6] and makes excellent meals with their meat. But these are the less interesting hunts, those which require neither skill nor hunting knowledge. The fauna of the country is rich enough to give him scope for some brilliant exploits. On the coast, web-footed birds abound. As one goes further inland a great number of birds belonging to different classes is found, in particular white parrots with yellow heads,[7] cockatoos, wild hens, turtle doves, pigeons and ostriches.[8] The pigeons and turtle doves nest in the woods and the savages eat their chicks when they are about to take wing. Once these birds have abandoned their nests they hunt them, in the same way as other birds, with their arrows.

But pigeons are sometimes hunted in another way as well. These birds flock together in such large bands that arrows, which could only hit one bird at a time, are put aside in favour of a more expeditious method. As we see in the Pyrenees, where they are known by the name of woodpigeons, these flocks, dense and numerous, will often fly across very narrow paths through the mountains. The hunter climbs a tree and lies in wait on a level with their flight path. If the flock passes within reach, he will strike out as they fly past using a stick which he has ready to hand. With his blows raining down on them, the number of victims mounts rapidly and the ground is soon covered with the birds.

In the 1970s Chase recorded information provided to him by senior men about the traditional activity of beating down

Torres Strait pigeons (*Ducula spilorrhoa*) at a mountain pass. He notes: 'The site for this is famous — "Night Island Gap" — a gap in the Chester Range about opposite Night Island. Certain strategically placed trees were "owned" and inherited by families.'[9]

Thomson describes the flocking of the pigeons (which he refers to by the earlier species name of *Myristicivora spilorrhoa*) and its significance to the Cape York coastal peoples:

'They appear in flocks in September and early October, and move down the coast in ever-increasing numbers. The coming of the "White Pigeons" is one of the events of the year to the sea-faring aborigines of this coast, and is correlated with the ripening of the fruit of the Wongai. ...

'On the east coast, the birds were encountered in great flocks on the mangrove-fringed, scrubby islands close to the coast — particularly on Hannibal Island, near Cape Direction, and on Chapman, Night, Hannah, and Burkitt Islands north of Princess Charlotte Bay. Each day the birds visited the mainland in flocks and scattered to feed in the scrubs or jungles. In the late afternoon, they gathered together in large flocks, and returned to the islands flying low over the sea.

'When lying in a lugger on Night, Hannah, and Burkitt Islands, the birds could be seen fluttering in incredible numbers, like snowflakes, over the dull-green mangrove thickets, and at a distance of about half a mile their loud call notes merged into a confused roar like a chorus of frogs from a swamp in the distance.'[10]

But the big hunt, the one that demands both skill and cunning and cannot be undertaken without the help of a dog, is the ostrich hunt. We know the method used for this in other countries. This bird, which can reach up to six feet tall in some cases, is an expert runner. If it were to compete on turf no horse could outpace it. Therefore the Arabs, mounted on their steeds, would pursue it in vain if it ran ahead in a straight line. Unfortunately, it almost always runs in circles. The hunter, who knows its habits, makes his move accordingly. Instead of following it step by step, he cuts across the diameter of the circle while the ostrich runs around the circumference. Covering much less ground than the bird, he will finally tire it out and lay hold of it.

The hunting method of the savages of northern Australia is completely different from that of the Arabs. Since they have no horses, it is impossible for them to outrun a bird whose agility on its feet is remarkable. They go about it quite differently and set up an ambush. I have said that wild dogs are very common in Endeavour Land. There are also dogs which are perfectly trained and which could compete with our best pointers.

Rigsby and Chase remark that in the past Sandbeach People obtained dingo pups to train as hunters and companions and that dogs had (and have, although the dogs they now keep are of European origin) personal names.[11] The wild dog, or dingo, also has important totemic sites in this region.[12] Thomson notes that 'a dog has a place in the kinship system; it is piado (son or daughter, man speaking) to a man, and mampa (son or daughter, woman speaking) to his wife'.[13]

Feeding them is not a heavy burden on those who own them: they take the place of cats and live on rats of which they consume an amazing amount.[14] When he goes off hunting, the savage is always accompanied by his faithful Achates.[15]

As soon as he detects the tracks of an ostrich, the hunter lies in ambush while the dog, going in search of it, does not take long to track it down. Seeing the dog, the ostrich, far from taking flight, runs at it and makes it beat a retreat. If the ostrich does not continue its pursuit the dog goes back on the offensive and provokes it by barking. The ostrich again gives chase and the dog again takes flight, moving nearer and nearer to the place where its master is hidden. This game is continued until, after countless twists and turns, the ostrich finds itself only a few metres from the hunter. The hunter then lets fly his arrow, and the man and dog immediately rush upon the poor wounded creature, which soon dies under the force of their blows.

There are two species of ostrich, one black, one white. The black ostriches keep to the mountains; the white to the plains.

It is not clear which birds are being referred to as the black and white ostrich. From the description of the habitats it would seem that Pelletier's black ostrich is the cassowary and the white ostrich the emu. While the plumage of emus can be quite dark, it is lighter than that of cassowaries, which is black.

Wolfgang Laade recorded a story about the different plumages of Cassowary, *kutini* and Emu, *nampi* [*nhampi*], and why the cassowary lives in the hills and the emu on the plains, from Nancy Pawlo of the Pascoe River who was told the story by her father, Charlie King, from Night Island:

'Once Cassowary and Emu (both females) lived together. At this time Emu had the red stuff on her head, like fowl. So one day Emu asked the Cassowary to pick the lice from her head. Cassowary did that. He [sic] grabbed the red stuff, run away and put it on her own head. Emu was thinking of revenge.

One day she went out with her chicken and came back with only two. The others she had left hidden somewhere in the bush. Cassowary asked her, "Where are your chicken? You had many. You come back with two only." Emu answered, "I made a big fire. When it was hot I put all my chicken into it and left only two." Cassowary thought "I will do the same." And so she went out with her chicken, made a big fire and when it was hot she pushed all her chicken into it and left only two.

'The Emu went out again and took her children out of the bush. She painted them nicely with white lines from the corners of the eyes to the ears. So they went back to the camp and made a big noise, "li li li li li li li". Cassowary was surprised and asked, "Where did you get these chicken from?" Emu answered, "These are my chicken. I did not kill them. I have only fooled you as you have fooled me before." The Cassowary was very angry and went away.

'They never lived together again. Emu lives now on the plains and Cassowary on the hills.'[16]

Thomson notes that the cassowary is found 'only in the densest tropical jungles or scrubs of the east coast, where the cover is so dense that the sun never really penetrates, where water is plentiful, and the atmosphere humid'.[17] The strength and aggressiveness of the cassowary made it a dangerous bird to hunt: 'On account of the esteem in which the flesh of this bird is held by the aborigines, and the difficulties and dangers surrounding its capture, elaborate rituals and tabus are associated with the eating of its flesh.'[18]

The savages only hunt the black ostriches. [However, Thomson reports that the emus 'are much prized, and are assiduously hunted by the aborigines, who kill large numbers of them'.[19]]

The eggs of the ostrich, as well as its meat, are a much sought-after food. The eggs are very big; no fewer than fifteen are laid. [While the emu lays five to eleven eggs, the cassowary only lays three to five.[20]] The ostrich lays them in a place that is exposed to the sun and only sits on them during the night. Those of the white ostrich are thought to have abortifacient properties. The pregnant woman is therefore very careful not to eat them. Only men and old women dine on them.

The right to eat the white ostrich and its eggs is forbidden to children and young people. [Thompson notes that, as with the cassowary, there are restrictions on who can eat the emu.[21]] One must have reached adulthood to be allowed to do so. It is expressly forbidden for anyone below adult age to touch this food. Those who are rash enough not to obey this injunction are liable to incur the same punishment inflicted on young people who eat the fish reserved for the old people.[22]

The hens do not just build nests, but veritable edifices. They are not less than two or three metres high. About twenty workers are involved in their construction. The *troutrous* — the name given to these fowl — pile up on the ground such a large heap of leaves and branches that fifteen or twenty birds will come to lay their eggs there in summer. If the natives have not interfered with the nest, the hens return to it the following year. The eggs are red, almost the size of our goose eggs. Each hen lays twelve to fifteen eggs.

Pelletier's *troutrou* is *tuutu* in Kuuku Ya'u. The species is *Megapodius Freycinet*, the Scrub Fowl.[23]

Pizzey's *Field guide* notes the following in relation to the breeding habits of a related species of Scrub Fowl, *Megapodius reinwardt*:

'Nest: enormous mound of earth and vegetation or of sand, some up to 12 m in diam. and 5 m high but usually much smaller; particularly when new. Eggs: yellowish white to pale-pink, becoming stained pale-brown or dark red-brown. Laid singly in deep excavations in mound; at times in decaying leaves in fissures in sun-heated rocks or in sand. Number uncertain.'[24]

Thomson photographed a huge Scrub Fowl mound on the banks of the Stewart River, Charlotte Bay.[25] It measured more than 82 feet across, the diameter of the egg cavity was 30 feet and it was almost nine feet high.[26]

They do not need incubating; the heat of the nest is sufficient to make them hatch. This heat is such that if one breaks up the nest a thick smoke issues from it that is probably produced by the decomposition of the plants from which it is made.

The search for hens' eggs is entrusted to the women. To get to them they must delve into the huge mass I have just described so that when they come out again their bodies are covered in feathers and a rather unpleasant-smelling coating.

The search for turkeys' eggs is much the same as it is for the hens' eggs. However, the *vounetas* do not put so much work into their nests as the *troutrous*. The edifice built for the eggs is less massive and one can get to them more easily. It is in spring, in the rainy season, that the eggs are laid.

Thompson found no equivalent for '*vouneta*' among his informants, but Chase notes that this is probably the Scrub Turkey (*Alectura lathami*) which is *nyacha* in the coastal languages.[27] Donald Thomson gives *wornta* for brush turkey, with the alternative *n'yätjä*.[28] The latter corresponds to *nyacha*, making Thomson's *wornta* and Merland's *vouneta* a likely match.

Pizzey's *Field guide* lists this species as the 'Brush-turkey' and notes the following in relation to breeding habits:

'Mound averages approximately 4 m across by 1–2 m high, but very variable; of leaves and other plant material mixed with earth, kept friable by constant turning over. Material typically raked downhill to mound, baring ground. Male does most construction, regulates temperature at about 35°C. Eggs: white, fragile; average clutch 12–16; laid singly, at intervals of days. Incubation period about 7 weeks.'[29]

Kangaroos, which are almost only found in Australia, are very numerous in Endeavour Land. There are several species of them, which are distinguished from each other by their shape, their size, and the nature and colour of their fur.

Hale and Tindale note that the agile wallaby (*Macropus agilis*) was the most common in their study area and that people at Port Stewart hunted three species of wallaby.[30]

They, too, are very agile; they can leap not fewer than seven or eight metres in a bound. A man hunting them with nothing but his arrows and his dog would therefore be very likely to find himself engaged in a futile struggle, so he will use fire more often than his usual weapons.

The kangaroos normally keep to the tall scrubland, grouped in small herds. When the dog has drawn attention to the presence of the kangaroos, the hunter sets fire to the scrub right around the perimeter of the terrain where they are situated.

Chase and Sutton describe firing of vegetation from August onwards as the dry season advances:

'At this time progressive drying of the landscape allows burning off of the small isolated grassplains in the coastal hinterland, and these firings are carried out systematically as part of game drives for wallabies and other small animals, and to attract birds such as ibis who rapidly arrive to feed on the disturbed insects and grubs.'[31]

As soon as it smells the flames the kangaroo leaps forward to get across the circle which surrounds it; but it cannot do so without causing a good deal of burning to its skin. The sensation of pain overcoming its sense of caution, it stops to lick the affected areas. The hunter takes advantage of this to penetrate it with his arrow. How many loving mothers, more concerned about the young ones they carried in their abdominal pouches than about themselves, have met their death in this tragic fashion while devoting their attention to them!

Another quadruped of the same kind, the possum, is also found in large numbers in these parts; it is not nearly as strong as the kangaroo and scarcely bigger than a cat. The savages hunt possum and like to eat it; but of all the animals found in their country the kangaroo is the one whose meat is the most sought-after. The Europeans who have eaten it find that it is similar to venison.

The possum Pelletier refers to is most likely the Common Spotted Cuscus (*Spilocuscus maculatus*) or, in Kuuku Ya'u, *ampuyu*. Possums are not recorded in the Night Island area.[32] Chase and Sutton note: 'At the end of the dry season when creeks, rivers and waterholes are at their lowest, the riverine vine forests were combed for cuscus, cassowary and echidna.'[33]

Narcisse Pelletier did not hunt. The tribe to which he belonged only devoted their time to fishing. For this activity, the savages have none of the numerous contraptions which we use. They have no nets, no lines, no lobster pots and no baits to attract fish. They only use their normal weapon, the arrow, but one whose barb is made from three or four splayed branches finished with sharp tips and hooks, as can be seen in the plate included in the appendix.[34]

Hale and Tindale were much impressed by coastal people's fishing abilities with their spears:

'One day we watched a man, with a fishing spear in each hand, walking along a low cliff overlooking the sea. A mullet flashed out from under the rocky ledge, and in a wink the man had thrown his two spears, using each hand in turn; both spears transfixed the fish. When conditions are favourable a man, working in shallow water with a single spear, will, in an hour or less, capture as many fish (small sharks, mullet, and so on) as he can carry.'[35]

Nets were used for fishing in the Princess Charlotte Bay area, south of where Pelletier lived, as can be seen from Thomson's photographs of people fishing with large nets in the Stewart River estuary, Port Stewart.[36]

Fishing, but now with hook and line, for fresh and saltwater fish, remains a key pastime both at Lockhart River and Port Stewart, and provides significant food to the diet of people there. The preferred saltwater species are barramundi and salmon; the freshwater jewfish are used to make a broth.[37]

Among the many fish found on the coast, there are three — the grey mullet, the sea bass and the thornback ray — that Pelletier had encountered before leaving the port of Saint-Gilles.

Chase and Sutton note that:

'In the late dry period from October to December, large shoals of mullet (e.g. *Valamugil seheli*) arrive in the estuaries and were speared from the shallow sandbars at creek and river mouths, and at the same time beaches and islands were combed for turtle eggs.'[38]

The Thorny Ray (*Urogymnus asperrimus*), *yakathi* in Kuuku Ya'u, is the most highly prized of the ray species for eating in this region.[39] Thompson lists fourteen types of ray with their Kuuku Ya'u names.[40]

For fishing, the savages take to canoes. There are usually three men to a boat. One man is positioned at the stern, one at the bow and the third in the middle. When a fish is within reach the fisherman does not always throw his arrow, rather he spears it holding his weapon in his hand. Sharing of the fish is done according to the position that each man occupies in the canoe. The man at the front has the upper section, the next man, the middle section, and the last, the tail section.

Thomson similarly describes the strict protocol of sharing out the dugong meat according to the participants' position in the canoe and says that the distribution is similar for a turtle. He includes a diagram showing how the dugong is cut into six named portions, noting that the distribution of these portions depends upon the number of men involved in the catch. If the canoe owner has not been part of the expedition the shares may be divided four ways with the canoe owner receiving the choice, upper part of the dugong. 'The main object in sharing the animal,' writes Thomson, 'is to ensure a fair division of fat and flesh. Fat is so greatly prized that the test applied almost invariably by a native to decide whether an animal is good or not is to look for the presence of fat.'[41] Chase reports that this method of apportioning cuts of dugong meat was no longer practised when he was undertaking his fieldwork in the 1970s.[42]

Hunting for cachalot is more difficult and demands more attention.[43]

A detailed account of the hunt for the dugong, *watayi* in Kuuku Ya'u — its technology, the associated ritual and magic, the great prestige of the dugong hunter, the distribution of the highly-prized meat — and the central role the hunt plays in the societies of the Sandbeach People, all passed over in Merland's brief description, is given by Thomson in his classic article 'The dugong hunters of Cape York'.[44]

Dugongs (*Dugong dugon*) are massive (weighing up to 400

kilograms), long-lived (70 years or more) marine mammals, more closely related to elephants than to whales and dolphins. They have tusks, as well as flippers and tails, but no dorsal fin. The majority of the world's dugong population, threatened elsewhere, lives in northern Australian waters. They are not fast breeders. Their diet is mostly seagrass and they mainly graze in shallow water but can dive deeply.[45]

The arrow used for this ends in a sharp-pointed iron prong and fits into a socket at one end.

The weapon which Merland describes here using the French word *flèche* is the detachable head harpoon used by coastal groups of Cape York for hunting turtle and dugong.[46]

A rope made from liana is attached to the prong. When the cachalot is harpooned the wooden shaft is removed with a rotating movement, and the fish is then followed, the harpooner holding on to the rope.

Thomson obtained a dugong rope from Princess Charlotte Bay which was 199 feet long but weighed only four and a half pounds. The men made the ropes from the bark of *Hibiscus tiliaceus*, which produces a very light, strong and elastic rope. Rope-making was a highly skilled and time-consuming craft, which meant that the ropes 'were highly valued by their owners'.[47] Thomson includes this Kuuku Ya'u myth about the first dugong rope:

'In the days of the *wulmpamo* [*wulmpamu*] (totemic ancestors) lived Katarra [*Katara*] (silver gull), now a sea bird. Katarra saw that there were plenty of dugong and turtle and he wanted to catch them. At length he thought of using a harpoon, and making a rope to hold it.

'Katarra looked about until he saw the big leaf of the *kopoi* [*kupuy*] (*Hibiscus tiliaceus*).[48] He took the bark and stripped it, and began to roll the fibre on his leg as women make string, but it was no good. Then he tried to make it with his hands. At last he tied the fibre to a stick and steadied the rope with a strand held with his foot, over which he threw his wooden shuttle.

'When his rope was finished he went out to catch turtle with it, and all the people cried out, "You have found a good rope; it is strong and good for us all — let us all use it." And so it has been handed down.

'Katarra made a great coil of rope and it was turned to stone and remains to this day as a rock at Wällämbiloŋ (Temple Bay). After this Katarra went away and was turned into a *min'ya* [*minya*] (animal), *katarra*, the silver gull, as we see him now.'[49]

When the men have reached the fish, they secure its tail to stop it thrashing, and they dispatch it by striking it on the head with sticks. [In Thomson's account the dugong hunters hold the animal's head under water and drown it after passing a rope around its tail.[50]] The whales that are found along the coast of Endeavour Land are much smaller than the enormous cetaceans that are encountered in other waters. As for the sharks, which also prowl these shores, they are left in peace and they are asked to grant the same favour to the swimmers.

Thomson's article pays homage to the bravery and prowess of the dugong hunters in the face of considerable danger at sea. The understatement of Pelletier's account of a highly skilled activity in a hazardous marine environment may reflect a similar attitude to that of the men Thomson met at Port Stewart, as he describes in the following anecdote:

'When a canoe in which we were crossing the Stewart River, near the mouth, had swamped in rough water, the natives insisted on remaining with it until they could safely beach it. When at last we reached the bank with the craft, I asked the *täŋokonji* [*tangukuunchi*, owner of the canoe][51] if he had not been afraid of crocodiles and he replied simply that it was "bad luck" to think about them; if we had thought about crocodiles then they would have come up. This is typical of their attitude towards sharks and other dangers associated with shipwreck — which is necessarily a familiar experience to these people.'[52]

I spoke of sharing the catch; this is not done until after it is cooked.

With dugong at least, both Thomson[53] and Chase[54] report that the animal was butchered and shared out before cooking. Thomson writes of the cooking:

'When the distribution of portions has taken place, the flesh, including the blubber and hide, is generally cut up into long narrow strips, which are at once boiled in *kauwi* [*kawi'i*] (large bailer shells), the chief cooking vessel of the sandbeach people. In this condition the flesh remains tolerably fresh for two or three days. After a dugong has been killed these strips of cooked meat are to be seen here and there about the camp on top of the bark wurlies, where they are placed out of reach of the dogs, to be eaten whenever the owner is hungry.'[55]

Pelletier and Sassy did not forget about their family; they always kept a large portion for them.

This comment does not convey either the size of the dugong, and hence the quantity of meat it yields, or the complexity of the distribution process which Thomson described for an earlier period. Chase, speaking of distribution practice at Lockhart River in the 1970s, writes:

'I have watched many distributions of dugong meat, and the loud speeches, seemingly careless generosity, and complex pattern of people being called up (with apparent reluctance on the part of the recipients) to receive meat, reflects the highly intricate nature of social relations which exist in kin-based societies.

'Distribution of dugong meat must always be by conspicuous giving, never by selling for money. The one time I saw an attempt to sell, the man was publicly vilified as being "like a European" or like an Islander, and not behaving like a "proper sandbeach man". Distribution of this meat follows a pattern of *primary*, *secondary* and *tertiary* distribution throughout the community ...'[56]

The least fortunate fishermen, those who have only obtained an insufficient supply of fish, will often ask those most favoured by chance to give them some of theirs. If they are refused there will be heated debate, and sometimes there will be an exchange of blows.

The sea does not only provide fish to the fishermen. Also to be found are numerous shellfish, oysters, huge and succulent lobsters, and prawns, but in small quantities. When the tide is low people will search for these creatures in the crevices of the rocks.

The big sea turtles are only found on the small islands or in their vicinity. They provide a considerable dietary resource as some of them weigh up to two hundred pounds and they are highly fertile. Indeed, they do not lay fewer than a hundred eggs. The outer coating of the eggs is soft, and they are larger than hens' eggs. Their taste is very pleasant and they make the most delicate of dishes.

Some days before the eggs are laid, which usually takes place towards springtime, the female turtle no longer seems to be able to move freely. At this time she is often accompanied by several males who by turns support her on the surface of the water. This is the moment when she is easiest to approach.

Thomson provides more detail about turtle breeding habits:

'October and November are the principal breeding months of the green turtle. At this season the animals are copulating and may be seen swimming or basking on the surface of the water, or drifting with the tide. During this period they lose their accustomed wariness and may be very easily approached in canoes, or even taken by swimming. These pairing turtles are distinguished by a special name, *penti* [*piinti*].[57] But the name *penti* must not be used in turtle hunting when the animals are sighted or they will submerge; an alternate term, such as *kulkorro* [*kulkuru*] may be used, or nowadays, the English words "turtle fast." If they are able to secure only one of a pair, the natives invariably choose the female and let the male go, for the immature eggs of which the female is full are greatly relished.'[58]

The fisherman, armed with a pike whose tip is made of iron, attacks and finally skewers her. When he encounters a turtle on land, he begins by turning it over on its back, less to stop its progress, which is very slow, than to focus his attack on the ventral region, whose resistance is less than that of the carapace.

There are five species of turtles found on the coast of Endeavour Land: the largest which I have just mentioned, is called *occapau*. The others are named *troucoullou*, *kakarré*, *paillut* and *eerre*.

Linguists have found no term for any turtle species corresponding to *occapau*. In Kuuku Ya'u the Green Turtle (*Chelonia mydas*) is *tukulu* which corresponds to Merland's *troucoullou*. Thomson notes that the Green Turtle is 'the most abundant and most valued species.'[59] The description Merland gives for the '*occapau*' actually concurs with Thomson's description of the breeding habits and the resulting hunting patterns for the *tukulu*. Hale and Tindale's word list suggests a match for *kakarré* as they gloss the word *karkara* from Umpila as 'turtle shell' or 'hawksbill turtle'.[60] David Thompson, however, gives *kuynangkay* in Kuuku Ya'u and *yakarungu* in Umpila for the Hawksbill Turtle (*Eretmochelys imbricata*).[61] Another Umpila match in Hale and Tindale's list could be *eira*, corresponding to Merland's *eerre*, which they gloss as the term for the Leathery Sea Turtle (*Dermochelys coriacea*).[62] A possible match for Merland's *paillut* is *paa'ayi* which Sutton has recorded as 'female turtle mature, has reproduced (generic)'.[63] The loggerhead turtle (*Caretta caretta*) is also hunted. This species is *lupu* or *wapun* in Kuuku Ya'u and *wapun* in Umpila.[64]

When the sea is calm, one day is spent fishing and the next is devoted to rest, to repairing the canoes and to making new arrows. [Thomson comments that it takes several weeks to make a canoe but they need frequent repairs and are not long-lasting.[65]] When the weather is bad, the people fall back on the food that they get from the land.

Fishing is not only done in the daytime, but sometimes at night as well, by the light of the moon and the stars; it is not always without danger.

Thomson writes:

'Dugong hunting is usually carried out in the daytime, the party making for the deep water offshore on the lookout for a school of dugong. But sometimes, especially in the calm at the end of the south-east trade season, the hunting is carried out on moonlight [sic] nights, when the animals come inshore to feed. This hunting in the moonlight is believed by the natives to be the cause of premature greyness.'[66]

Rigsby and Chase note that another method of dugong hunting by night, not mentioned by Merland, was from platforms built over shallow feeding grounds.[67] Thomson observed one of these platforms, at Cape Direction, but believed that the technique had been recently introduced from the Torres Strait.[68]

One evening when Pelletier and Sassy were fishing, and had taken a very large turtle, a storm burst over their heads. They had lost sight of shore and, in order to reach it more quickly, they sought to lighten the canoe by tying the turtle to the outside of the boat. This movement, or something else, caused the canoe to tilt excessively and it capsized. The two fishermen were lucky enough to unfasten the outriggers, with which they kept themselves afloat. Hours later, with the weather clearing, they could see land and finally reached the shore. When they arrived back, there was great consternation throughout the tribe. It was a night of festivities, but their absence had given rise to the fear that they might not be seen again, and the singing and enjoyment had changed to weeping and wailing. Two of their companions were looking for them, torch in hand, thinking that they would only find their bodies, when finally they saw them returning safe and sound. We can imagine the joyful reception that greeted them and the note of pleasure on which the festivities were resumed. Never was dancing so lively, never did the expression on people's faces change more rapidly from that of deep sadness to one of even greater happiness.

Three days later, when the wind had begun to blow towards land, the canoe came to shore without having suffered too much damage.

Fishing is exclusively the preserve of the men; women never take part in it. They once used to go and collect the catch, but after an incident which caused great concern among the population the women no longer take this risk. One day when the catch had been abundant and the husbands had returned to land, leaving their wives to bring back the fish which they had caught, ten women boarded a canoe and landed on the little island where the men had left the fish.[69] Barely had they set foot on shore when they noticed an English ship which was heading in their direction. Very frightened by the sight of it, and not having time to get back to their canoe, they made a hasty escape and hid in the woods covering the island. The English landed straight away.

Nothing which had just occurred escaped the eye of the savages and they were therefore extremely fearful: they were convinced that their wives were going to be taken from them and that they would never see them again. When night had fallen, the men, taking the greatest precautions, went to the island. How great was their surprise and joy in finding their dear wives again! They soon consoled themselves about the loss of their canoes and the fish, which the English had seized.

Hunting and fishing would not be of much interest to Pelletier's tribe unless these activities provided them with the greatest pleasure they know — not only that of satisfying their hunger, but also of eating to excess. 'What time should I take my meals?' an Athenian asked Diogenes.[70] 'If you are rich eat when you want to; if you are poor eat when you can,' replied the Cynic. If Pelletier had asked the same question of someone of his tribe the savage would have added, 'Eat as much as you can.' Even if their cuisine is of the most basic sort, and their dinners do not shine next to the menus of Baron Brisse,[71] I very much doubt that there are gourmands to match them in France. [Thomson uses the word 'gorges' to describe the feasting on dugong in which only men take part and which follow very lean periods.[72]]

Although they have none of the utensils which we find indispensable for cooking our food, with the exception of a few fruits, they do not eat anything that is raw. They have found a way to make an economical oven of such simplicity that, when they need it, they make it then and there. This is how they go about it: having dug a hole of a certain depth in the ground and having partly filled it with peat, they lay across it several branches of a wood that does not burn easily and is strong enough to support the weight that is to be placed on top of it. How do they treat a bird or game with fur? After a preliminary operation which consists of plucking them or skinning and cleaning them, they are laid on a grill of this sort; the same goes for fish. On top, a kind of earthen roof is constructed in which an opening is made that acts as a chimney. Before doing this last part of the procedure, the cook has taken care to light his fire. The fire burns slowly and without throwing a flame; game and fish cook in the steam released by the peat.[73]

To obtain fire, the savages use a rather curious kind of light. They take a piece of white wood that crumbles at the merest touch. With the help of a stick of very hard wood sharpened to a point [*tiki*, 'fire drill'], they drill into the piece of wood with this improvised gimlet using rapidly rotating movements. This causes the wood to turn to dust, it starts to smoke and the fire is not slow in taking.

Hale and Tindale provide more detail on the firemaking process, noting that the people at Port Stewart

'make fire by twirling between the palms of the hands a thin stick (held in a perpendicular position), which has its lower extremity pressed firmly into a notch in the side of a similar wand laid on the ground and held in place with the foot. The twirling sticks are at first often five or six feet in length, but of course gradually become reduced with use. When not in use the ends of the sticks are protected in a sheath or case (as described by Roth); sometimes this case is embellished with a knob of wax, into which jequirity seeds (*Abrus precatorius*) are fixed. More rarely the sticks themselves have a scratched or carved pattern. A man rotating the upright stick places his hands near the top of it, and as it is twirled his palms travel down the shaft. With a quick movement he then brings them up again. During wet weather the process of firemaking is often tedious, and two persons may assist, one quickly continuing the twirling when the other tires. The firesticks are not resorted to unless absolutely necessary, and parties carry smouldering

Eucalyptus branches with them, even taking them from the islands to the mainland in their canoes, rather than be put to the necessity of generating fresh fire.'[74]

I said a moment ago that the savages had no cooking utensils, but I was mistaken: they have a shell wide and deep enough to cook in it fish of medium size.

Thomson notes that large bailer shells [*kawi'i*] served as the coastal peoples' main cooking vessel.[75] These shells were also used as water containers and crafted into the oval-shaped counterweight of the spearthrowers.[76]

Some animals demand special attention. Crocodiles, for example, must first of all be turned over on their back and put on the burning embers in this position. It is only after they have been burnt that the scales can be removed. Once this preparation has been done, they are cooked in the normal way.

But it is the large turtles, the *occapau*, this dish to which the savages are especially partial, which demand, in order to be well prepared, exceptional care.

First of all, the head must be cut off and the digestive tract removed by pulling on the upper part of it. It is of considerable size both in length and width. In order to coagulate the blood, which if allowed to flow would fill the entire space that was occupied by the alimentary canal, blazing hot stones are inserted into it. After this, the body of the turtle is divided into several portions which are cooked on stones as well. Finally, the carapace is removed, much care being taken to lose nothing of the oil which is found underneath. This oil is then poured into the intestines, where it is kept for several days.[77] When mixed into it, the oil gives a very pleasant taste to a kind of puree which the savages consume in quantity.

Thomson describes turtle and dugong oil being used in a preparation of the flesh and liver of stingrays, or eaten with the *mai'yi* [*mayi*, vegetable food] prepared from mangrove fruit (see below). It was also mixed with the resins used in making spears and other implements.[78]

This puree is made from the fruit of a tree that grows on the water's edge; it is white in colour, quite thick and contained in a pod. The savages crush it, thin it with water and lay the resulting paste on the sand in the sun. The paste cooks from the heat of the sun without the need for fire.

Chase notes that this is probably the fruit of various edible mangrove species. Hale and Tindale observed the making of a mangrove 'mash' and describe the process in detail, but do not refer to the paste being 'cooked' in the sun:

'The fruits are collected at low tide, for the trees apparently grow towards the middle of the swamps. When camp is reached a small, hot fire is made, and for thirty or forty minutes stones are heated therein. The fire is then raked out, and the mangrove fruits are thrown in amongst the hot stones, which are distributed evenly amongst them with a stick. The heap is then covered with a piece of paper-bark, and this in turn is covered with a layer of sand an inch or so in depth. The mass is left undisturbed for about an hour, after which the covering is taken off, and the roasted fruits (now brownish-grey instead of green) are removed. When they are cool enough to handle, the tops are pulled off and thrown away, after which the fruits are picked up, one or two at a time, pounded between two stones, and thrown into a baler-shell. They are next tipped into an open-work basket and taken to the beach, where a large container is filled with sea-water. With the basket standing in the salt water in this dish, the woman vigorously kneads the crushed mass; the water becomes yellow and then milky as the floury contents of the fruits pass through the open meshes of the basket. After fifteen minutes or so of kneading, the husks are thrown out of the basket, and the floury sediment in the dish is allowed to settle, a rising scum on the surface being skimmed off meanwhile. The water is then carefully poured off, and the sediment similarly washed in a further change of sea-water. After the second "pouring off" the thin, mushy sediment is tipped into a closely-woven dilly-bag, which is squeezed to get rid of excess water, and finally undergoes two washings in fresh water, with much kneading between each. This mangrove fruit mash resembles paper-pulp of a greyish colour, but is eaten with evident enjoyment when other food is scarce.'[79]

The savages have two reasons for gorging themselves on turtle meat: firstly, they satisfy their love of eating and, secondly, if they kept a store of the meat it would give them little pleasure, being soon spoiled by the flies which would come and lay their eggs on it.

They never add any condiments to their meals even if their menu is not very extensive. Although salt is found in abundance in the crevices of the rocks, they never use it. One of their great treats is biscuit, which they sometimes obtain from the English in exchange for fish or shellfish.

Mostly they will only drink pure water, but sometimes they drink honeyed water. They could make the latter their normal beverage as bees are plentiful in their country.

They have never tasted wine, but they do have vines, although the grapes are so bad they do not even eat them.

The savages do not gather as a family to have their meals and give themselves up, *inter pocula et scyphos* [over a drink], to the pleasures of conversation. They eat separately, wherever they happen to be, cutting up the animals they have cooked with a knife, sharing them between those who have taken part in the hunt or the fishing, and having no other implements than their hands to put the pieces into their mouths. Before putting their catch on the fire, they always give some to their old parents and often to the infirm. The women eat last, and if any food remains, which does not always happen. The fishermen and the hunters give each other gifts of food and thus vary the foods they eat.

Merland gives the impression of an absence of commensality in Uutaalnganu routine, probably because of Pelletier's social status as an unmarried man. In fact, as Thomson explored in an early article, hearth fires were the 'centre of family life' and represented the daily pattern of social interaction. He describes how each family group, a man and his wife, or wives, and children, had its own fire around which not only the cooking of meals but family life was centred, thus 'shared only by those between whom a special bond exists'. The single men and the single women in their separate camps had their own fires, and communal meals involving both sexes occurred rarely, on ceremonial occasions. During the dry season the people dispensed with their bark shelters and even their windbreaks constructed of branches. Men would never approach another family's fire when women were present: 'Even the long discussions that take place at night are carried on by shouting from fireside to fireside, or at fires at which the men only forgather.'[80]

The description Thomson wrote for *Walkabout* of a day in camp on the Stewart River estuary provides an evocative complement to Merland's prosaic account of subsistence activities in this chapter:

'I lived for nearly a year with the Yintjingga, and as I write I can still see the broad reaches of the Stewart River estuary. Let us look at one of these camps of the Malkanidji [Sandbeach People] in the late afternoon, when the women are returning to camp with the harvest of vegetable food gathered during the day. The division of labour between the sexes is strongly emphasised among these people, and while the men are the hunters and fishermen, providers of most of the flesh food, particularly of larger animals, upon the women falls the burden of gathering and preparing the vegetable food which still forms the principal food supply of these people.

'Usually the camp is deserted during the day, when it is given over to scavengers. First come native-reared dingoes, which fight and snarl over the bones and hide left from the last dugong feast, or the carapace of a green turtle. Aloft, a crow or two caws hoarsely with brazen cries that suggest throats dry and parched, with cruel, white, expressionless eyes; while kites and whistling eagles, scavengers all, wheel over the tree-tops, waiting. But as the afternoon wanes and the shadows lengthen, and the sand ceases to glare in the sun, the scene changes. Towards four o'clock, the women converge on the camp from the day's foraging, carrying on their heads, or in baskets slung down their backs, great loads of shellfish or of the vegetable foods that are being harvested at the current season of the year. In addition, they carry rolls of paper bark that will be used in preparing the food or serve as sleeping mats for their families at night. Some of the women also bear water vessels of wood or bark on their heads, the water prevented from slopping over by small leafy branches placed in the vessel. Slowly, the tired people, accompanied by the younger girls and smaller children, reach the camp, and make at once for their own fireside, where they set to work on the preparation of the evening meal. To these people, this is the principal meal of the day. Fires are soon lighted and the smell of cooking food fills the air to the accompaniment of the thumping of the heavy mallets used in pulverizing nuts, fruits, and roots, which are often hard and fibrous. About sixty or seventy vegetable foods, including fruits, are eaten in the course of the year by these people, but of these probably less than a dozen can be regarded as staple foods harvested in large quantities.

'Among the vegetable foods eaten by the Yintjingga are at least three species of mangrove, generally the cotyledons or seed-leaves or the hypocotyl. These, and many other of the vegetable foods gathered by the women, necessitate elaborate and often prolonged techniques for preparation, some of them to leach out poisonous materials. ...

'Meanwhile the men, who often hunt in parties or carry out organised drives for fish or large game, are also returning to camp, bearing the results of the day's hunt. Wallabies and the larger kangaroos, and game such as emu, jabiru and native companions, are generally partially cooked and quartered in the bush after the hunt and brought back to camp in this condition. The food is now shared out by the hunters among those to whom they have an obligation, defined by kinship, to provide meat, and it is then cooked again.

'In suitable weather, when the dugong comes inshore to feed on the sea grass in sheltered bays along the coast, the dug-out canoes are manned.'[81]

CHAPTER 10

Industry

Necessity, they say, is the mother of industry. Now, as the only compelling need felt by the savages is that of hunger, we should not be surprised that the great industries of the civilised peoples are completely unknown to them, and that once they had the things that were essential for them to procure an adequate diet they worried little about much else. But as all industries are interrelated and are built on mutual borrowing, and as it is difficult for one to survive without the assistance of the others, incredible efforts were needed to succeed in producing the tools for fishing and hunting when all they had at their disposal was what nature provided.

Imagine that if in our case we were to say to our most resourceful fellows: 'There is the sea and there are the tall trees growing along the coast. To sail upon the sea you must make boats using their trunks, but to do so you will have none of the tools used in the shipyards. You will lack even the most basic material which is used to make them, namely iron.' I very much doubt that the most skilful worker would attempt such a task. But savages, who have no conception of the marvels which excite our enthusiasm, who have not attended any kind of technical school or ever set foot in a workshop — men whose minds are course and uncultivated — will accomplish a task which modern genius and the spirit of invention would shrink from undertaking.

These men, however, found large shells on the shore, they serrated their edges with hard, thin stones, they sharpened them by grinding and they made saws and blades from them. Using these very primitive instruments they would fell trees of huge size, from which they cut planks about eight metres long on average, hollowed these out, pushing their sides apart to give a certain width to the boats, and launched them into the sea. They then took up their positions on board, sometimes numbering ten or twelve men to a boat.

When, later on, the frequent passage of the English meant that there were wrecks along the coast, and they came by barrels with rings made of iron, they replaced the shells with the saws and the knives that they were able to make from them. Even though they still left much to be desired, these new tools had a huge advantage over the previous ones. Thanks to them the construction of canoes became very much easier and took much less time.[1] Instead of several months, the time two men had needed to make a canoe seaworthy, it now took no more than a few days. When the tree had been hollowed out, a great fire was lit around it to make the wood more pliable. Then the sides were pushed apart and pieces of very strong wood were inserted between them. Once these things had been completed all that remained to do was to provide the canoe with an outrigger, a kind of broad floating device, firmly fixed to its planking,[2] which helps greatly in keeping it afloat. It takes seven or eight men to launch the canoe into the sea. The fishermen propel it with rods and oars.

The canoes used by Sandbeach People were double outrigger canoes. Thomson writes:

'A sea-going canoe is usually 24–30 feet in length and is manned by at least three or four men, sometimes more, if the vessel is a large one. Each part of the canoe is named, and the members of the crew are named according to the positions that they occupy in the craft.

'... The *paän* [*pa'an*], or bow of the canoe (literally the head,), does not taper to a sharp wedge-shape but is rounded in front, cut away at the waterline, and carries an overhanging flat platform called *yata*. On the starboard side, a round wooden peg about ten or twelve inches in length is driven through the hull close to the gunwale, to form a rest for the *warnagädji* [*waanakachi*, "dugong spear"] (long harpoon), the other end of which rests upon the forward *punta* [*palnta*, "upper arm"] (literally arm), the wooden boom to which the floats of the outriggers are secured. The short, barbed harpoon head is not fitted to the *warnagädji* until the quarry is actually sighted but is attached to the long rope, one end of which is secured to the port side of the canoe where it is passed through a hole specially made for it, and the remainder coiled on the bottom of the vessel in front of the harpooner. The harpooner's ordinary station is from a quarter to half way from the bow to the forward *punta* (boom), according to the size of the vessel and the number of men forming the crew. When the crew consists of three men only, the second is seated in the *pala'pala*, and is known as *yi'adjikonji* [*yi'achikuunchi*] (literally, to him belongs the middle).[3] The helmsman's station is just in front of the stern *punta*. He is called *koti'konji* [*kutikuunchi*] (literally, to him belongs the stern).'[4]

Rigsby and Chase report that while wooden dinghies began to be used in the 1930s, at Lockhart River outrigger canoes continued to be made and used until the 1950s.[5] The last outrigger canoe made at Lockhart River (and by a Night Island man) was made for the University of Queensland Anthropology Museum in the early 1970s.[6] As well as this canoe in Brisbane, another canoe from this area is held in Museum Victoria's Donald Thomson Collection.

The making of the arrows is even more important than the building of the canoes as the arrow is the only device used for fishing and without it the canoe would be completely useless.

We saw in Chapter 3 that Pelletier was envied for his skill in making spears. The value the coastal peoples put on their weapons is described by Thomson, who notes the work and time that goes into the making of a harpoon. Implements are 'valued according to the skill with which the material has been selected, the perfection of the technique employed in its manufacture, and the amount of time that has been required to make it'.[7]

The savages make several kinds of arrow, all basically similar; the biggest have the thickness of a candle and are about 1.85 metres in length.

Thomson describes ten harpoons of varying lengths that he obtained from Sandbeach People in 1929. The longest was 398 millimetres in length.[8] Hale and Tindale provide photographs and detailed descriptions of spears used in fighting, hunting and fishing by the coastal peoples.[9]

Apart from the tip or the head, they are made of three pieces of wood joined to each other. The piece to which the arrowhead is fitted is about 20 centimetres long; it is made of light wood and is of a smaller bore than the next piece into which it fits. This piece is 1.3 metres in length; it is of hard, heavy wood. To this piece is added a third which is of light wood, 35 centimetres long, and the distal end of which is pierced by a lengthwise hollow. Into this hollow fits a small round peg with a pointed end, not more than five centimetres long.[10] This peg, fixed at an acute angle on to one end of the part called the bow by the savages, is attached to the arrow by thongs, which prevent it from coming out of the socket.[11] The bow is formed from a small piece of wood four or five centimetres wide by 70 centimetres long; on its free end it is finished with a shell. The bow does not run parallel to the arrow. The part where the shell is positioned is a little further from the arrow than the part containing the plug. The gap is barely five or six centimetres at its widest.

Merland uses the term *arc*, 'bow', for this weapon but the bow was not used on Cape York, or anywhere on the Australian continent. The description corresponds to the spearthrower or *yuli*. Hale and Tindale note that the spearthrower was used by all of the different coastal groups at Princess Charlotte Bay and provide this description of how it was made, also mentioning its other use to parry spears:

'The spear-throwers are cut from hardwood trees, and are flat and usually rather wide; a hardwood peg (with a nick to receive the slightly hollowed end of the butt of the spear) is fastened against one end with gum and twine, while at the opposite end is a rather large baler shell ornament, the making of which occupies considerable time. Two pieces of shell are roughly chipped to shape, and are then ground to an oval form on stones, sand and water assisting the operation; next the convex outer face is polished on a smooth rock, using finer sand as an abrasive, until it is pure white. The shells are then placed, one on each side and with the concave or inside faces opposed, at the "grip" end of the throwing-stick, and fastened with beeswax, which fills the gaps between them. A charm is frequently concealed within the adhesive between the two shells. The thin "grip" portion near the shell ornament is coated with bloodwood gum, and sometimes also bound with string. The shell ornament may also be bound across with wallaby or kangaroo sinews. During combat the spear-thrower is used to divert, or parry thrown spears, the flat of the implement guiding the spear to one side or over the shoulder.

'... The Princess Charlotte Bay people depend only on their

throwing sticks to protect themselves from spears, and the baler shell ornament is said to prevent it from slipping out of the hand when thus used.'[12]

The arrow is thrown using two hands. While the right hand raises the weapon, the left hand holds the bow near the shell, imparting a movement which is transmitted to the peg, changing its angle to the wood of the bow from acute to obtuse. As the right hand lets go, the peg, with a sharp movement, returns to its original position;[13] the arrow is then released and thrown into the distance. The different pieces which are used in the making of an arrow adhere together by means of a material that is so adhesive that, even though it might break, the pieces will never come unstuck. [This is most likely the resin from *Canarium australasicum* (*yinchanyu*, 'gum tree') which is the favoured spear adhesive in this area.[14] Thomson describes the use of this resin in weapon making.[15]]

Before the sea brought them glass from bottles and iron, the savages used ostrich and kangaroo bones to make the barbs, getting them very sharp by means of grinding their edges. Today these barbs are made solely of glass or iron. [As well as harpoons with barbs of iron or wire, Thomson describes one harpoon whose barb is of wallaby bone and two with barbs of the same wood as used for the shaft.[16]] They vary slightly in shape and composition, just as the arrow varies in its dimensions according to its intended use. The barb is never poisoned.

The fishermen also make pikes which they use to spear the large fish. They bear some resemblance to those we use ourselves. The lithograph I have put before the reader, which Monsieur C. Marionneau has been kind enough to provide, will give a better idea of the weapons used in hunting, fishing and warfare than any further descriptions I could provide.

It now remains for me to say just a few words about some other industries which, in the lives of the savages, are of much less importance. Let me however draw attention to the making of razors, using pieces of glass, from which sharp blades are made. With these razors they manage to shave and to cut their hair. We should note, too, the ropes made with lianas, the baskets for carrying yams and the cradles for the newborns. This work falls to the women.[17]

Hale and Tindale describe the netting stitches used to form the mesh of the bags they collected at Princess Charlotte Bay and note that the twine used in bags, as in other things, is frequently that of the *Livistona* palm, with wattle barks also being used. As to size and use, they write: 'The bags are of all sizes, from three inches to two feet in diameter; some are of fine mesh, and used (like certain baskets) as strainers; larger ones are utilized for collecting screw palm nuts and similar foods; others are employed as "carry-alls" for desirable odds and ends.' They examined the contents of one of these dilly bags and found that it contained: 'three spear-smoothers of hardwood; a sheath studded with jequirity seeds, for the ends of firesticks; prepared wattle-bark and grass for string; wallaby sinews; beeswax and gum; fragments of red ochre; and a small quantity of string made from grass.'[18]

In this region there is a type of wood whose bark is so soft that when it is placed in the bottom of the cradles their little children can settle there as if they are lying on feathers.[19]

This is a very short chapter but I can find nothing further to add to it. I cannot see among these tribes any other branch of industry which seems to be even in the embryonic state, unless, from the agricultural viewpoint, we wish to consider the care the savages take in firing the woods where the yams grow so that the tubers of these plants develop more extensively and their crop is more plentiful.

Chase and Sutton describe a different management practice in relation to yams. Vegetable foods are the staple of the diet and yams of different species are the most important of these. Yam scrubs lying within a group's territory are recognised as being owned by that group. One prolific yam, *thampu* (*Dioscorea sativa*), was carefully managed as a resource to ensure its supply through the dry season, while 'a specific gathering technique which left the top portion of the tuber together with the vine undisturbed on the ground ready for regrowth' aimed to encourage continuing supply of the yam in the following seasons.[20]

So it is that time has passed over these peoples without changing the way they are, without multiplying their needs, without their minds having been broadened, without any appreciable progress being made. Will it always be like this? No, certainly not. Civilisation is spreading from the south of Australia towards the north. Like a rising tide, it first of all invades the lands along the coast. Before very long, barbarism will have disappeared from there. But how will this great work be achieved? Will the savages greet it as a blessing or reject it as a scourge? Will the changes to customs, tastes and beliefs come about through force or persuasion? Will holy voices penetrate into ignorant and rebellious souls? Will the pleasures of material wellbeing and the delights of the body be enticing enough to generate new needs in men who only know the crudest need of all?

Judging the savages of Endeavour Land by what happens elsewhere one might doubt it, and yet, if they had people to guide them and a complete set of tools, what might we not expect them to produce with their manual dexterity? Let houses be built for them and let the plough, tilling the soil, give them abundant crops. If they are so fond of biscuits, let them be taught to make bread, and let their grasslands be covered with our cattle. Let their children be given the milk which can only yield an inadequate supply during the five years at their mother's breast. Let their natural distrust be overcome through the benefits they receive. Then, it seems to me, it would be very difficult for the contact with civilised men not to exercise a powerful attraction over natures more coarse than wicked.

But the first element of civilisation, that which no society worthy of the name can be without, must be looked for in higher realms. We must think of the soul before taking care of the body and instil in it great and generous beliefs. But how do we go about a task of this kind when these people have no beliefs?[21] How do we cultivate a soil that has never produced anything? How do we sow the seed where no one has been able to penetrate before?

All of this is perhaps less difficult than we might imagine. If the peoples of whom we are speaking had, rather than the absence of any belief, beliefs that were false and deeply rooted, in order to destroy these there would need to be an initial struggle in which victory could only be achieved with considerable effort. Here, by contrast, it is not a question of destroying but only of building; and, since I have just been talking about uncultivated fields, I should say that it is much easier to till bare soil than to clear land where the brambles have put down deep roots. The future will provide the solution to the problem. God willing, may we one day find the bearers of civilisation and the receivers standing side by side and taking each other's hand, with the former opening up a new era to the latter, and both of them forming a true alliance, rather than seeing the tribes abandon their territory at the approach of the victorious enemy and flee into the interior, taking with them ignorance and barbarism!

Chapter 11

Pelletier's return to France

Pelletier lived with the savages for seventeen years; he had adopted all the ways of his tribe and his naturalisation was complete. He was no longer a Frenchman, he was an Australian.[1]

For fear that he might try to escape, the natives had long been careful to keep him away when they had dealings with the whites. On only one occasion had he seen other white men, who, on reaching land, gave gifts to the blacks in exchange for those they received from them. In vain had he wanted to approach them; he had been kept away from them. If, when the sea was calm, his brothers of the tribe sighted a foreign boat, they always made towards it with the same aim, but at such times Pelletier remained on land.

However, with time, the misgivings of the savages had ceased, and they no more feared that Pelletier would make his escape from them than he dreamt of doing so himself.

Such was the mutual trust which existed between Pelletier and his tribe when, on 11 April 1875, an English ship, the *John Bell*, cast anchor in sight of land. Maademan, Pelletier and some other men of his tribe were on the little island where the women had hidden in the woods during the landing that had been so frightening for them.[2] The longboat of the *John Bell* headed in their direction. So that they would be favourably received, the captain of the ship had seen to it that there were only Negroes on board, his crew being made up partly of men belonging to that race.[3]

Imagine their amazement when they saw a white man in the company of the blacks! Having presented Pelletier's father with valuable gifts, having given him tobacco, for which the men of his tribe have become very greedy, pipes, biscuits, a knife and a necklace, they returned to their ship and informed the captain of the strange encounter they had just made.

The captain then ordered them to return to the place they had come from, dangle in front of the savages the most dazzling objects they had ever seen, offer them to Pelletier if he wanted to come and get them, and, once he had set foot on board, hold him prisoner and take him off with them.

This scheme was executed as planned. His father, seeing the wonders displayed before him, and considering the offer made to Pelletier to obtain them and the signs of friendship which were lavished upon him, could not hold out. He said to him that he had to do all that he could to get hold of such fine gifts, advising him to swim away as soon as he had received them if the sailors wished to detain him, and to bring back to him what he could.

Pelletier had little trust in this arrangement; behaviour which was perhaps not as benevolent as it appeared inspired in him only minimal confidence and he wondered if all these friendly gestures were not just a front which the blacks, who belonged to a race of cannibals, were using to lure him into a trap and seize hold of him. Apprehensive of the sad fate which perhaps awaited him, he hesitated, but in view of Maademan's express command he had to obey.

Scarcely had he set foot on board than his fears intensified: the sailors indicated to him, with revolvers in their hands, that he was not to move, and the longboat headed towards the *John Bell*, which had remained at its moorings.

Before reaching the ship, the crew members gave him clothing and helped him to get dressed. It had been so long since he had lost the habit that he found himself very awkward in his movements once he was wearing clothes. However they were now coming up to the *John Bell*. Once there, Pelletier, seeing himself in the company of whites, began to feel more reassured. The captain was very attentive towards him and he was not long in realising that instead of the death he feared, it was his freedom which was being given back to him. But it was impossible for him to make himself understood: no one on board spoke French, and besides, he had completely forgotten his mother tongue. His country of origin therefore remained completely unknown until the word 'Frenchman', uttered in English by way of a question, came back to him and, understanding its meaning, he nodded affirmatively.

The *John Bell* was sailing for Somerset. During the journey Pelletier took a pen and, tracing characters on the paper almost at random, succeeded in remembering some words of his language. The first lines that he wrote were absolutely incomprehensible and, although the conversations that he had with some Frenchmen once he had arrived at Somerset had awakened in him the memory of the words which he had forgotten, the letter that he addressed to his parents on 13 May 1875 is not a model of style, spelling or penmanship.[4] I believe that it is not without interest to reproduce its facsimile, while pointing out that the heading, 'Somerset, cap York', and the date, 13 mars [March] 1875, where the word 'mars' should be replaced by the word 'mai' [May], are not in Pelletier's handwriting (see the Appendix).[5]

From Somerset the *John Bell* left for Sydney,[6] called at Brisbade [sic] in passing, and arrived at its destination on 25 May. Sydney belongs to England but this great city is populated by citizens who have come from every corner of the globe. Pelletier found there many French people, became the object of general curiosity, and was courteously welcomed by our consul,[7] who had him photographed.[8] He remained in Sydney for 38 days, during which the frequent contacts he had with compatriots completely restored his memory of his language. This can be judged by the extract from a second letter which Pelletier wrote to his parents on 6 July [1875] (Appendix).[9]

However imperfect this letter may be, we can see just how much progress Pelletier had made in less than two months.

Finally, in October, some days before leaving Noumea for France,[10] he wrote his parents a third letter where the progress observable in the second is still more pronounced (Appendix).

Marchand, whom Pelletier talks about, was a young soldier from Saint-Gilles who was serving in Noumea.[11] His meeting, so far from his country, of a fellow countryman, had been a very pleasant experience for Pelletier. It had brought back to him all his memories of his early childhood. From then on he could think of only one thing: he wanted to see the authors of his days again as soon as possible, having long been tormented by anxiety as to whether they were alive, and who, Marchand had told him, were in good health at the time that he had left France.

While Pelletier's thoughts travelled over that great distance which separated him from the country of his birth, his father and mother were no less impatient to see him again, the son they had wept over for so many years. His first letter, of 13 May, had not reached them until 21 July, and they held so strongly to the idea that he was dead that they wondered if it really was from their child or if someone had not taken a horrible pleasure in playing with their suffering. This cruel uncertainty lasted no more than 24 hours. The next day the good news was confirmed in an official way. The Pelletier couple received the *Bulletin français*,[12] which included an extract from the English newspaper *The Times*, in which was told the story of Narcisse Pelletier and his deliverance. It was only then that his mother abandoned the mourning dress she had been wearing for seventeen years and that her heart, so long haunted by sadness, was filled with joy.

Narcisse Pelletier left Noumea on 7 August, on the *Jura*, on which his friend Marchand was also travelling; he arrived at

Toulon on 13 December. One of his brothers came to collect him. From Toulon he went to Paris, where he had been summoned by people who were particularly interested in him. He received the best of receptions and returned with the hope, which is soon to be realised, of obtaining from the government a position offering him an adequate living in the present and guarantees for the future.

On 2 January he made a triumphal entry into Saint-Gilles. The whole population had come out to meet him, and his childhood friends smothered him in their embrace. I shall refrain from evoking the tender scene which deeply moved the hearts of one and all when he threw himself into the arms of his parents: no description could do it justice. Opposite their modest dwelling a bonfire awaited the new arrival and, when he came to light it, prolonged shouts of 'Long live Pelletier!' were heard. His father's house was too small to receive all those who wanted to come inside and, for fear of mishap, he was obliged, to his great regret, to shut the doors.[13]

The next day a solemn mass of thanksgiving for this happy event was celebrated in the church of Saint-Gilles, which was filled by the throng. The priest who celebrated the mass showed his emotion as he spoke, and his hand which, 32 years previously, had on the same day[14] poured the baptismal water on to Narcisse Pelletier's forehead, called down upon his head God's blessing from above.

Phare de l'Aiguillon, Pointe de l'Éve, the lighthouse on the northern side of the estuary of the Loire, where Pelletier was employed as lighthouse keeper after his return to France. Courtesy of the Écomusée de Saint-Nazaire.

SAINT-GILLES-SUR-VIE. — Les quais

A 19th century view of Saint-Gilles-sur-Vie showing the church of St-Gilles near where the Pelletier family lived. Courtesy of the Mairie de Saint-Gilles-Croix-de-Vie.

The quay of the harbour office of Saint-Nazaire where Pelletier was employed as a clerk at the time of his death. Courtesy of the Écomusée de Saint-Nazaire.

Mouth of the harbour of Saint-Nazaire where Pelletier was employed as a signalman at the time of his marriage. Courtesy of the Écomusée de Saint-Nazaire.

APPENDICES

APPENDIX I

Musical Observations about the songs of Narcisse Pelletier

I have been asked to note down some of the songs of the savage land where Pelletier lived for so long and to add any reflections this kind of music might suggest to me.[1]

These tunes or these songs — is such an ambitious name really appropriate here? — were not easy to collect since Pelletier, who has no musical knowledge, would change his rendition each time, to such an extent that deciding between different versions became very difficult. His voice, while quite true, was not at all stable. Consequently his singing would wander off, never remaining the same from version to version. The rhythm, even though a natural and formative element, which predominates in any rudimentary music, was itself frequently difficult to make out because of its lack of definition.

But it could not have been otherwise when, naturally, no Conservatory or school of Solmization existed in the far-off place from where this young and interesting sailor has so fortunately returned.

I therefore lacked any reliable means of verification or sure guide.

Nevertheless, in presenting the transcription in the way that I have — meticulously and with the greatest attention — I believe that it is as exact and close a match as possible to what I heard from Pelletier's singing.

I have had to find and adopt the version which the singer found the most familiar.

I therefore vouch for this faithful reproduction, as, besides, any musician who might come to know Pelletier will be able to ascertain.

Once I had achieved this, I was not satisfied with the vocal — I dare not say melodic — line alone. In order to give more character, variety and contrast to these uniform and primitive tunes, I was led to harmonise them in the simplest way, that is in the plagal style which, being that of the music of his childhood and most distant from our modern tonality, must best suit the case in question.

A musical base of this kind did not, undoubtedly, include any accompaniment. But if there was not a great deal of point in undertaking this work, it presented no less numerous difficulties for that.

These I forced myself to overcome because, in my view, it was very important to impart a little interest to these songs which individually were formless, somewhat monotonous in character and had no more tonality than structure.

I was therefore keen to add an accompaniment to them. The choice of single harmonising chords seemed to me to correspond best to our more or less accurate ideas about the music of early times. Considered rationally, this music must have been without accompaniment and, as civilisation acted upon it, there came, first of all, *duets*, or two-part harmonies, followed by the ear, becoming more demanding, needing more and more complicated combinations.

I hope thus to have succeeded in giving a form with variations to each of these clumsy and unformed songs, and which, without harmonic support, our developed sense of hearing would not easily have accepted.

Thanks to this accompaniment I was able to take advantage of every instance of *rhythmic patterning* that presented itself to further accentuate it. What resulted was therefore more *regular* and especially more *musical*.

I did not think I was obliged to have recourse only to the chords of three sounds, the *raw state*, which produced a monotonous series that was too heavy. One will find some early inversions which, with the *triads* (chords of three notes) in their basic state and some little *pedals* — none of this departing from the style adopted — have left me a much broader field.

Although the sense of tonality is totally unknown in the land where Pelletier lived, it seemed to me preferable to equip the key with a *flat* since, according to my academic adaptation, here we are always in *F major*, or in *D minor* (without an audible note: *C sharp*). Then this avoids the very frequent repetition of the flat before the *B*.

As to the movements indicated, I have done more than simply guess them, as they are the expression of what I heard. In any case, these movements are in a rational relationship with the form and the relative difficulty of execution of each of the accompaniments.

Without claiming to set myself up as a teacher and here give a lesson in harmony which would be rather inappropriate, let me say, however, to those of my readers who, having some knowledge, might criticise me for having written in the third song, from the second to the third beat of the second bar, *two fifths*, admittedly by *contrary* motion, that these are completely acceptable in this context. Moreover, these perfect fifths do not form an *actual sequence*, the first finishing one phrase and the second beginning another. The strict rules of counterpoint only exclude those which are found in the *extreme* and clearly *consecutive parts*.

I thought it was important to establish these distinctions.

The words, with the exception of those to the *Hiento para gallinand*, mean nothing to Pelletier himself, and I have been obliged merely to write down the sounds or the syllables with a wholly invented spelling, intending only to give the best equivalent of the proffered pronunciation. These words belong to the traditions of another tribe and it is odd that Pelletier did not seek to find out their meaning. This particularity suggests therefore, in the case of the first, third and fourth songs, a much vaguer and less identifiable provenance. This is not the case with the *Hiento* which, it will be noticed, has much more melodic clarity and rhythmic character, which would prove that Pelletier's companions are better musicians and composers than their neighbours. *Hiento* means 'pieces of wood', [*yunthu*, 'waterlily, edible root'], *para*, 'the white men' [*para*, 'white man/woman'] and *gallinand*, 'to take away' [*kalinan*, 'carry-we']². The natives had seen the Europeans cut down trees and load them on board. Thus the quite unexpected circumstance of a ship having anchored off these strange shores and taken on a provision of wood had become an event worthy of being celebrated in a memorable song and handed down for posterity.

This could refer to the cutting of wood for use on the luggers and to 'smoke' the bêche-de-mer, or to the cutting of sandalwood, which started as an industry in Cape York around this time.³

The four songs when set down are all similar to a degree; but two of them finish in exactly the same way and so, to add some variety, I have taken pains to change their final harmonies.

Pelletier, who — like all those who have lived alone for a long time or with beings who converse rarely — is not very communicative and has given me very few details about his refrains, so I am sorry not to be able to enter into more interesting explanations about them.⁴

The first and third songs are dance tunes.

The *Hiento* (second song) is sung at night.

La ponghé lapon (fourth song) is an invocation to the moon.

The natives keep the beat alternately with their hands and on the knees. In this way they will repeat these and other tunes over and over again through the long night hours, in order to stay awake and not to be taken unawares by the enemies who prowl around in the vicinity.

Chase notes that a song style used for these purposes among the Umpila and possibly among the Uutaalnganu was called *kilamungu*. These songs could recount events in the past days or perhaps a favourite 'yarn'. Or they could be ceremonial songs connected with the initiation ceremonies. The words of these songs may not be understood.[5]

It remains for me to express some reservations and to put forward some hypotheses about the authenticity and the true origins of Pelletier's songs.

First of all, the strange combination of circumstances which has brought us these airs, so little meant to be harmonised in this way, is cause enough to muse and wonder.

I would have liked to find intonations that were less defined, less similar to our musical system, odder and starker, in a word, offering more signs of their exotic origins.

These tunes have, rather, a liturgical character. They are reminiscent of church plain-song and especially of Breton choruses.

Pelletier was born a stone's throw from Brittany. At the age of at least twelve, after attending the communal school for a long time, he embarked as a cabin boy. He had heard the sacred hymns of the church of his village; he had attended the feast days of his country, its big gatherings, its celebrations with singing and dancing. Is there not therefore some childhood memory, some recollection of these first and indelible impressions, in the tunes he brought back?

My musician's convictions and sensibility compel me to express these doubts.

Indeed, the singing of savages is, generally, nothing more than a kind of uniform murmuring, without very distinct intervals, in a simple rhythm interspersed with guttural cries.[6]

From that, how can we accept the relatively tonal and melodic music of Pelletier as indeed being that of this barbarous people? And in that case, since the natives have songs distinct enough to be noted down, how is it that they do not also possess some instrument to produce sounds other than those of the voice or a rhythmical beat? When I questioned Pelletier on this subject he claimed that there were no instruments of any sort in his tribe, that he had never seen any, except for sheets of metal washed up by the sea, these having been turned into makeshift percussion instruments on which they beat time as loudly as they possibly could.

There is no mention of the ceremonial drum whose use by the Kuuku Ya'u in their *ukaynta* ceremonies was recorded by Thomson.[7] Thomson, in line with his evolutionary views about the transmission of cultural and technological elements from what he saw as the more advanced societies of Torres Strait and New Guinea to Cape York, viewed the drum as part of this Papuan influence. This was despite the denials of Kuuku Ya'u people who, moreover, 'were quick to admit, and even to point out, obvious recent introductions from Torres Straits, which they looked upon with a slightly contemptuous air as "another fashion".'[8] And in fact Thomson gives linguistic reasons for the drum having been, as he sees it, introduced to the mainland some considerable time ago.[9] The reason Pelletier did not mention the drum as a musical instrument is no doubt related to the location of his estate in the centre of Uutaalnganu territory, in which case Garnier's description of the makeshift percussion instruments would tie in with the following observations of Thomson's:

'The drum is unknown to the Yänkonyu [i.e. Uutaalnganu]

on the southern boundary of the K<u>o</u>k<u>o</u> Yaʼo territory, and to the Kanju to the west. Among the Sandbeachmen of these tribes, however, the *y<u>u</u>kkʼo aʼ<u>i</u>nyuʼg<u>o</u>* [*yuku aaʼinyuku*][10], the so-called 'corroboree sticks,' used by all the tribes on Cape York Peninsula to beat time at dances, are supplemented occasionally by a portion of an old canoe used as a sounding log. But this is in no sense a drum; it is not deliberately manufactured for this purpose and it carries no tympanum.'[11]

If I could get a listener to hear these tunes, without any explanation, it is certain that he would barely suspect their savage provenance.

The erudite observer will distinguish amongst them one song in particular, in our minor mode, which is quite singular, and hard to explain here: these natives, while they cannot have a very sensitive ear, nevertheless show a marked predilection for the typical minor third, suggesting a more advanced degree of perception and civilisation.

There must surely be some savage songs which proceed only by semitones, and I even think that the *chromatic* form better translates the confused murmurings, the vague articulations which are particularly characteristic of vocal production in the inferior beings. Therefore it is curious that in Pelletier's tunes there is not a single semitone. Nor is any similar interval present in anything which he sang to me. My attention having been awakened to this, I would not have let pass unnoticed a semitone interval which would certainly have struck me. The resulting music, if however we can call it that, and its scale, if one exists, would be made up of a scale of rising and falling sounds, all invariably composed of the whole tones alone.

Would not such an observation confirm the view that the more civilised the ear becomes, the more it is inclined to accept more refined intervals in music? It is thus that the ancient Greeks, undoubtedly as a result of a greater acuity of hearing, had a musical system with more complicated subdivisions and with much smaller intervals than ours.

When faced with the overly distinct tempo of the following songs, one can imagine how very perplexed and unsure I have been, and how I have wondered whether they were not rather Pelletier's unconscious recollection of the tunes of his native land or of the liturgical forms of his parish church which had later become confused with the language, the words and the kinds of more or less fixed sounds of the savages with whom he lived for many years.

To give another explanation of these precise intonations, one could equally suppose that they had come from a civilised being who, thrown by a shipwreck onto that unknown beach, had spread among the inhabitants, and left with them, these vestiges of European music.

Again, I owe these reservations, and the admissions that I have just made, to a desire for sincerity and to respect for my art.

And since we are talking about savages, let me speak about those whom I have seen myself, when I was just a child. This was a long time ago now, in New Orleans, in the State of Louisiana.

As I remember them, the Chactas[12] of Louisiana were taciturn and grave. Their customs had been mellowed by their vicinity to the town where they came to bring the game they had hunted and the fruits they had gathered in their woods. We often saw them coming along loaded with game (as they are dogged and skilful hunters), huge palm leaf baskets filled with ripe blackberries, and shoes of supple, yellow hide, or *moccasins*, made with some skill, that they were coming to sell. They were followed by their wives who had regular and childlike features, big doe eyes and small, white, even teeth, all of this giving much grace and attractiveness to their countenance which is brought out by the vermilion that they use to paint their cheeks. Their feet are extremely small. Despite the tattoos, their features are still pretty.

They have a certain air of modesty about them. Their chest and arms are loaded with necklaces of glass beads of every colour. We find, then, that even in the tall grasses of the bayous[13] and in the middle of the lonely forests, feminine wiles claim their due.

These savage women are called Taicas.[14] The men make them their slaves, their beasts of burden. It is the women who carry the cooking pot in one hand, in the other their husband's gun, and on their backs carry the child in a basket or in the woollen blanket which they skilfully drape around themselves, while other children trot along on their little feet beside them, and their husband walks along by himself in front, grave and proud in his freedom.

The Chacta women are small and graceful, the men tall and well-built. Their ears are made longer by crude metal ornaments.

These savages wear their hair straight, long and natural (that goes without saying), and falling on their shoulders. Besides their guns, they are very skilful with their bows and arrows. They are supple, agile and reserved, will endure any ordeal, and do not seek beyond the freedom of the deep and mysterious woods. Their primitive nature is one of goodness and from that time one could venture among them without fear. Increasingly, the Chactas are disappearing. Today it seems that they are coming into New Orleans wearing modern trousers and sporting our silk hats.

If only God had willed it that Pelletier had landed in their tribe! Because if they are serious and sparing in their words, to a degree that one would think they were mute, at least they are harmless. With them his situation would have been bearable and his captivity much shorter, because of the closeness to a large town.

What trials this unfortunate man has endured! How many times must he have dreamt of his home and family and thought of it as paradise!

It seems to me that these memories could not have been wholly extinguished as, at the time of his abandonment among the natives of Australia, he was, if I am not mistaken, fourteen or fifteen years old. At that age one has complete recollection, especially of one's mother, young sisters and little brothers, and his thoughts and the things he missed must often have led him to God. The unhappier he was, the more he must have dulled his pain with the vague memories of the songs of his native land and of those of the church of his village in the Vendée.[15]

Let me therefore insist on my conviction that, undoubtedly, it is here, in part, that is to be found the source of the musical phrases, melancholic and imprinted with a certain religious feeling, which I have learned from Pelletier.

The true savage never sings a tune whose intonations are quite perceptible and easily noted. The monotonous and guttural sounds that he articulates are made to irritate rather than to charm the ear. In spite of his taste, sometimes quite passionate, for music, the results that he obtains are in no way satisfying. In vain will he blow into a shell or a reed, or get the single string of his lyre to vibrate, or beat the taut skin of his drum, for the sounds that he produces will always be discordant. Rather it is a mixture of more or less rapid clucking and yapping that constitutes his music, which seems to be an imitation of the sounds familiar to his ear.

The singing of the Chactas of New Orleans for their part, although they were in contact with a civilisation that must have influenced them, had nothing tonal or finished about it when, gathering together in bands, they would come into town to celebrate their feast days and, drinking great quantities of tafia, give themselves up to their songs and dances.

But I have come to the end of my conjectures about the real provenance of the kind of music brought back by this adventurous, and now so happily repatriated, young sailor.

With their vocal line alone these tunes would have little import. But presented with this accompaniment, they acquire, I believe, a certain character; they take on a kind of far-off flavour, and, in these different ways, they will perhaps offer some interest to musical readers.

EDOUARD GARNIER

APPENDIX II

Four songs taken down from Narcisse Pelletier and set to music by
Edouard Garnier

Appendix III

Transcription and translation of Pelletier's three letters to his
family after his recovery[1]

Letter One

Somerset Cape York
13 May 1875

papa nanan gene seui par nore ge se sui vivan narcise getente abore
du saint paule de boredaut gavé fée novorage dans lur le roce du
suovage de lile les ginoï dans lile reter be noroire tue turoi ge suis
venire dans un petite batou dans une ille des sovage ge veis garcée de
lau a boire le capitene paretire dans le petite batou ge carece de leau
dans les boua ge ver rate dans boia ge vais leure les soivage q[t?]uoi
viv[n?]i sur sa cote venire qui nave trove le souvage donere a boire et
a nange in a pa tuèe ge donne la nait in apa donne du nale ge suis
retait dans le bois bien lontain ge-téte perecée nore gav veè o garant
fant et garant boire gaveè becoup dé nale

papa mama I am not dead I am living narcisse I was on board the
saint paul of bordeaux I had been shipwrecked in [?] the rock of
the savage of the island the chinese in the island stayed and died [?]
killed I came in a little boat to an island of savages I had looked for
water to drink the captain left in the little boat I looked for water in
the woods I stayed in woods I then see the savages who live on its
coast come who had found me the savage gave food and drink he
did not kill I give my hand he did not hurt me I stayed in the wood
for a very long time I was almost dead I had o great hunger and
great drink [thirst] I was in a lot of pain

I

Somerset Cape York
13 May 1875

papa nanan gene seul pap nore ge se
sui vivan narcise getenté abore Du saint
paule de boredant gaveffée mvorage
dans lur le roce du suovage de lile
les ginoï dans lile reter le morovre
me turoi ge suis vemire dans un
petite batou Dans une ille Des sovage
y geveis garcée de lau a boire le capitene
paretire dans le petite batou ge carece
de leau dans les boua ge vo rate dans
boica ge vais leure les sovage tuoi
viai sur sa cote venire qui nave
trove le souvage donore a boire et
amange in apa tuée ge Donne la
nait in apa donne du nale ge suis
rebait dans le boit bien tendain
ge tete perecé more gave tvée o
garant fant et garant boire gavée
becoux dé nale

LETTER TWO

Narcisse Pierre Pelletier
Le 11 juliette 1875

Mon cher Père et Ma cher mère et maisfrère, je vous ècrie une autre foi. je vous enbarsse De tout Mon cœur. ci vous ête vivant. je suis arriver à noumèa le consule de sydney Ma envoyez. Je suis A bord du'un navire De guere. je partirait Dans un mois à bord du autre navire qui est venu il y a trois jour, je me Porte Bien jai toujours mal à la gambre Droits. il y à Bien longtemps que jai mal, jaivait ut Bien de la misere avec eux. il mon en Poissonnez la gambe. Mais seulement je me Porte Bien.

Je vous dit Bonjour
Narcisse Pierre Pelletier

Narcisse Pierre Pelletier
11 July 1875

My dear father and my dear mother and my brothers, I am writing to you again. I embrace you with all my heart if you are alive. I have arrived at noumea the consul of sydney sent me. I am on board a war ship. I will leave in a month on board another ship which came three days ago, I am well I still have pain in my right leg. I have been in pain for a long time, I had much misery with them. They poisoned my leg. But even so I am well.

I send you greetings
Narcisse Pierre Pelletier

II

Narcisse Pierre Pelletier
le 11 Juliette 1875

Mon cher Père et Ma cher mère
et maisfrère, Je vous écrie une autre
foi. Je vous enbarsse De tout Mon
cœur. ci vous été vivant. Je suis arriver
à nouméa le consule de sydney. Ma
envoyez. Je suis A bord du'un navire
De guere. Je partirait Dans un mois
à bord Du autre navire qui est venu
il y a trois Jour, Je me Porte Bien
J'ai toujour mal à la gambre
Droits. il y à Bien longtemps que J'ai
mal, J'avait ut Bien de la misère
avec eux. il mon en Poissonnez la
gambre. Mais seúlement Je me
Porte Bien.

Je vous dit Bonjour
Narcisse Pierre Pelletier

LETTER THREE

*Mon cher père et ma chère mère et mes chère frère Je vous embrasse
de tout mon coeur, je vous écrie de mes Nouvelles, je me porte bien.
et Nous sommes arriver à Ryogenaire. le 14 octobre, je ne suis pas
bien à bord. Avec les maîtres, je mange avec les matelots à la racion
Il n'ont pas piéte de moi. de la soufrance que j'ai Eut de puis le temps
que jai resté avec ces sauvages. Mais je suis pas mal avec les matelots.
il y à 2 Mois que nous étions partit de Nouméa.*

Pelletier
Narcisse Pierre Naufragé

My dear father and my dear mother and my dear brothers I send
you all my love, I am writing to you with my news, I am well. and
we have arrive at Rio de Janeiro. on 14 October, I am not happy on
board. With the petty officers, I eat with the sailors on rations They
have no sympathy for me. for the suffering that I have had since
the time I stayed with these savages. But I do not get on badly with
the sailors. it was 2 months ago that we left Noumea.

Pelletier
Narcisse Pierre Castaway

III

Mon cher père et ma chere mère et mes chère, frère
Je vous embrasse de tout mon cœur, je vous écrie de mes
Nouvelles, je me porte bien et Nous sommes arrivés à
Rzogenain le 14 octobre je ne suis pas bien à bord
Avec les maîtres, je mange avec les matelots à la racion
Il n'ont pas pitié de moi de la soufrance que j'ai
eut depuis le temps que j'ai resté avec ces sauvages.
Mais je suis pas mal avec les matelots. il y à 2
Mois que nous étions partit de Nouméa.

Pelletier
Narcisse Pierre Naufragé

APPENDIX IV

Drawings of weapons made of wood

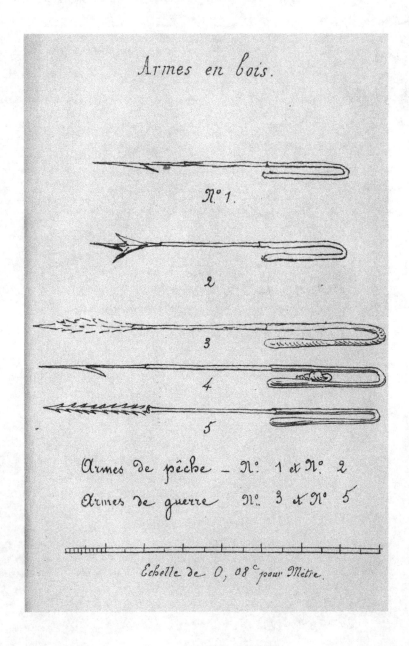

Armes en bois.

N.º 1.

2

3

4

5

Armes de pêche — N.º 1 et N.º 2
Armes de guerre   N.º 3 et N.º 5

Echelle de 0, 08ᶜ pour Mètre.

APPENDIX V

*Extract from a letter dated 30 May 1923 written
by Sir John Ottley to H. J. Dodd giving an account of
his meeting and conversations with Narcisse Pelletier
on board the* Brisbane *in 1875*[1]

In April 1875 I travelled from Calcutta to Rockhampton on a visit
to relatives. From Singapore I came on by an Eastern Australian
steamer the name of which I have forgotten.

On arrival at Thursday Island,[2] Narcisse Pelletier was put aboard
our ship for conveyance to Sydney, where he was to be handed
over to the French Consul, for repatriation to his own country. We
were informed that when the pearling schooner John Bell put in at
Night Island for wood and water, it was observed that there was a
white man amongst a number of blacks. On the assumption that
this white man was detained against his will, and that he would
naturally wish to get away, the skipper sent boats on shore with
a view to trading for the white man. Eventually they succeeded
in separating him from the blacks and having got him into one
of their boats gave him some food. As the blacks were clearly
unwilling to let their white companion go the sailors motioned to
him to sit down whilst they kept the blacks off by making a show
of firing their guns. This maneouvre [sic] proved successful, and
they were enabled to take the rescued man off to the John Bell
where they gave him clothes and took him to Thursday Island
whence as already mentioned he was placed on board our steamer
for conveyance to Sydney. As a matter of fact Narcisse Pelletier
subsequently explained to me that the men of the John Bell had
quite misunderstood the position of affairs. It was true that the

blacks were unwilling that he should be carried off, but it was equally true that he himself had no desire to leave the tribe.

Unfortunately he knew no English, and was unable to talk to the seamen — moreover he gathered that if he did not sit still or if he attempted to escape they would shoot him. In short his view evidently was that instead of being rescued he was kidnapped on the 11th April 1875. I have said that Narcisse Pelletier knew no English but a still greater difficulty was that when he was put aboard our ship he had to all intents and purposes forgotten his own mother tongue[.] It is true he remembered his name, and this gave a clue to his nationality but beyond this almost the only intelligible thing he could say was 'je ne sais pas' (I don't know). Now it so happened that I had been educated for some years in Paris, and that consequently I possessed an exceptionally good knowle[d]ge of French, whereas no one else on board could speak that language really fluently. It thus came about that Pelletier became as it were my special charge. I have been told that in an article on the case of Narcisse Pelletier published in the London 'Times' shortly afterwards the writer said that I was probably the only Englishman who could claim that he had taught a Frenchman his own language.[3] Of course I did nothing of the sort. What really happened was that by constantly talking to him in French, I succeeded in opening up the floodgates of Pelletier's memory, and this brought to the surface a whole host of words that had long been disused and temporarily forgotten. Anyway he was a marvellously apt pupil for before we parted he was not only discoursing volubly in French but had also to a great extent recovered his knowledge of reading and writing and had acquired as well a certain number of English words in addition. I remember for instance how interested and amused he was at discovering that while 'glass' in English meant 'verre' in French, the French word 'glace', was called 'ice' in English. I may add that whilst Pelletier was picking up his French and English, I was trying to learn as much as possible of the language of the tribe with which he had passed so many years[.] I was not very successful as I only managed to record about 100 words for by the time I had secured these Pelletier professed to have forgotten the remainder. The theory was that he could not hold two languages and that as his French came to the surface so did the native language sink out of sight and memory. If however Pelletier has gone to his black friends I am inclined to think that he had definitely made up his mind to give us no more information regarding the tribe and the language. The following account of Narcisse Pelletier's adventures up to the time of his landing in Australia in 1858 was taken down by me after he had recovered sufficient French to enable us to converse fairly freely. It appears that his father was one Martin Pelletier, a cobbler of Saint Giles [sic] près de l'isle Dieu [sic][4] near Bordeaux and that as a youngster Narcisse was sent to sea. In 1858 he was a cabin boy on board the 'St. Paul' of Bordeaux which was conveying some 300 Chinese coolies from China to Australia. One dark night the vessel struck a reef in the Louisiades group of islands. The Captain and crew got away in the boats, Pelletier and the coolies being left to make their way to land as best they could along the coral reef. Later on, distrusting the Chinese, the Europeans made for a neighbouring island where they were attacked by the natives, and compelled to return leaving three of their number (the second officer, a seaman, and an apprentice) in the hands of the enemy. Pelletier said that he himself was struck on the head by a stone but ma[n]aged to get off with the others. Once back on their original island with the Chinese, the Europeans decided to get away quietly in the night, and to make for the Australian coast in the hope of either falling in with an English settlement or else meeting with some Englis[h] vessel. Having overheard the discussion Pelletier followed the others down to the boat, and managed to get away in the one commanded by the Captain. I gathered that the boats became separated so that all that Pelletier knew was what happened to the boat in which he was.[5] He had no idea of the length of the voyage, but the shipwrecked men were evidently short of food, whilst their supply of water ran out some three or four days before they sighted land. Subsequently as we went down the coast Pelletier pointed out to us the place they had landed at and this was identified by our ship's officers as 'First Red Rocky Point' and a little south of Cape Direction. Raging with thirst the crew left the boat and searched for water. They eventually found a small quantity which was at once used up by the men, leaving none for young Pelletier, who was already nearly dead from exhaustion. Their thirst being assuaged to a certain extent, the Captain and his men — some eight in all — rapidly retraced their steps to the boat and sailed away, leaving the young cabin boy to his fate. This was the last that Pelletier ever saw of his shipmates, and of course he knew nothing more of any subsequent adventures they may have had. It was rumoured aboard our steamer that a story had been current in Australia of a boatload of wrecked French mariners having reached New Caledonia many years previously. In the absence of authentic information it is impossible to say whether this was or was not the captain's boat.[6] To return to Pelletier's story, it appears that some blacks happened to cross the white men's trail, and following it up found the almost dying boy lying by the side of the dried up water hole.[7] As we steamed down the coast Pelletier pointed out to us both the place where he first landed in 1858 and also Night Island — whence he was taken away in 1875. I made pencil sketches of both localities as seen from the deck of our steamer and I attach tracings of the same in the hope that they may be recognisable by those who happen to know the coast of Northern Queensland.[8] So far as we could ascertain Narcisse Pelletier mush have been about 14 or 15 in 1858 when he was a cabin boy on board the 'St. Paul' so that when we made his a[c]quaintance in 1875 he would have been about 31 or 32 years old and if he is still alive he must be now somewhere about 80 years of age.

The accompanying two photographs show what he was like in 1875 [see front and back covers]. The one naked to the waist shows the bars of raised flesh on his chest and shoulders and also the pierced lobes of his ears. The other shows him as dressed in the slop clothes served out to him. He was about middle height, broad shouldered, and evidently immensely powerful. His forearms were covered with a thick growth of hair. The thick pieces of wood some inches long that he was said to have worn in his ears when originally found had been removed prior to his coming on board our steamer.[9] They had been [sic] probably been annexed as curios by some one who had come across him before we met him.

The photographs do not of course enable one to realise the colour of his body which had been burnt by the sun to a deep red tan. As regards the bars of raised flesh on his body and shoulders he told me they had been made by scratching or cutting with a sharp tool — I believe a shell — and then pinching up the flesh in front of a fire. I gathered it was a very lengthy operation and must have been very painful, but he seemed to be rather proud of the result and we were not sure that it did not denote some sort of rank in the tribe.[10] The photographs show that he had a really splendid head and that he had a very determined look. On the whole he was fairly goodtempered whilst with us though occasionally there were indications that his temper might easily be aroused. On one point I was quite satisfied — namely that it would be an exceedingly evil day for his old captain, should he ever have the misfortune to come across the cabin boy he had deserted so many years before. Pelletier never disguised his intention of killing him if he ever ever [sic] had the chance. Pelletier's eyesight was little short of marvellous. I well remember that one day when steaming off the part of the coast that he knew so well he suddenly pointed out some apparently minute specks on a distant island and stated that they were canoes or dugouts belonging to a certain enemy tribe of blacks that he named. We were quite unable, even with our most powerful glasses, to make out what these specks really were, and it was not till we had steamed much closer that we were able to satisfy ourselves that the objects were really canoes of some kind. It was evident therefore that his naked eyesight served him better than our strongest field glasses. The truth I suppose is that for many years Pelletier had been compelled to depend to a great extent not only for his food but also for his safety on the keenness of his sight and hearing and that thus by constant exercise both these senses had been sharpened to an extraordinary degree as compared with those of Europeans, especially town bred ones. I have mentioned that Pelletier evidently possessed great strength. I once asked him if the blacks were strong and his reply was 'yes,' but 'I am very much stronger.' From this remark and from what he let drop at other times we came to the conclusion that he was quite a personage in his tribe, though he always asserted that no chief or headman was acknowledged. In one respect only did he admit that the blacks with whom he lived could do anything better than he could. This was in the matter of swimming. That he himself was a really fine swimmer was evident from what he told us of some of his feats but he always said that the blacks could beat him in this respect. We were somewhat surprised to find that though he had gone about stark naked for so many years yet he seemed to feel the cold very much when wearing clothes. He frequently shivered on deck when we were under steam and invariably took refuge on the lee side of the smoke stack. It seemed to me that he disliked the draught caused by our steaming. He certainly was never comfortable in his clothes and I fancy he often wished to get rid of them. At times I found him a serious nuisance owing to the fact that he had no notion of private property and seemed to think that we ought to hold things in common. Coming down to my cabin he used calmly to annex anything that struck his fancy and shewed his annoyance when I took things from him and locked them up in my trunks. A really singular feature of his case was the apparent impossibility of linking him up in any way with his early life in France. For instance he admitted he not only had a father and mother but also several brothers an[d] sisters[11] and yet when it was suggested to him that he would like to see them all again his invariable reply was 'they are all dead, for it was so long ago.' It was useless to point out to him that though possibly his father and mother might be dead there could be no reason to assume that his younger relatives had also died. Seeing that he himself was alive and well he might surely assume that some at any rate also still survived. To all these arguments he still replied 'they are all dead, it was so long ago.' He appeared to have lost all conception of the Deity or of religion in any shape or form. Eventually I managed to make him remember the existence of his parish priest (M'sieur le Cure) and to admit that he had been confirmed but all this meant nothing to him and were mere words without any meaning. In short his early life and all that it meant had apparently been completely wiped off the slate of his memory. On the other hand he was extremely reticent as to his life among the blacks and gave us little or no information when we pressed him for interesting details as to their customs[,] manners and beliefs[.] On one occasion I was asked by Sir Arthur Gordon (one of our passengers and the Governor Elect of Fiji) to ascertain what truth — if any— there was in the rumours current, that cannibalism was practised by, at any rate some of the blacks of North Queensland. To this Pelletier gave very vague replies, that left us under the impression that he knew more than he chose to confess and wound up the conversation with the final remark that 'ce n'est pas joli' which we took to mean that it was not a subject that he cared to discuss. We gathered that the various tribes of blacks inhabiting this part of the world hold very little intercourse with each other. Each tribe occupies its own tract of country and any intrusion on this is promptly resented, quarrels being apparently very frequent. The particular tribe to which Pelletier belonged call themselves the 'MUCKUDDUMAH' and are located on the coast some 40 or 50 miles south of Cape Direction. Another neighbouring tribe is known as the 'EHCHAHNS'. It would seem that all these tribes spend their lives in hunting, fishing, and fighting and never attempt any kind of cultivation. As to their beliefs and customs Pelletier either could not or would not tell us anything beyond the fact that there were no marriage ties in the sense that these are understood by civilised nations. The weapons used by the tribe would seem to be a spear (eehley) [*yuli*, 'woomera', 'spearthrower'][,] knife (tahweer) [*thawura*, 'knife'][,] throwing stick (kalkah) [*kalka*, 'spear' (generic)] and a three pronged harpoon (tayah) [*thaya*, 'spear, for dugong']. I append a list of words in Mukkudumah [sic] language that I was able to obtain from Pelletier. They may prove of use to some one going into their country. This ends Sir John Ottley's narrative of his knowledge of Pelletier but in his letter to me [i.e. to H. J. Dodd] that gentleman writes, 'Now for a word about the alleged return of Pelletier. I do not rule this out as impossible or even very improbable — because as I have shewn — he evidently did not want to leave the tribe and I am now inclined to think that if the canoes we saw off the coast had belonged to his own instead of to an enemy tribe he would very likely have gone overboard there and then and made a dash for freedom.'

APPENDIX VI

From The Times, *21 July 1875, 'Seventeen years among savages' by Arthur Hamilton-Gordon*

SEVENTEEN YEARS AMONG SAVAGES.

(FROM A CORRESPONDENT.)

S.S. BRISBANE, KEPPEL BAY, MAY 20.

On the 11th of April in the present year the John Bell schooner, engaged in the bêche de mer fishery, anchored at Night Island, a small island off the north-east coast of Queensland, in lat. 13deg. 10min. south, long. 143deg. 35min. east, about three miles distant from the mainland, to which boats were despatched from the ship in search of water. The sailors sent on this duty encountered in the bush a party of aboriginal blacks, with whom they found a white man, who was, like the blacks, perfectly naked, and appeared to be completely identified with them in language and habits. On these facts being reported to the master of the John Bell, he determined to make an effort to rescue the man, and with this view sent on shore the following day a large supply of articles of barter, which it was endeavoured to explain to the natives were intended to be exchanged for their guest or captive. The white savage was induced to enter one of the ship's boats, where he was given biscuit to eat and told to sit still, muskets being at the same time pointed at the natives and fired over their heads to induce them to retire, which they were very unwilling to do without being accompanied by the white man, whom they begged to return with them. This, he has since explained, he wished to do, but was afraid of the guns held by the sailors, and thought that they would shoot him if he tried to leave the boat, where he had been bidden to remain.

The John Bell brought her prize to Somerset, the settlement at Cape York, where he was clothed and cared for by the resident magistrate, Mr. Aplin. For some days after his arrival he sat the greater part of the day perched on the rail fence of a paddock "like a bird," as an eye-witness describes it, casting quick, eager, suspicious glances around him on every side and at every object which came within his view, rarely speaking, and apparently unable to remember more than a few words of his own language, although he said enough to show that he was a Frenchman, and wrote down on paper, in a stiff, upright French hand, his own name and a few almost unintelligible sentences, which were subsequently found to contain a short account of his history. On the return to Cape York of Lieutenant Connor, R.N., who speaks French fluently, a good deal more was extracted from the savage, and it appeared that his name was Narcisse Pierre Peltier, or Pelletier, son of Martin Peltier, shoemaker at St. Gille's, Department of Vendée, France. At the age of 12 Narcisse Peltier embarked as cabin-boy on board the St. Paul, of Bordeaux. This ship sailed from China for Australia in the year 1858, having on board some 359 Chinese Coolies. She never, however, reached her destination, having been wrecked one dark night on a reef off Roussel Island, in the Louisiade Archipelago. The captain and sailors got off in three boats and made for the main island, while the Chinese, with whom was Narcisse, walked along the reef to a small island situated upon it. An attack was subsequently made by the natives upon the captain's party, which was compelled to retreat to the island where the Chinese were, leaving in the hands of the savages the second officer, a sailor, and an apprentice. Distrustful of the Chinese, and totally unprovided with means of conveyance for so large a number, the captain and European sailors determined to abandon them secretly and escape in their boats, making for the Australian coast, in the hope of falling in with some English settlement or European vessel. This plan they accordingly carried out in the night. They had intended also to leave behind the boy Narcisse, but he had discovered what was contemplated, and followed the crew down to the boats, into which they did not refuse him admission. How long their voyage lasted is uncertain. They subsisted on a paste of flour and water, and such sea birds as they could catch, which were devoured raw. Two or three days before they reached the Australian coast their supply of fresh water failed, and when at length they made the shore, which they did at First Red Rock Point, south of Cape Direction, lat.

13deg. 4min. S., long. 143deg. 32min. E., their first thought was the alleviation of their thirst. Leaving the boat, they wandered along the shore, until at length they found a small quantity of water, the whole of which was eagerly drunk by the men, leaving none for the poor little cabin-boy, half-dead with hunger, thirst, exposure, and fatigue, and whose feet were cut to pieces by the sharp coral of the reef. Their thirst having been quenched, the captain and his men—eight in all—returned to their boat and sailed away again, leaving the boy to die by the empty water hole. They reached New Caledonia in safety, and there the captain reported the loss of his vessel and the hardships which he and his companions had undergone. He did not, however, report his abandonment of Narcisse Peltier.

The Chinese left at Roussel Island were, it was afterwards ascertained, gradually killed and eaten by the natives, with the exception of some 20, who ultimately escaped.

The career of the boy Narcisse Peltier would undoubtedly have come to a close even before his captain's arrival in New Caledonia had it not chanced that some blacks crossed the footprints left by the sailors in their search for water, and followed them up until they found the dying boy by the side of the dried-up well. They gave him food, which he describes as "des noisettes," and then led him away gently by the hand to their tribe, with which he has remained uninterruptedly until the present time, a period of no less than 17 years.

The opportunities for observation of the effects, physiological and psychological, of such a residence on one captured so young, and of his first renewed contact with civilized life, are of course rare, and the following notes, taken on board the mail steamer Brisbane, by which Narcisse has been sent from Somerset to be placed at the disposal of the French Consul in Queensland or New South Wales, may be of some interest.

Narcisse is a short, thick-set, active man. His skin is of a bright red colour, and glazed upon the surface by continued exposure to the sun. He is clean in his person, and says that the blacks among whom he has lived are so also—a statement apparently confirmed by the disgust he expressed for the Chinese on board the Brisbane, whom he styled dirty pigs ("des sales cochons"). Across his chest are two horizontal lines of raised flesh, about the thickness of an ordinary lead pencil. The upper one extends from nipple to nipple, the other, rather shorter, is about an inch lower. Above each breast are four short horizontal scars, one above the other, and on the upper part of his right arm a sort of gridiron has been scored, consisting of four vertical cuts enclosed in one passing all round them. These cuts were made with pieces of broken bottles obtained from ships, and the lips of the cut raised by continually pinching them up. No earth or other foreign matter had been introduced into the cut. These scars, he states, are made simply for ornament, and he is proud of them, or was so a short time since. The lobe of his right ear has been pierced and the flesh itself considerably drawn down, apparently between two and three inches. When found he wore a piece of wood in this aperture about half an inch in diameter and four inches long. This ornament he gave to one of the sailors of the schooner which brought him to Somerset. When speaking of the size to which the ear had been drawn down, he mentioned, with evident admiration, some men of his tribe who had trained the lobe of the ear down or nearly down to the shoulder. After having been on board the Brisbane a day or two, however, he came to the conclusion that the best thing he could do would be to have the lower part of his ear cut off, as not being "the right thing" in civilized society.

His nose is also pierced, and he was accustomed to wear in it a piece of white shell, probably that of the pearl oyster. When first found by the blacks he says he was very unhappy, often thought of his father, mother, and brothers, and longed to get away. In the course of time the recollection of them became less vivid and less painful, and he ultimately completely indentified himself with the tribe. He had never made an attempt to escape, as being alone he could not have managed a canoe out at sea, and though he had often seen vessels passing along the coast he had never been allowed to get near them, having been always sent by the blacks into the woods in the interior when they went on board a ship. It is not very clear how they came to allow him to be seen at last by the sailors of the John Bell.

When first recaptured he could hardly recall a

word of French, and the rapidity with which he has recovered " is remarkable. Even when he came on board the ....sbane a week ago his knowledge of his own language was very limited, and it was curious to see the manner in which a word or its meaning would suddenly recur to his recollection. He now speaks French fluently, and in proportion as it returns to him he forgets the language of his tribe, of which, however, about 100 words have been collected from him and taken down by Lieutenant Ottley, R.E. What is very much more remarkable, however, than his recovery of his mother tongue, is the fact that he has not lost the powers of reading or writing after a disuse of 17 years, during which he of course never saw a book, and, as he says, never wrote a line ; nor, indeed, did the blacks know that he possessed the power to do so. Very probably he did not know it himself. After two or three weeks residence at Somerset, however, he wrote, as has already been mentioned, a few almost unintelligible lines. Before coming on board the Brisbane he had much improved in intelligence, and pronounced correctly the names he saw written up on the boats and elsewhere about the ship. His progress since has been most rapid. He now spends a good deal of every day in reading, though whether he understands all that he reads may possibly be doubted, He displays considerable intelligence, but at the same time a childish dependance and imitativeness of others. That anything is done by *les autres* is sufficient to induce him to attempt it himself. He is generally good humoured, though with occasional fits of apparently causeless sulkiness ; he frequently coughs violently, and his habits of crouching about here and there are still those of a savage. He can count in French up to 100, having however at the first attempt stuck at 80, passing from 79 to 100 (" *soixante dix neuf—cent.*") The blacks, he says, have no names for the different numbers, and can only count by signs up to ten, signified by touching different parts of the body.

He is very bitter against the Captain of the Saint Paul for deserting him, but at the same time appears to be afraid of him. He speaks with kindness of his family, which he distinctly remembers, but always maintains that they must all, even including his younger brothers, be now dead, and it would appear as if, having no measure of the time

he has passed with the savages, the past appears to him at so vast a distance as to have given him the impression that he is extremely old, although in fact barely 30. He says he wished to remain with the blacks, and, although he acquiesced in his removal, he is evidently by no means as yet either happy or satisfied.

The name of the tribe with which he has lived is Macadama. They have no kings, chiefs, or leading men among them, all the males being equal. The men, he says, are strong, but observes with pride that he himself is very strong, much stronger than the blacks. On the other hand, though he says he is a good swimmer and diver, he acknowledges that in the water the blacks far surpass him. The tribe subsists chiefly on fish, turtles, turtles' eggs, alligators' eggs, and roots and fruits. Sometimes they hunt animals, but apparently not often. The occupation of the men is fishing, that of the women to gather roots, and sometimes also they get honey. They have no knowledge of nets, lines, or hooks. The larger fish are harpooned from canoes, the smaller speared with a three-pronged spear. The canoes are cut out of trees with knives formed of hoop iron obtained from barrels washed up from wrecks. Of this hoop iron also the heads of their spears and harpoons are made. Narcisse says he has himself constructed two canoes, which he has left behind him.

The women appear to be more numerous than the men, every man having from two to five women in his suite. Their position is a low one, as appears from the fact that although there are separate names for " man," " brother," and " son," there is only one word—" beycheynumma"—for " woman," " sister," and " daughter." The terms " husband ' and " wife" are of course unknown, as are the ideas which they imply. The relations of the sexes are strictly animal, and " might makes right." The men, he says, not unfrequently fight with spears for the possession of a woman, while the women fight among themselves about a man, their weapons being heavy staves, with which they beat one another about the head till the blood flows. These quarrels probably arise when a decided preference is shown to one woman over another by their lord. The men have no clothing whatever, not even opossum rugs or other covering at night; the women wear a fringe of cords extending from the waist to half way down the thigh. They have no houses or huts, but when it rains they put up some temporary shelter of branches of trees or bark. He maintains, however, that they never feel cold because they always have fires. On board he feels the cold bitterly and dislikes the wind. Like all savages he can make fire by rubbing together two pieces of wood. He describes the tribe he has been attached to as very peaceable, and says that he has never seen one of its number killed by another member of the tribe. Battles, however, sometimes occur between two tribes. He describes one in which he took a part. A tribe named the Echaus killed some of the Macadımas, upon which the latter retaliated by surprising the Echaus when asleep one rainy night and killing a large number. Two were speared by Narcisse himself.

The blacks have no knowledge of any Superior Being, and no form of religion of any kind whatever. The dead are tied up with cords after the fashion of a mummy, and exposed to the action of the sun either in the forks of trees or on a rough scaffold. He describes the treatment he has received from the tribe as having been uniformly kind, and he thinks they would treat any white man well. They are not afraid, he says, of white men, but of white men's guns. They are not cannibals nor does he think that any of the tribes of that region are so. He states that he has heard that in his tribe there was an old white man who had lived among them for many years and was at last drowned while out fishing. He does not recollect having seen this man himself, and is not sure when his death occurred.

An Australian correspondent writes to us on the same subject :—

"An interesting case of the naturalization of a white man among savages has just come to light. Seventeen years ago the French ship St. Paul, with 327 Chinese coolies for Australia, was wrecked on a reef off Rossel Island, in the Louisiade Archipelago, east of New Guinea. The coolies were landed on an island, where they were left by the captain. The story of the Chinamen is a short one, for, as the natives happened to be cannibals, it seemed good to them to fetch off two of the fattest every day and eat

them, so that when at last a ship came to fetch them away there were only 17 left. The boat containing the captain and his crew of eight Frenchmen made the coast of Australia near Cape Direction, on the Cape York Peninsula, and the captain and crew landed in search of water. Among them was a boy about 12 years old, named Narcisse Pelletier, of St. Giles, near Bordeaux, who cut his feet badly in walking over the rock, and was unable to keep up with the others; consequently, when the boat started on its course he was left behind, and remained three days alone on the coast. He was lying asleep under a tree when a gentle shaking made him aware that he was in the presence of three black men and two black women, who made signs of surprise and commiseration. They gave him some food, and led him away without any violence to their camp, where he was received by others of the tribe in an equally friendly manner. He became one of the tribe and adopted their way of living, which, as he describes it, is, perhaps, as primitive as any that can now be found. Shelter and clothing are dispensed with altogether, except that the women wear a small fringed girdle round the hips. Their food consists of fish, which they take entirely by spearing and harpooning, fruits, and a few animals. They use fire for cooking, obtaining it by rubbing two pieces of dry wood together. Their personal ornamentations consist of a few scars made by cutting the flesh with broken bottles and pinching up the incision repeatedly until a cork-like excrescence is formed. The design, as exemplified in his person, consists of two straight cords across the lower part of the chest, the longer of them about 10 inches in length, about a third of an inch thick in the middle, and tapering off to the ends, the other somewhat smaller; four or five short lines parallel to these and above them on each side of the front of the chest, all the lines being about an inch apart; some similar short lines or ' crackling' in front of the right shoulder, and a few slight ones in front of the left; besides that he has a hole through the lobe of the right ear large enough to hold a piece of wood of the size of a five-franc piece when stretched, and, finally, a hole through the division of the nose to admit a piece of bamboo as large as a common lead pencil just below the nostrils. They do not practise any other mutilation or modification of any part of the body, but they cut their hair (which is black and straight—not curled in the smallest degree) with broken bottles. The incisions applied to the women differ only in pattern from those of the men. When it rains heavily they try to shelter themselves with pieces of bark or branches, but they have not even the rudiment of a hut. They seldom stay long in one place. They have no stone implements in use ; their weapons and fish spears are tipped with iron, obtained from the hoops of casks picked up on the beach. Their language, about a hundred words of which have been written down from Pelletier's dictation, does not appear to have anything in common with Malay, or with any of the Papuan dialects, of which vocabularies are at hand. It abounds in nasal sounds. They are wholly unable to count, and have no words for numbers. Their relations between the sexes are those which obtain among animals other than man. The strongest take three or four women each, and fights for their posses- sion are of frequent occurrence. When a man for any reason is dissatisfied with or tired of his wife, he simply spears her, and there is an end of it. Domestic troubles are consequently of short duration. Neither cannibalism nor infanticide is practised by this tribe ; on the contrary, according to Pelletier's statement, they are rather good- natured people, and would be kind to any white man who came among them unarmed. Of any religion, or belief in the existence of any kind of unseen world, they appear not to have the slightest vestige.

Pelletier is, of course, a living curiosity. He is to be handed over to the French Consul at Sydney, who will, no doubt, forward him to France. What his ultimate fate may be, no one can say, but it is certain that if he is to thrive as a civilized man he will require a larger amount of dis- cretion than his training up to this point is likely to have given him. The position of a nine days' wonder must be a difficult one to fill satisfactorily. The showman will be lying in wait for him, and at each successive place that he reaches the idea of work, which at present does not seem to exist in his brain, will become further and further distant. He certainly has one great advantage in being able to read and write, and he is recovering his native language, which at first he appeared to have entirely forgotten, with surprising rapidity. The description given by those who saw him when he was first landed at Somerset a fortnight ago —he had been taken off, scarcely, it seems, with his own consent, by a coasting vessel's boat, which had gone on shore for water—is that he sat on a rail and stared about him like a bird, just as a black fellow does who is bewil- dered. The life of a cabin-boy up to 12, and of a naked savage up to 29 years of age, does not, indeed, seem likely to develope a French peasant lad into a very high type of humanity. But Narcisse, clothed and conversing with white people, appears by no means deficient in intelligence, and there is a chance for him yet, for at this very moment he is spelling out the pages of a French novel."

ENDNOTES

THE TWO LIVES OF NARCISSE PELLETIER

[1] See Chase, 'Belonging to country: territory, identity and environment in Cape York Peninsula, Northern Australia', 1984: 104, 108.

[2] Pelletier, *Chez les sauvages. Dix-sept ans de la vie d'un mousse vendéen dans une tribu cannibale 1858–1875*, ed. Philippe Pécot, 2001 (new edition).

[3] This geographical mismatch is puzzling. Details taken from the report of Pelletier's recovery published in *The Times* of 21 July 1875 (the article is reproduced as Appendix VI) were incorporated into the article published by the *Bulletin français* of 23 July 1875, which announced his imminent return. The *Times* report gives the locations of where Pelletier landed and where he was recovered, but this information was not included in the French article. Similarly, later reports that appeared in the French press and also drew their information from *The Times* do not specify where Pelletier was found on Cape York.

[4] The story of Eliza Fraser, the most famous of castaways who lived with Aboriginal people, is not comparable to these since she was recovered after only a matter of months. She is now 'a source of myth and legend', as her entry in the *Australian dictionary of biography* puts it, and the various accounts and representations of her experiences are contentious (http://www.adb.online.anu.edu.au/biogs/AS10171b.htm, accessed 4 December 2008).

[5] The new edition of Merland's book edited by Philippe Pécot does not contain the complete text of the original. Merland's discussion of linguistic theory at the beginning of Chapter 4, material that is not relevant to Pelletier's account, has been omitted, as well as some material from Garnier's musical appendix.

[6] See Rigsby and Peterson, 'Introduction', 2005; Peterson, 'Thomson's place in Australian anthropology', 2005.

[7] 'Across Cape York Peninsula with a pack team', 1934a: 22, 26.

[8] 'The masked dancers of I'wai'i. A remarkable hero cult which has invaded Cape York Peninsula', 1956b: 17, 18.

[9] 'Anthropology through a biological lens', 2005: 17.

[10] See Chase, *Which way now? Tradition, continuity and change in a North Queensland Aboriginal community* 1980b: 116; Rigsby and Peterson, 'Introduction', 2005: 4-5. Also Rigsby: personal communication.

[11] Peterson, 'Thomson's place in Australian anthropology', 2005: 33; Rigsby and Peterson, 'Introduction', 2005: 4–5.

[12] Rigsby and Peterson, 'Introduction', 2005: 6; Peterson, 'Thomson's place in Australian anthropology', 2005: 42.

[13] 'The Aborigines of Princess Charlotte Bay, North Queensland', 1933–36.

[14] 'Cultural continuity: land and resources among East Cape York Aborigines', 1980a: 84.

[15] See Bradley, *I didn't know that: Cairns and districts, Tully to Cape York, 1936–1946, service personnel and civilians*, 1995. More recently, in the vicinity of the Iron Range airport, one of Australia's worst civilian air disasters occurred in May 2005, when a twin-engined plane carrying 15 passengers crashed into a hillside on its approach to the airport, leaving no survivors.

[16] Cultural continuity', 1980a: 84.

[17] Hagan, *Lockhart River Community Plan 2004–2008. Empowering the community — working together*, 2005: 36.

[18] The art movement at Lockhart River was the subject of a major exhibition at the University of Queensland Art Museum held in Brisbane in 2007 and of a related publication, Butler, *Our way: contemporary Aboriginal art from Lockhart River*, 2007.

[19] See Chase, '"All kind of nation": Aborigines and Asians in Cape York Peninsula', 1981, for an account of the involvement of men from the Lockhart community in the lugger industry.

[20] See Thompson, *'Bora belonga white man': Missionaries and Aborigines at Lockhart River Mission*, 1995 (rev. ed.); Chase, 'Lazarus at Australia's gateway. The Christian mission enterprise in eastern Cape York Peninsula', 1988; Warby, *You - me mates eh! : a personal story of reconciliation and change among the Aboriginal people and missionary staff of Lockhart River Mission, Cape York Peninsula 1924–1960*, 2000.

[21] Chase, 'Lazarus at Australia's gateway', 1988: 131; *Which way now?* 1980b: 114–16.

[22] Chase here uses J. C. Anderson's concept of 'intervention complex' to characterise particular European activities aimed at intervening in Aboriginal societies in purposive ways, and, in the light of the Howard Government's Northern Territory Intervention in 2007, his prescient terminology (*The political and economic basis of Kuku-Yalanji social history*, unpublished PhD thesis, University of Queensland) discussed in 'Lazarus at Australia's gateway', 1988.

[23] 'Lazarus at Australia's gateway', 1988: 122, 136.

[24] See Sutton, 'After consensus', 2008a: 205.

[25] Chase, 'Thomson time', 1979.

[26] See Chase, *Which way now?* 1980b: 89.

[27] Haviland, *Old Man Fog and the last Aborigines of Barrow Point*, 1998: 190.

[28] See Chase, *Which way now?* 1980b: Chapter 10, on this point, and for an analysis of the impact of the successive phases of contact on the coastal peoples of north-eastern Cape York.

[29] See Chase, *Which way now?* 1980b, for a detailed examination of cultural continuity and change in the Lockhart River community.

[30] Pérocheau, *Dictionnaire historique des Vendéens célèbres additionné des incontournables*, 1994: 135.

[31] Rochas, 'Naufrage et scènes d'anthropophagie à l'île Rossell [sic] dans l'archipel de la Louisiade (Mélanésie)', 1861.

[32] Tylor, *Primitive culture: researches into the development of mythology, philosophy, religion, language, art and custom*, 1871.

[33] *The Times*, 21 July 1875. The title 'Seventeen years among savages' is the same title Merland chose for his book.

[34] Bowen Historical Society, *The story of James Morrill*, n. d.

[35] See White, 'The forms of wildness: archaeology of an idea', 1972: 4.

[36] See Bartra, *Wild men in the looking glass: the mythic origins of European otherness*, 1994.

[37] White, 'The forms of wildness', 1972: 26.

[38] Flannery (ed.), *The life and adventures of William Buckley*, 2002: 105.

[39] See, for example, Broca's *On the phenomena of hybridity in the genus Homo*, 1864 [1860]: 45.

[40] Verne, *Les enfants du Capitaine Grant*, n.d. [1868]: 363, 359.

[41] *Triumph in the tropics: an historical sketch of Queensland*, 1959: 178–9.

[42] This is what he reports in his letter to Dodd (Ottley manuscript), but the *Brisbane Courier* (24 May 1875) reports that he was on sick furlough. Ottley's letter is reproduced here at Appendix V.

[43] *Who was who, 1929–1940* (second edition), vol. 3, 1967: 1031.

[44] Ottley manuscript.

[45] David Moore, who undertook the task of transcribing Brierly's journals in which he recorded his interviews with Barbara Thomson, sees Brierly as quite exceptional for his time as an enlightened and interested observer of the Aboriginal people he met on his travels, and 'remarkable', too, in his attitude to Barbara Thompson (*Islanders and Aborigines at Cape York. An ethnographic reconstruction based on the 1848–1850 'Rattlesnake' Journals of O. W. Brierly and information he obtained from Barbara Thompson*, 1978: 4–5).

[46] *Brisbane Courier*, 24 May 1875; *Sydney Morning Herald*, 27 May 1875; *Sydney Mail*, 29 May 1875. These three reports are almost identical and are attributed to statements gathered from Pelletier by Ottley. References below to the *Brisbane Courier* article can be found in the corresponding articles in the other papers.

[47] In his report to H. J. Dodd (see below), Ottley states that he was the only person on board who spoke French fluently, which means that Hamilton-Gordon would have had to rely on him for information. He also mentions that Hamilton-Gordon asked him to put questions to Pelletier about cannibalism (Ottley manuscript).

[48] *The Times* does not name Hamilton-Gordon as the writer but simply gives its source as '(From a correspondent.) S.S. Brisbane, Keppel Bay, May 20.' The main part of the article is Hamilton-Gordon's. There is a second, shorter part by an unnamed 'Australian correspondent' (*The Times*, 21 July 1875). The draft of the article is included in the Stanmore papers held by the British Library (Hamilton-Gordon manuscript).

[49] *Who was who, 1929–1940* (second edition), vol. 3, 1967: 1031.

[50] The Cooktown Telegraph Station opened in 1875 and Dodd was appointed as an operator that year (Gribble, *What hath God wrought: the story of the electric telegraph, Queensland*, 1985: 447). My thanks to Leo Molony for this information.

[51] My thanks to Alan-Michel Misson de Saint-Gilles (whose great-grandfather, Elie Jean-Félix Pelletier, was one of Narcisse Pelletier's younger brothers) for supplying this information.

[52] *Saint-Gilles Croix-de-Vie, d'après les écrits de Marcel Baudouin. Miroir d'une mémoire*, 1986: 31. Havre-de-Vie was the dechristianised name given to the town of Croix-de-Vie during the Revolutionary period (Véronique Guilbaud: personal communication).

[53] Gaucher, *Saint-Gilles-Croix-de-Vie*, 1969: 10.

[54] Roussière, *A l'écoute de la Vendée*, 1975: 26.

[55] Baudouin, *Saint-Gilles Croix-de-Vie*, 1986: 56, 124.

[56] Jean Babin, then aged 63, is listed as 'mâitre de port', harbour master, and 'chef de ménage', head of household, in the 1861 Census of Saint-Gilles (extract from the Dénombrement de la population, Année 1861). My thanks to Véronique Guilbaud for supplying this and other archival information relating to Pelletier and the *Saint-Paul*. The information about Pelletier's voyages was transcribed by Roland Mornet from Pelletier's maritime service record held at the Service Historique de la Marine at Rochefort (manuscript, Registre des mousses des Sables, La Chaume, Moricq, Ile d'Yeu, cote du Service Historique de la Marine de Rochefort, 3P7 50, folio 267, no. 53).

[57] Pinard's full name is recorded as 'Em^{el} Sévère Ph^{pe}' on the disembarkation roll of the *Saint-Paul* dated 1860, at Marseilles (extract from the 'Désarmement' of the *Saint-Paul* supplied by Véronique Guilbaud).

[58] Gittins, *The diggers from China: the story of the Chinese on the goldfields*, 1981: 42.

[59] See ibid.: Chapter 4.

[60] Liep, '"This civilising influence": the colonial transformation of Rossel Island society', 1983: 120.

[61] Armstrong, *Rossel Island: an ethnological study*, 1928: 109.

[62] Charles Card's diary, cited by Goodman, *The Rattlesnake. A voyage of discovery to the Coral Sea*, 2005: 220.

[63] See Chapter 2, n. 1 for more details on this point.

[64] Ottley writes: 'Subsequently as we went down the coast Pelletier pointed out to us the place they had landed at and this was identified by our ship's officers as "First Red Rocky Point" and a little south of Cape Direction' (Ottley manuscript) and again: 'As we steamed down the coast Pelletier pointed out to us both the place where he first landed in 1858 and also Night Island — whence he was taken away in 1875'.

[65] My thanks to John Liep for his comments to me on Pinard's lack of geographical precision, starting from the time of the shipwreck, which the captain assumed had happened close to Adele Island but that in fact occurred 25 kilometres further west, off the north-east coast of Rossel Island (email, 18 September, 2006). Rochas refers to Pinard's difficulties in taking navigational readings from the sun's position in the three days before the shipwreck because of the weather ('Naufrage et scènes d'anthropophagie', 1861: 82).

[66] *Univers illustré*, 7 August 1875.

[67] Ibid.: 83 (my translation).

[68] Ottley manuscript.

[69] See Chase's ethnographic commentary.

[70] Chapter 3.

[71] See Loos, *Invasion and resistance: Aboriginal-European relations on the North Queensland frontier 1861-1897*, 1982: Chapter 6, on the sea frontier in North Queensland, and Ganter, *The pearl-shellers of Torres Strait: resource use, development and decline 1860s-1960s*, 1994.

[72] Chase, "'All kind of nation'", 1981: 10.

[73] *The Times*, 21 July 1875.

[74] See Chase, "'All kind of nation'", 1981 for discussion of the impact of the lugger industry on the Lockhart Community and the attitudes of older Lockhart men to their past involvement in the industry, particularly their nostalgia for the period when they went to sea on Japanese boats.

[75] Aplin manuscript, 'Report on the pearl fisheries of Torres Strait', Somerset, 3 March 1875. Aplin was the first Government Geological Surveyor of Southern Queensland. His briefly-held post at Somerset was to be his last; he died there in September 1875. See Woods, 'C. D'Oyly H. Aplin, First Government Geologist for the Southern District of Queensland', 1964.

[76] Ottley manuscript.

[77] Aplin manuscript, Letter to the Colonial Secretary, Somerset, 11 May 1875.

[78] See Chase, *Which way now?* 1980b: 155–158.

[79] David Thompson notes that 'Amglo', with its particular cluster of consonant sounds, is not a word or name that would be found in the Uutaalnganu language (personal communication). A possible correspondence to Aplin's 'Anco' is the name Ankum or Angkum, a place name referring to a particular waterhole in the southern part of the Uutaalnganu lands.

[80] Aplin manuscript, Letter to the Colonial Secretary, Somerset, 11 May 1875.

[81] *The Times*, 21 July 1875.

[82] Ibid.

[83] The entry from the section of a notebook headed 'Recollections of Johnny Maori', reads 'Narcisse Peltier: French cook at Somerset tried to talk to him but he could only talk mainland' (MacFarlane manuscript, 'Early days of Thursday Island').

[84] MacFarlane does not mention that he himself had some contact with Night Island people as he was involved with the establishment of the Lockhart River Mission in 1924 which was situated in Uutaalnganu territory.

[85] *Cummins & Campbell's Monthly Magazine*, December 1948.

[86] *Sydney Evening News*, 22 May 1875.

[87] Sharp, *Footprints along the Cape York sandbeaches*, 1992: 77; Mullins, *Torres Strait: a history of colonial occupation and culture contact, 1864-1897*, 1995; Chase, 'Lazarus at Australia's gateway', 1988: 124.

[88] Samuel McFarlane manuscript.

[89] Page 169, diary entry for 4 February 1927. Transcribed by Peter Sutton, Mortlock Library, State Library of South Australia, 28/2, 2/3, 11/3 1994. SA State Library Manuscript code: PRG 13, series 3.

[90] Baudouin manuscript.

[91] Email to S. Anderson, 13 March 2004. He continues: 'At that time, the oldest people in Lockhart River would have been born in the late 1880s and 1890s, and I would not have expected this event to have necessarily survived in the oral stories. Other well-documented events from the 1860s and 1870s for this region were equally unknown to the then old people at Lockhart River. My experience was that unless it was a personally remembered event, or unless it was a major story repeatedly told by a parent or close relative, then it did not survive in the group memory. I did get an account of [the explorer] Logan Jack's first trip into the McIlwraiths in the 1870s, from a man whose father had been a young man then, and who repeatedly told a story of the first sight of horses, their spear throwing, and subsequent retaliation by shooting'.

[92] Chase, *Which way now?* 1980b: 348.

[93] *Brisbane Courier*, 24 May 1875.

[94] Ottley manuscript.

[95] Ibid.

[96] Ibid.

[97] Ibid.

[98] *Brisbane Courier*, 24 May 1875; *The Times*, 21 July 1875.

[99] Ottley manuscript.

[100] *The Times*, 21 July 1875.

[101] Ibid.

[102] Ottley manuscript.

[103] Ibid.

[104] *Brisbane Courier*, 24 May 1875.

[105] Ottley manuscript.

[106] Ibid.

[107] To use the title of an article by Barry Hill, inspired by the figures of William Buckley and T. G. H. Strehlow, in which he discusses the possibilities and impossibilities of doing so ('Crossing Cultures', 2003).

[108] Aplin manuscript, Letter to the Colonial Secretary, Somerset, 11 May 1875.

[109] *Brisbane Courier*, 24 May 1875.

[110] Baudouin manuscript.

[111] See Flannery (ed.), *The life and adventures of William Buckley*, 2002: xi.

[112] Bowen Historical Society, *The story of James Morrill*, n. d., n. p. (the quotation is from Morrill's 'Note' which precedes Chapter 1 of the publication).

[113] Gregory, *Narrative of James Murrells' ("Jemmy Morrill") seventeen years' exile among the wild blacks of North Queensland*, 1896: 31.

[114] Ibid.: iv.

[115] My thanks to Peter Sutton for his remarks on this question.

[116] Moore, *Islanders and Aborigines at Cape York*, 1978: 10, 313.

[117] Ibid.: 292.

[118] This is the term used by Donald Thomson ('The hero cult, initiation and totemism on Cape York', 1933a).

[119] See Rigsby and Chase, 'The Sandbeach People and dugong hunters of Eastern Cape York Peninsula: property in land and sea country', 1998: 48; Thompson, 'Bora is like Church', 1985: 2-3.

[120] Chase, *Which way now?* 1980b: 199–200.

[121] See Thompson, 'Bora is like Church', 1985: 7.

[122] Thomson, 'The hero cult, initiation and totemism on Cape York', 1933a: 460-1.

[123] The *Times* report states: 'The blacks have no knowledge of any Superior Being, and no form of religion of any kind whatever' (21 July 1875). See Chapter 5 for similar comments by Merland.

[124] See, for example, Pruner-Bey, 'L'homme et l'animal', 1865; Broca, 'Discours sur l'homme et les animaux, 1866; Martin De Moussy, 'La religiosité est-elle un des caractères spéciaux du genre humain?', 1866.

[125] Thomson, 'The dugong hunters of Cape York', 1934b.

[126] See Chase, *Which way now?* 1980b: Chapter 6.

[127] Ibid.: 209.

[128] Ibid.: 267–8.

[129] Ibid.: 194–7.

[130] Ibid.: 184.

[131] *The Times*, 21 July 1875.

[132] Ottley manuscript.

[133] Ibid.

[134] See Bowen and Bowen, *The Great Barrier Reef: history, science, heritage, 2003*: 120; *Australian dictionary of biography*, online edition, http://www.adb.online.anu.edu.au/adbonline.htm, entry for George Poynter Heath (1830–1921), accessed 7 November 2008.

[135] *Australian dictionary of biography*, online edition, http://www.adb.online.anu.edu.au/adbonline.htm, entry for Harold Heneage Finch-Hatton (1856–1904), accessed 7 November 2008.

[136] Finch-Hatton, *Advance Australia!: an account of eight years' work, wandering and amusement in Queensland, New South Wales and Victoria*, 1885: 14.

[137] *Australian dictionary of biography*, online edition, http://www.adb.online.anu.edu.au/adbonline.htm, entry for Sir George Ruthven Le Hunte (1852–1925), accessed 7 November 2008.

[138] *Cooktown Herald and Palmer River Advertiser*, 19 May 1875, 'A Chinese Lady'.

[139] *Queenslander*, 29 May 1875, 'Shipping intelligence'.

[140] *Brisbane Courier*, 26 May 1875.

[141] *The Illustrated Sydney News New South Wales Weather Almanac* for 1874 lists Simon as the Consul of France at 284 Pitt Street (p. 40) and for 1875 at 227 George Street (p. 14).

[142] Broc, *Dictionnaire illustré des explorateurs français du XIXe siècle*, vol. 2 (Asie), 1992: 416.

[143] The report is contained in the article by Charles Letourneau mentioned above and constitutes the major part of it. It is not clear to whom the report was addressed. Simon concludes by stating that Pelletier is now back with his family and that he has forwarded other information to the Ministry of the Navy.

[144] Samuel McFarlane manuscript.

145 Letourneau, 'Sur un Français nommé Narcisse Pelletier', 1880: 713.

146 Ibid.: 714.

147 Manuscript, Service Historique de la Marine de Rochefort, cote 3P2 37, 1862, Dépêches ministérielles les Sables, no. 70 du Registre. Interestingly, an earlier note added to Pelletier's naval record has it that 'his death is not certain — his young age leads one to think that he would have been adopted by the indigenes of Cape Flattery' (manuscript, Service Historique de la Marine de Rochefort, cote 3P 7 50, Registre des Mousses des Sables, La Chaume, Moricq, St Gilles, Ile d'Yeu).

148 Entry for Alexandre Henri Lamartinière in *Dictionary of Australian artists online*: http://www.daao.org.au/main/read/3825, accessed 7 December 2008; entry for Charles Henry Kerry in the *Australian dictionary of biography* online edition: http://www.adb.online.anu.edu.au/biogs/A090578b.htm, accessed 7 December 2008.

149 *La Presse Illustrée*, 7 August 1875. The article provides no new information about Pelletier and is based, not completely accurately, on the earlier article in *The Times*.

150 *Melbourne Herald*, 21 March 1961; *Holy Name Monthly*, October 1969; *Canberra Times*, 16 May 1992.

151 See Chapter 3 for Merland's account of how Pelletier believed this wound was inflicted upon him while he was sleeping as a punishment.

152 *Jura* manuscript.

153 He was admitted for a 'sore on his thigh' while the hospital doctor records the 'recognised illness' as being a 'specific ulcer on the right leg with two venereal testicles'. Under 'Observations' the record reads: 'has been pricked by a bone by the savages of Australia' (Hôpital Beaujon manuscript).

154 Flannery (ed.), *The life and adventures of William Buckley*, 2002: 182.

155 Information obtained from letters transcribed by Roland Mornet at the Service Historique de la Marine, Rochefort. One letter is from Pelletier, dated 26 January 1876, and written from Nantes to 'Monsieur le Ministre' in which he refers to the petition he had made in an earlier letter. The other letter, dated 29 January 1876, from the 'Ministre de la Marine et des Colonies pour le Ministre et par son ordre le Commissaire général Directeur des Services Administratifs' to 'Monsieur l'Administrateur de l'Inscription Maritime à St Gilles Croix de Vie' attaches the first letter and refers to Narcisse Pelletier's petition to gain employment as a lighthouse keeper in the earlier (and missing) letter.

[156] 'Narcisse Pelletier', 1876a: 18 (my translation).

[157] The archives of the Service des Phares et Balises at Saint-Nazaire, which may have contained this information, were destroyed along with much of the town during World War II. Oral history is supported by a contemporary source, the anthropologist and museologist Ernest Hamy, who, in 1880, was reported as saying that he believed Pelletier was the keeper of the lighthouse at Saint-Nazaire (Letourneau 1880: 715).

[158] *Journal des Sables*, 6 June 1954.

[159] Letourneau, 'Sur un Français nommé Narcisse Pelletier', 1880.

[160] Ibid.: 711.

[161] Ibid.: 712.

[162] *New York Times*, 3 August 1875.

[163] Letter dated 9 November, 2005 to S. Anderson from Bureau's biographer, Gildas Buron.

[164] Letourneau, 'Sur un Français nommé Narcisse Pelletier', 1880: 716 (my translation).

[165] Baudouin, 'L'homme sauvage de Vendée', 1911: 157; Baudouin manuscript.

[166] See Lane, *The wild boy of Aveyron*, 1976.

[167] Hervé, 'Le sauvage de l'Aveyron devant les observateurs de l'homme (avec le rapport retrouvé de Philippe Pinel)', 1911.

[168] Baudouin, 'L'homme sauvage de Vendée', 1911: 158. (my translation; his italics).

[169] Ibid.: 157–8.

[170] *Journal illustré*, 8 August 1875, 'La capture de Narcisse Pelletier'.

[171] Pajot, *Personnages pittoresques de Nantes et de Loire-Atlantique*, 1999 and *Nantes-sur-mer. Histoires de l'eau de la Loire à l'Atlantique* 2002; Marlex, *La vie à Saint-Nazaire au 19e siècle*, n.d. n.p.; Bouchon, *Un Mousse oublié. Narcisse Pelletier, Vendéen*, 1997: 47.

[172] It is worth noting that Pelletier's name is most often spelt correctly in Australian reports but it sometimes appears as Peltier or Pellatier.

[173] See various permutations of the story in *Cummins & Campbell's Monthly Magazine*, December 1948; Cilento and Lack 1963 [1959]: 33; *Melbourne Herald*, 21 March 1961; *Holy Name Monthly*, October 1969, vol. 38(9); *Sydney Sun*, 5 August 1974; *Courier Mail*, 27 December 1995; *Smith's Weekly*, 25 February 1922 and 17 November 1923.

[174] *Smith's Weekly*, 25 February 1922; Cilento and Lack 1963 [1959]: 33. The latter give the date of Owens' encounters with this man as 1910.

[175] *Smith's Weekly*, 17 November 1923.

[176] Entry for Louis de Rougemont in the *Australian dictionary of biography* online edition: http://www.adb.online.anu.edu.au/biogs/A080309b.htm, accessed 7 December 2008.

[177] Howard, *The fabulist: the incredible story of Louis de Rougemont*, 2006: 14.

[178] There are three very similar versions of this work published under different titles (Rouillé, *De Vendée en Australie: l'aventure de Narcisse Pelletier mousse vendéen*, 1967; *Le sauvage blanc : de Vendée en Australie,* 1980; *La prodigieuse et véritable aventure d'un mousse vendéen,* 2002).

[179] Bouchon, *Un Mousse oublié. Narcisse Pelletier, Vendéen,* 1997.

[180] Trogoff, *Mémoires sauvages,* 2002.

[181] The extract is a composite taken from Lumholtz, *Among cannibals. An account of four years' travels in Australia, and of camp life with the Aborigines of Queensland,* 1980 [1889], combining part of Chapter 12 (pp. 153–80), mainly concerning the position of women, and most of Chapter 22 (pp. 293–7), concerning cannibalism.

[182] See Poignant, 'Captive Aboriginal lives: Billy, Jenny, Little Toby and their companions', 1993 and Anderson, 'Clichés of Australian Aborigines: photography and raciology, Paris, 1885', 2006. When 'Jenny' and 'Billy', the subjects of the photographs on the cover of the new edition of Merland's book, were photographed, they and a young boy named 'Little Toby' were the only surviving members of the original nine of their countrymen and women who made up Cunningham's troupe.

[183] The *Sydney Shipping Gazette* gives the name of the schooner as the *Prince of Denmark* (3 January 1859 and 24 January 1859) and the name of the captain as Captain McKellar (24 January 1859).

[184] *Sydney Shipping Gazette,* 3 January 1859. Rochas gives the rescue date as 11 October (1861, p. 85).

[185] Rochas, 'Naufrage et scènes d'anthropophagie' 1861: 85 (my translation; his italics).

[186] Guillou, 'Le naufrage du *Saint Paul* en 1858', 1981: 33.

[187] Rochas, 'Naufrage et scènes d'anthropophagie', 1861: 87.

[188] Ibid.: 88.

[189] *Sydney Morning Herald,* 27 January 1859.

[190] Rochas, 'Naufrage et scènes d'anthropophagie', 1861: 91.

[191] Prideaux (*Somerset, Cape York Peninsula, 1864–1877, from spear to pearl-shell*, 1988: 43), who apparently obtained his information from the papers of John Jardine, an early and notorious settler in the Somerset region, refers to the men more probably as Tan-Tan and Pa-Qui.

[192] Misspelt there as Pirow.

[193] Edwards was the 'first recorded commercial fisherman in Torres Strait waters', having set up a bêche-de-mer station on Albany Island in 1862 (Chase, "All kind of nation"', 1981: 7).

[194] *Port Denison Times*, 25 November 1865.

[195] E.g. Priday's article in the *Pacific Islands Monthly* is headed 'NG's Most Celebrated Cannibal Feast' (1959: 83).

[196] See Urry, 'W. E. Armstrong and social anthropology at Cambridge 1922–1926', 1985: 413.

[197] Liep, '"This civilising influence": the colonial transformation of Rossel Island society', 1983: 120.

[198] Haddon in Armstrong, *Rossel Island*, 1928: xiii.

[199] Armstrong, *Rossel Island*, 1928: Chapter 9.

[200] Ibid.: 110.

[201] Ibid.: 111.

[202] This extract is from *Annual Report on British New Guinea*, 1892–93, pp. 5–7, quoted by Armstrong, *Rossel Island*, 1928: 211.

[203] Entry for Sir William MacGregor (1846–1919) in the *Australian dictionary of biography*, online edition, http://www.adb.online.anu.edu.au/biogs/A050184b.htm, accessed 21 January 2009.

[204] This extract is from *Annual Report on British New Guinea*, 1900–1, pp. 21–22, quoted by Armstrong, *Rossel Island*, 1928: 215.

[205] *Brisbane Courier Mail*, 31 January 1996; Liep, '"This civilising influence"', 1983: 122.

[206] Osborne, 'Bits of the "St Paul" are still there. But there have been other wrecks on Rossel', 1959: 53.

[207] This extract is from *Annual Report, Papua*, 1911–12, pp. 19–20, quoted by Armstrong, *Rossel Island*, 1928: 229.

[208] *The Bulletin*, 7 December 1960.

[209] Ibid.: 11.

[210] Ibid.: 13.

[211] See Leys, *The wreck of the Batavia and Prosper*, 2005. In a later discussion of the *Saint-Paul* tragedy, Ruhen puts forward the theory that most of the Chinese sailed away from Rossel Island to evade the interest they owed their agents in Hong Kong and to set up a new life in New Guinea. He suggests that 'the Greek' stayed behind and set up a reign of terror among those who were left. Again, there is no evidence for this suggestion, and the number of craft the Chinese would have had to build to make their departure would have been considerable (*Mountains in the clouds*, 1963: Chapter 1).

[212] Liep, email to S. Anderson, 10 November 2004.

[213] Liep, '"This civilising influence"', 1983: 120–21.

[214] Ibid.: 121.

[215] David Thompson: personal communication.

[216] My thanks to Lucy Hobson of the Lockhart River Community who informed David Thompson of this expression in Kuuku Ya'u (personal communication).

[217] Bowen Historical Society, *The story of James Morrill*, n.d., n.p.

[218] Moore, *Islanders and Aborigines at Cape York*, 1978: 80.

PAMA MALNGKANA: THE 'SANDBEACH PEOPLE' OF CAPE YORK

[1] See Chase and Sutton, 'Australian Aborigines in a rich environment', 1987.

[2] The naming of dialectal and other groups here is complex, sometimes using geographic referents such as 'east' and 'west', 'on top' and 'down below' (referring to hill people and coastal flatland people), and also the verb forms in different dialects for 'look' and 'eat' (*yangkunyu* is one of these). There is no known meaning today for the words 'Uutaalnganu' and 'Umpila'. The name 'Kuuku Ya'u' means literally 'to talk THIS way' as opposed to *kuuku iyu*, 'to talk THAT way'. The word for the inland dialect, Kaanju, has as a primary meaning, 'the peg at the rear of the woomera which engages the rear of the spear'.

[3] *Kinship and behaviour in North Queensland. A preliminary account of kinship and social organisation on Cape York Peninsula*, (ed. Scheffler), 1972.

[4] Rigsby and Peterson (eds), *Donald Thomson: the man and scholar*, 2005.

[5] For further discussion on Thomson's views on these connections, see Chase, 'Anthropology through a biological lens', 2005.

[6] See ibid.

[7] See their 'Aborigines of Princess Charlotte Bay, North Queensland', 1933–36.

[8] These are held by the Australian Institute of Aboriginal and Torres Strait Islander Studies in Canberra.

[9] I avoid the term 'tribe' here. It is a difficult term without a precise and agreed meaning in anthropology. Difficulties with the term are compounded by the fact that its use in Aboriginal English displays various meanings depending on context. Among the people at Lockhart it can mean people from a language/dialect territory, the smaller family group associated with an estate within this territory, or even a wider cognatic family grouping across several of these estates. Sometimes people will even talk of a Lockhart 'tribe' as opposed to other community-based populations.

[10] See 'References' in Rigsby and Peterson (eds), *Donald Thomson: the man and scholar*, 2005 for a listing of some of Rigsby's papers.

[11] *Which way now? Tradition, continuity and change in a North Queensland Aboriginal community*, 1980b.

[12] See Bibliography.

[13] See Bibliography.

[14] Anthropologists use this term to refer to a group which, though ideally seeing itself commonly affiliated by descent through the male line from an apical male ancestor, actually allows for some genealogical 'slippage' by readjusting after an anomalous membership. Thus a male may in fact be affiliated to the estate through descent from a woman of the group, or even from another group, through various reasons of necessity or choice, and his descendants will continue as members. Descent in this case is more a matter of affiliation at any particular generational level, rather than application of the patrilineal model rigidly down all generations. This is of course a matter of adjustment to real life events rather than application of an inviolable model.

[15] 'Aboriginal territorial organization: estate, range, domain and regime', 1965: 12.

[16] The term 'moiety' is an old English word for 'half'. Anthropologists use it to describe these dual systems where, through descent, people belong to either one or the other of two named categories. Indeed the system extends in this area to include all animals and major plants and even the territory of the family

estates (see Chase, *Which way now?* 1980b). Elsewhere in Aboriginal Australia there can be further division of each moiety again into two (the semi-moiety system) and in central Australia a similar system that categorises people and animals into eight categories, known as sub-sections.

[17] *Kinship and behaviour in North Queensland*, 1972. See also Chase, *Which way now?* 1980b.

[18] See Thomson ibid.

[19] See Thomson, 'The joking relationship and organized obscenity', 1935b.

[20] *On Aboriginal religion*, 1966.

[21] *The Australian Aborigines: a portrait of their society*, 1972: 109.

[22] We do not have space here to go into detail regarding these, but again, the various papers written by Donald Thomson for this area provide more information. For discussion on how these beliefs and rituals operate in the contemporary communities, see Chase, *Which way now?* 1980b.

[23] See Hynes and Chase, 'Plants, sites and domiculture: Aboriginal influence upon plant communities in Cape York Peninsula', 1982. This article provides detailed data on the wealth of edible plant species within the immediate environs of a major camping site in Kuuku Ya'u territory, a situation that is replicated frequently elsewhere along this stretch of coast.

[24] Chase and Sutton, 'Australian Aborigines in a rich environment', 1987.

[25] Jukes, *Narrative of the surveying voyage of H.M.S. 'Fly'…during the years 1842–1846*, vol. 1, 1847: 106–113.

[26] *The Great Barrier Reef: history, science, heritage*, 2003.

[27] Jack 1915, v. 2: 210, quoted in Chase, *Which way now?* 1980b: 96.

[28] See Australian Government, Department of the Environment and Heritage, Report, *Assessment of the Queensland east coast beche-de-mer fishery*, 2004: 3, http://www.environment.gov.au/coasts/fisheries/qld/east-coast-beche-de-mer/report.html, accessed 20 June 2008.

[29] He is better known as the husband of Mary Watson who perished in a floating tank with her child and Chinese assistant after Aborigines attacked his bêche-de-mer station on Lizard Island in 1881. He was fishing at Night Island when the attack took place.

[30] Queensland Government Environmental Protection Agency, http://www.epa.qld.gov.au/projects/heritage/index.cgi?place=600421&back=1, accessed 9 January 2009.

[31] Douglas 1890, quoted in Chase, *Which way now?* 1980b:

[32] Parry-Okeden 1897, quoted in Chase, *Which way now?* 1980b:

[33] See Chase, *Which way now?* 1908b:

[34] *The World's News,* 17 November 1923, 'Away out on the Barrier. Where the dead ships lie'.

[35] *The tin scratchers*, 1959: Chapter 4.

[36] See Chase, *Which way now?* 1980b: 107–12.

[37] There were exceptions, the most notable being the superintendence of John Warby in the 1950s.

[38] See Sutton, 'After consensus', 2008a.

[39] The only piece of information that could be at odds with this is to be found in Aplin's report where he refers to the statement Captain Frazer made to him about Pelletier's recovery. Frazer stated that Pelletier told him that the Aboriginal people who rescued him after he had been left behind 'took him to the tribe after 6 days' walking'. Given that Frazer's report was made within only weeks of Pelletier's reacquaintance with Europeans — he was taken on board the *John Bell* on 11 April 1875 and delivered to Somerset by Frazer on 5 May where, as far as we know, he encountered French speakers again for the first time — information recorded from him by Frazer may not necessarily have been accurate (Aplin manuscript, Letter to the Colonial Secretary, Somerset, 11 May 1875).

[40] Personal communication.

Introduction

[1] *Univers illustré*, 7 August 1875, 'Pierre Pelletier: Le sauvage d'Australie'.

[2] I have been unable to find any record of papers that Constant Merland may have left. It would be particularly interesting to see the notes made by Pelletier himself which Merland mentions here.

Chapter 1

[1] In fact church records of the Diocese of Luçon concerning Saint-Gilles indicate that Pelletier was born on 1 January 1844, his baptism being recorded for 3 January 1844 following his birth 'avant-hier', the day before yesterday (extract

from records of the Diocèse de Luçon supplied by Véronique Guilbaud).

[2] This is the seaside resort of Les Sables-d'Olonne, situated to the south of Saint-Gilles-Croix-de-Vie.

[3] The north-western coast of the Balkan Peninsula.

[4] 'Sidney', as Merland spells it, stands for the colony of New South Wales.

[5] See the introductory essay for a discussion of the attitudes Merland reveals in the terminology he uses throughout *Dix-sept ans* to refer to Aboriginal people, and in this chapter to the inhabitants of Rossel Island or Yela. Words such as 'savage' are offensive but they were typical of the usage of the era in which he wrote.

[6] Rochas, 'Naufrage et scènes d'anthropophagie à l'île Rossell [sic] dans l'archipel de la Louisiade (Mélanésie)', 1861.

[7] Rochas seems to have substituted the French name 'Danemark' for the English 'Denmark', and the error has been repeated by Merland. The *Sydney Shipping Gazette* (3 January 1859 and 24 January 1859) records the name of the ship as the *Prince of Denmark*. Holthouse describes the ship as a whaling schooner which itself was wrecked, on the Chesterfield Reef in the Coral Sea, on 19 March 1863 (*Ships in the coral*, rev. ed., 1986: 176). With echoes of the fate of the Chinese left in the Louisiades, the crew made a boat from its timbers and the men sailed for Brisbane 'leaving eleven native members of the crew on the reef with provisions for about eighteen months' (Loney, *Wrecks on the Queensland coast, 1791–1992*, 1993: 58).

[8] The *Sydney Shipping Gazette* of 24 January 1859 gives the name of the captain of the *Prince of Denmark* as Captain McKellar. Captain J. B. Bennett was in command of the ship when it was shipwrecked in 1863 (Holthouse, *Ships in the coral*, 1986: 176).

[9] This is an error. In fact the ship arrived at Port-de-France in New Caledonia, now the capital Noumea, which took this name in 1866.

[10] European fascination with cannibalism in the 19th century is no doubt responsible for this highly coloured and no doubt fanciful account of the deaths of the Chinese.

[11] See the introductory essay concerning the later recovery of two more Chinese survivors.

CHAPTER 2

[1] The exact number of men who left the Louisiade Archipelago is not known because of discrepancies in the various accounts of the shipwreck and the later

rescue of the French crew. Both Ottley in his letter to Dodd (see Appendix V) and the report in *The Times* (Appendix VI) say that when Pelletier was left behind at Cape Direction eight left in the boat, supporting Merland's figure of nine men. In Rochas's report, however, the captain is said to have left Rossel Island with his remaining crew of eleven men ('Naufrage et scènes d'anthropophagie à l'île Rossell [sic] dans l'archipel de la Louisiade (Mélanésie)', 1861: 83). Rochas mentions the disappearance of Pelletier (ibid.), the death of one man the following day at sea (ibid.) and the death of another man when they were moved by their captors from the island they had landed at in the Home Group to the mainland (ibid.: 85). But he notes that seven men finally arrived at Port-de-France (ibid.: 81), which leaves two men unaccounted for out of twelve. The *Sydney Shipping Gazette* reports that the captain and eight of his men were recovered by the *Prince of Denmark* and that one of them died on the same night he was taken on board (24 January 1859). A report that appeared in the *Port Denison Times* (25 November 1865) states that the captain and his crew of ten left Rossel Island. Including the man who died after boarding the *Prince of Denmark*, a figure of eleven men leaving the Louisiades would account for all of the men, recovered, dead or missing, if Rochas's figure of seven men arriving at Port-de-France is correct.

[2] This is incorrect. It was in fact Cape Direction, considerably further north. See the introductory essay and Chase's ethnographic commentary for a discussion of the location of the landing place.

[3] In fact he was fourteen years old when he landed at Cape York.

[4] This is the Wongai plum (*muungkala*). Throughout the annotations to the translation I have used David Thompson's study of Kuuku Ya'u and Umpila, *Lockhart River 'Sand Beach' Language: an outline of Kuuku Ya'u and Umpila*, 1988b, as the source of indigenous terms unless otherwise stated. Uutaalnganu is a dialect closely related to Kuuku Ya'u and Umpila and falls between these dialects in terms of their geographical distribution. See Thompson's map of dialect distribution (ibid.: 3).

[5] Merland uses the term *flèches* ('arrows'), throughout the book, although the weapons of the coastal peoples are in fact spears. It is clear from his usage of the word, as well as from the drawings of spears, the *armes en bois* or 'wooden weapons', which appear at the end of the book (see Appendix III), that he is quite aware of the kind of throwing weapons used by Pelletier and his group. The most likely reason Merland chose this term was that the spears are projected by a *yuli*, or spearthrower, and that he had no obvious terms at his disposal to describe this mechanism other than 'bow' (*arc*) and 'arrow' (*flèche*). The word *propulseur* which can be used for 'spearthrower' only came into French in 1846 and then in the sense of 'thruster' or 'booster'. Its ethnographic

sense is more recent still. I have therefore translated the term *flèche* as 'arrow' to reflect Merland's own usage, but readers should be aware that his 'arrows' refer to spears.

[6] This tree is *muungkalmulu*, the suffix *–mulu* indicating a close association, 'mate for' as Sandbeach People would say. Chase recorded this term from Michael Sandy, an Uutaalnganu man (personal communication).

[7] *Which way now? Tradition, continuity and change in a North Queensland Aboriginal community*, 1980b: 156. See also Chase and Sutton, 'Australian Aborigines in a rich environment', 1987: 80.

[8] Personal communication.

[9] We saw in the introductory essay that Aplin, in his report to the Colonial Secretary, noted Pelletier's new name as 'Anco' (Aplin manuscript, Letter to the Colonial Secretary, Somerset, 11 May 1875).

CHAPTER 3

[1] See the introductory essay.

[2] See Chase, *Which way now? Tradition, continuity and change in a North Queensland Aboriginal community*, 1980b: 157–8.

[3] 'The dugong hunters of Cape York', 1934b: 241.

[4] 'Australian Aborigines in a rich environment', 1987: 76.

[5] *Which way now?* 1980b: 156 n. 4. For a comparative discussion based on historical sources of how Aboriginal people in the area from Cairns to Cardwell just before European settlement seasonally exploited the environment, and of their associated residence patterns and ceremonial behaviour, see Harris, 'Adaptation to a tropical rain-forest environment: Aboriginal subsistence in northeastern Queensland', 1978. Harris concludes that the subsistence system for these people was maintained 'at a level that can be characterized as intensive, selective foraging with a broad-spectrum pattern of resource use' (p.132), a description which could equally be applied to the subsistence pattern of the Sandbeach People.

[6] *Which way now?* 1980b: 133.

[7] See Wilson and Swan, *A complete guide to reptiles of Australia*, 2003: 430.

[8] Rigsby notes that Thomson's 'Ngumai' corresponds to the Umpila *ngamay*.

This term, which is used at Port Stewart, is the Umpila word for the aggressive King Brown snake (personal communication).

[9] As recorded by Rigsby.

[10] 'Observations on the venom of a large Australian snake, *Pseudechis Australis* (Gray)', 1930: 134.

[11] 'Notes on Australian snakes of the genera *Pseudechis* and *Oxyuranus*', 1933b: 858.

[12] Ibid.

[13] Ibid.: 856.

[14] Thompson provides ten Kuuku Ya'u terms for types of snake, as well as the generic term *ira* for 'snake' and the term *yumachi* for 'black-headed python' (*Lockhart River "Sand Beach" language*, 1988b: 69).

[15] Hale and Tindale's article 'Aborigines of Princess Charlotte Bay, North Queensland' (1933–36), from which I quote a number of times as commentary to this translation, is copiously illustrated with photographs and diagrams. I have not included the authors' references to their 'figures' in my quotations as this would be misleading. The reader is referred to their article for illustrations, in particular of items of material culture.

[16] 'Aborigines of Princess Charlotte Bay', 1933-36: 133–4.

[17] This is possibly a rendering of the Umpila word *pantikuma* or *puntikuma* meaning 'everybody' or 'many' (Thompson: personal communication).

[18] This name is not in fact a group name but refers primarily to a major site and, applied from this, to the estate where the site lies. It is situated at Dinner Creek, just south of Cape Direction. See Chase's ethnographic commentary.

[19] Chase, 'Cultural continuity: land and resources among East Cape York Aborigines', 1980a: 85. Chase describes the mechanics of the patrilineal estate groups and the estates over which they had custody in more detail in his ethnographic commentary. See also his 'Belonging to country: territory, identity and environment in Cape York Peninsula, Northern Australia', 1984: 112–3.

[20] See Rigsby and Chase for a description of clans, clan estates and the moiety system of Cape York Sandbeach People ('The Sandbeach People and dugong hunters of Eastern Cape York Peninsula: property in land and sea country', 1998: 196–7).

[21] Ibid.: 197.

[22] 'Belonging to country', 1984: 110–1, maps 2a and 2b.

[23] Ibid.: 110.

[24] Ibid.: 110–1. See also Thomson ('The hero cult, initiation and totemism on Cape York', 1933a: 460) on the the moiety system. Today, the moiety division is a frequent theme in the paintings of Rosella Namok, the renowned Lockhart River artist. See Butler, *Our way: contemporary Aboriginal art from Lockhart River*, 2007: 93–4.

[25] Merland's description virtually mirrors those of Australian Aborigines that appeared in the French and English anthropological journals of the day (and was very likely taken almost verbatim from one of them rather than from Pelletier). These invariably antipathetic portrayals were based on the reports of explorers and settlers that in turn harked back to the famous derogatory description of Aborigines by William Dampier who, in his *New voyage round the world* (1968 [1697]: 312–14), had set the tone for what became an enduring racial stereotype.

[26] Ottley manuscript. See Appendix V.

[27] 'The Sandbeach People', 1998: 200–1.

[28] 'Belonging to country', 1984: 107.

[29] 'Cultural continuity: land and resources among East Cape York Aborigines', 1980a: 85. The subject is discussed in detail by Chase in *Which way now?* 1980b: chapter 7.

[30] 'The Sandbeach People', 1998: 205.

[31] *The Times*, 21 July 1875. See Appendix VI.

[32] Chase: personal communication.

[33] Chase and Sutton, 'Australian Aborigines in a rich environment', 1987: 72.

[34] 'Aborigines of Princess Charlotte Bay, North Queensland', 1933–36: 125, and figs 155, 156.

[35] Rigsby and Chase, 'The Sandbeach People', 1998: 214 n. 32.

[36] Ibid.

[37] 'Belonging to country', 1984: 115–6.

[38] See Chapter 6 for more about such significant graves.

[39] See Warby, *You - me mates eh! : a personal story of reconciliation and change among the Aboriginal people and missionary staff of Lockhart River Mission, Cape York Peninsula 1924 – 1960*, 2000 and Chase, *Which way now?* 1980b: 119–22 on the Lockhart River Christian Co-operative established under Mission auspices in 1954 in an attempt to generate employment and income and push the community towards self-sufficiency.

[40] *Speak you so gently*, 1959: 71.

[41] See Chase, *Which way now?* 1980b: 225–9.

[42] Ibid.: 168–9. See also Thomson, 1935b, 'The joking relationship and organized obscenity'.

[43] *Which way now?* 1980b: 197.

[44] Ibid.

[45] See ibid.: 140–2 on moieties.

[46] 'Ceremonial presentation of fire in North Queensland', 1932: 163.

[47] Quoted in Hagan, *Lockhart River Community Plan 2004–2008*, 2005: 40.

[48] *Which way now?* 1980b: 182–3.

[49] Chase: personal communication.

[50] 'Aborigines of Princess Charlotte Bay', 1933–36: 135.

[51] Chase, Thompson: personal communication.

[52] This practice, referred to by anthropologists as the levirate, is by no means confined to Aboriginal societies.

[53] *Which way now?* 1980b: 194–7.

[54] Pelletier also praised the swimming abilities of his companions to Ottley (Ottley manuscript. See Appendix V).

[55] *Children of the wilderness*, 1983: 18.

[56] *The Times*, 21 July 1875.

[57] Personal communication.

[58] 'The hero cult, initiation and totemism on Cape York', 1933a: 468.

[59] Thompson notes that the 's' sound does not occur in the Sandbeach languages but can be used in singing as a substitute for the sound 'ch'. So the name could be 'Chachi' (personal communication). Chase has recorded 'Chachil' as a man's name (personal communication).

[60] Chase, *Which way now?* 1980b: 196.

[61] Ibid.: 258–9.

[62] 'The hero cult, initiation and totemism on Cape York', 1933a: 475.

[63] The malleoli are the small knobs of bone on either side of the ankle.

[64] Personal communication.

[65] Chase, *Which way now?* 1980b: 193.

[66] Ibid.: 194.

[67] Chase: personal communication.

[68] Rigsby: personal communication.

[69] 'The dugong hunters of Cape York', 1934b: 240.

[70] 'The hero cult, initiation and totemism on Cape York', 1933a: 509.

CHAPTER 4

[1] The few pages of theoretical discussion at the beginning of this chapter show the great interest in the science of language and particularly the question of the origin of language that flourished in France during the first half of the 19th century (see Auroux, 'La question de l'origine des langues: ordres et raisons du rejet institutionnel',1989), but they also show the kind of misconceptions held about non-European languages in the period before linguistics emerged as a discipline in its own right. Some of these are Merland's own misconceptions where he reveals his confusion in considering a language of which he has no knowledge and assumes to be 'primitive'. For example, he is surprised on the one hand at the richness of the vocabulary of Pelletier's adoptive group and the fact that the language is not monosyllabic, but asserts on the other that 'I am far from wishing to claim that it might be compared with that of civilised peoples'. But other misconceptions appear to stem from his summary of Letellier's thesis (see below) about the evolution of language — and with which he takes issue after considering Pelletier's information about the language he had learned. Merland's references to African tribesmen 'who, in the depth of the night, cannot carry on extended conversations' and to remote tribes having vocabularies of less than two hundred words stand out particularly as prejudiced and ill-informed.

[2] This is a reference to Charles Louis-Augustin Letellier, a scholar of philology and the author of numerous works that have now left no lasting impression. His particular interest seems to have been the creation of an a priori universal language (see Porset, 'Langues universelles, langues philosophiques, langues auxiliaires au XIXe siècle. Essai de bibliographie', 1979 for references).

[3] My thanks go to David Thompson and Athol Chase, and to Bruce Rigsby, Peter Sutton and Clair Hill for their subsequent input, in providing possible/probable Kuuku Ya'u or Umpila equivalents for the vocabulary items that Merland collected from Pelletier and transcribed, using no apparent

system, to produce a word his French readers could attempt to pronounce. His transcriptions show particular difficulties with initial consonants and with unfamiliar consonant sounds such as '*ng*' or '*ch*'. The transcription of vowels is variable. Not all of the words listed by Merland can be matched to an equivalent, either because his idiosyncratic transcriptions make this impossible or because the words were peculiar to Pelletier's language group. Thompson, in his study of the Kuuku Ya'u and Umpila languages, provides vocabularies of English-Kuuku Ya'u and Kuuku Ya'u-English, with Umpila variants (*Lockhart River "Sand Beach" Language: an outline of Kuuku Ya'u and Umpila*, 1988b). He points out that Kuuku Ya'u and Umpila 'are closely related coastal dialects' where 'a list of 500 common words has 87% common' to both dialects (ibid.: 1).

[4] 'The joking relationship and organized obscenity', 1935b: 482. In standard Sandbeach language orthography *tuntoi* would be transcribed as *tuntuy* (Thompson: personal communication). Apart from the initial consonant, this approximates to Merland's French transcription.

[5] 'Aborigines of Princess Charlotte Bay, North Queensland', 1933–36: 163. It was in fact Tindale who compiled the vocabularies. See Rigsby, 'Genealogies, kinship and local group composition: old Yintjingga (Port Stewart) in the late 1920s', 1999: 119 n. 12, and 'The languages of eastern Cape York Peninsula and linguistic anthropology', 2005: 140 n. 9, for the sources of Tindale's vocabularies from which the word list in Hale and Tindale's article was constructed. One informant was Mick Tuckandidgee, another was Alec Markwell, a boat captain, and the third known informant was Thommy Thompson (Rigsby: personal communication).

[6] Rigsby and the linguist Geoffrey O'Grady recorded *nhiiyi* (Rigsby: personal communication).

[7] 'The hero cult, initiation and totemism on Cape York', 1933a: 477, 481. In standard Sandbeach language orthography Thomson's term would be transcribed as *puchan* (Thompson: personal communication). We can see that Merland's French transcription is similar to *puchan*.

[8] 'Aborigines of Princess Charlotte Bay', 1933–36: 161. In standard Sandbeach language orthography Hale and Tindale's *tjotjo* would be transcribed as *chuchu* (Thompson: personal communication). The resemblance between their transcription from Umpila and Merland's French transcription is apparent.

[9] Rigsby and O'Grady recorded *tha'u* (Rigsby: personal communication).

[10] Neither Pelletier nor Merland could be expected to have been able to conduct an expert linguistic analysis of the language, hence the misapprehensions contained in this summary. Those interested in the structure

of Kuuku Ya'u and Umpila should refer to Thompson's description of the language (*Lockhart River "Sand Beach" Language*, 1988b). One dimension of these languages which is not mentioned at all in Merland's account is the existence of a respect language used between kin in partial avoidance relationships, namely father-in-law and son-in-law, as described by Thomson (1935b: 481–482). To use this special language is described as talking 'one side'. The son-in-law must address his elder through an intermediary, usually a child or dog, using parallel terms that are restricted to the important aspects of life. Peterson notes that Thomson was the first person to report on these Cape York respect languages ('Thomson's place in Australian anthropology, 2005: 33).

[11] As recorded by Chase. Rigsby, however, records *kuupi*, 'sweetheart', with a long vowel and similarly –*kuupi* in compound words (personal communication). See also Thomson, 'The hero cult, initiation and totemism on Cape York', 1933a: 503 n. 1.

[12] 'Aborigines of Princess Charlotte Bay', 1933–36: 156-8.

[13] Ibid.: 158. Photographs of a number of message sticks are included in the article (ibid.: 157).

[14] In French: 'Le vrai peut quelquefois n'être pas vraisemblable'. The citation is from Nicolas Boileau's treatise in verse, *L'art poétique*, Canto 3, l. 48 (1966 [1674], ed. G. Picot: 72).

[15] The story as Merland tells it has a legendary, and cautionary, flavour. In the *Times* article Pelletier's reference to a previous white man in the area is more factual: 'he has heard that in his tribe there was an old white man who had lived among them for many years and was at last drowned while out fishing. He does not recall having seen this man himself, and is not sure when his death occurred' (*The Times*, 21 July 1875, see Appendix VI).

[16] 'The hero cult, initiation and totemism on Cape York', 1933a: 461.

[17] Personal communication.

[18] John Warby was Superintendent of the Anglican Lockhart River Mission from 1951 to 1960. See his memoir *You - me mates eh! : a personal story of reconciliation and change among the Aboriginal people and missionary staff of Lockhart River Mission, Cape York Peninsula 1924 – 1960*, 2000; Thompson, '*Bora belonga white man': missionaries and Aborigines at Lockhart River Mission*, 1995.

[19] *Which way now? Tradition, continuity and change in a North Queensland Aboriginal community*, 1980b: 88-9.

CHAPTER 5

[1] 'The hero cult, initiation and totemism on Cape York', 1933a.

[2] 'Notes on the boras at Lockhart River Mission, Cape York Peninsula, north-east Australia', 1970.

[3] *Which way now? Tradition, continuity and change in a North Queensland Aboriginal community*, 1980b.

[4] '*Bora is like Church*', 1982; 'Bora, church and modernization at Lockhart River, Queensland', 1988a; '*Bora belonga white man': missionaries and Aborigines at Lockhart River Mission*, 1995.

[5] Chase and Sutton, 'Australian Aborigines in a rich environment', 1987: 79.

[6] 'The hero cult, initiation and totemism on Cape York', 1933a: 507.

[7] Ibid.: 507, 507 n. 1, 479 n. 2.

[8] Rigsby notes that Umpila speakers at Port Stewart say *mirpi* (personal communication).

[9] 'The hero cult, initiation and totemism on Cape York', 1933a: 498. Thomson defines the word *mumpa* as 'Cry, or exclamation, made when a meteorite is heard; it is supposed to be the sound made when the *mipi* of a dead person returns to its own country' (ibid.: 524). Rigsby has recorded *mumpa* as 'shooting star' in Umpila at Port Stewart (personal communication).

[10] *Which way now?* 1980b: 187.

[11] The concept of the transmigration of the soul.

[12] Jones, 'Images of natural man', 1988: 57.

[13] 'Stories about feeling: Dutch–Australian contact in Cape York Peninsula, 1606–1756', 2008b: 51.

[14] Jones, 'Images of natural man', 1988: 57.

[15] 'Stories about feeling', 2008b: 54.

[16] Chase: personal communication.

[17] 'The hero cult, initiation and totemism on Cape York', 1933a: 493–9; 'The masked dancers of I'wai'i. A remarkable hero cult which has invaded Cape York Peninsula', 1956b: 19.

[18] Thomson, 'The hero cult, initiation and totemism on Cape York', 1933a: 498.

[19] 'The dugong hunters of Cape York', 1934b: 238-9.

[20] Ibid.: 251 n. 1. W. Lloyd Warner records similar rainmaking and rain stopping rituals for Yolngu people in north-east Arnhem Land where rainmaking could be practised by anyone but would be performed usually by ceremonial clan leaders when the dry season continued for too long. The simple procedure involved shaping a bundle of green grass into a human image, digging a hole and then burying the bundle (*A black civilization: a social study of an Australian tribe*, 1958, rev. ed. [1937]: 208–9).

[21] The mention of iron blocks and metal levers in the explanatory myth seems anachronistic.

[22] 'Cultural continuity: land and resources among East Cape York Aborigines', 1980a: 85. See also Thomson, 'The hero cult, initiation and totemism on Cape York', 1933a: 502.

[23] Chase, *Which way now?* 1980b: 116–7.

[24] 'The dugong hunters of Cape York', 1934b: 251.

[25] 'Aborigines of Princess Charlotte Bay, North Queensland', 1933–36: 141.

[26] Ibid.: 144.

[27] *Which way now?* 1980b: 194.

[28] Ibid. See also Thomson, 'The dugong hunters of Cape York', 1934b: 240.

CHAPTER 6

[1] University Gallery, University of Melbourne, *Mortuary objects from North East Arnhem Land and Cape York Peninsula: the Donald Thomson Collection. August 3 – September 16, 1983*, 1983: 6.

[2] The terms used in this passage are not from Kuuku Ya'u or Umpila. The first two terms mentioned by Hale and Tindale are in Flinders Island language (for which there is no indigenous term per se). For 'opamaka', which Hale and Tindale describe as 'rectangular tablets', Sutton has recorded *opamakal* with the gloss 'resin bat'. For their 'iyawur', 'ceremonial net dress', he has recorded *iyawurr* with the gloss 'fishing net, fence'. However he has not recorded a term in Flinders Island language corresponding to Hale and Tindale's 'akwama'. The term he recorded for 'mourning cap' is *alangarr* (personal communication).

[3] Since, in Chapter 9, Pelletier reports that fishing nets were not used by the group he lived with, this item of mourning dress may not have been part

of Uutaalnganu mourning practice. Hale and Tindale's photograph of this garment is from Flinders Island (1933–36: 96, fig. 73). Rigsby notes that Donald Thomson photographed the same use of old fishing nets as mourning attire at Port Stewart in 1928 (personal communication).

[4] 'Aborigines of Princess Charlotte Bay', 1933–36: 95–6.

[5] See Thomson, *Kinship and behaviour in North Queensland*, 1972: 10.

[6] Personal communication. Chase photographed this women's dance in 1972. See *Which way now? Tradition, continuity and change in a North Queensland Aboriginal community*, 1980b: facing p. 238.

[7] Ibid.: 185–6. See also Thomson's description of mortuary practices and behaviour, and a burial he observed at the Stewart River in his article 'Ceremonial presentation of fire in North Queensland', 1932: 165.

[8] Although no Kuuku Ya'u or Umpila equivalent has been found for this term, Merland may have misunderstood the context in which Pelletier used it. Thompson has recorded a similar-sounding term from his informant Ronald Giblet, *mani kalku*, meaning 'medicine man' (personal communication), though other informants at Lockhart River give 'medicine man' as *nhuyun* (Thompson, Hill: personal communication).

[9] 'The dugong hunters of Cape York', 1934b: plate XXXI, fig. 2.

[10] Ibid.: 253 n. 1.

[11] Personal communication.

CHAPTER 7

[1] Merland's quotation from Voltaire's tragedy *Zaïre* (Act 4, Scene 2, line 1182), first performed in 1732, is not quite apposite. Set during the Crusades, the play presents the sultan Orosmane, fictitious Turkish ruler of Jerusalem, who is betrothed to a French captive, Zaïre. When Zaïre discovers her origins she must choose between her love for Orosmane and her newfound duty to her kin, country and religion. The 'art' of the quotation does not refer to cosmetic enhancement but to psychological artifice which is foreign to the pure-hearted Zaïre. See Voltaire (ed. Jacobs) 1975 [1775].

[2] *The Times*, 21 July 1875. See Appendix VI.

[3] *Kinship and behaviour in North Queensland*, 1972: 56, Plate 1.

[4] 'Aborigines of Princess Charlotte Bay, North Queensland', 1933–36: 139.

[5] Ibid.: 142–4.

[6] Ibid.: 143–4.

[7] Ibid.: 140–1.

[8] Ibid.: 142. The article contains photographs of all of these types of necklace.

[9] Ibid.: 140.

[10] Merland describes emus, or possibly cassowaries, as ostriches here and in a later chapter.

[11] Personal communication.

[12] *The Times*, 21 July 1875. See Appendix VI.

[13] Merland must in fact be referring to the Enelhit people of the Paraguayan Chaco known as the Lenguas or Lengua Indians. See Wilbert, 'Lengua', *World Culture Encyclopedia*, http://www.everyculture.com/South-America/Lengua. html, accessed 15 November 2007. These people wore thick drum-like discs, larger than the earplugs of the Uutaalnganu, in their perforated earlobes (Hawtrey, 'The Lengua Indians of the Paraguayan Chaco', 1901: 283).

[14] Hale and Tindale, 'Aborigines of Princess Charlotte Bay', 1933–36: 140. There is a photograph of a man wearing one of these nose-pegs at fig. 201.

[15] See Chapter 5.

[16] Ibid.: 83.

[17] Personal communication.

[18] 'Notes on the boras at Lockhart River Mission, Cape York Peninsula, northeast Australia', 1970: 306.

[19] 'Aborigines of Princess Charlotte Bay', 1933–36: 76–7.

[20] *The Times*, 21 July 1875. See Appendix VI.

[21] Congestive reddening of the skin.

[22] A bacterial infection causing intense reddening of the skin, also known as St Anthony's Fire.

[23] 'Australian Aborigines in a rich environment', 1987: 72.

[24] 'Aborigines of Princess Charlotte Bay', 1933–36: 87–9.

[25] See Chase *Which way now? Tradition, continuity and change in a North Queensland Aboriginal community*, 1980b: 226–29.

[26] Ibid.: 227.

[27] *Lockhart River "Sand Beach" Language: an outline of Kuuku Ya'u and Umpila*, 1988: 140.

[28] 'The hero cult, initiation and totemism on Cape York', 1933a: 495 n. 1.

[29] See the commentary about percussion instruments in Garnier's 'Musical observations', Appendix I.

[30] 'Aborigines of Princess Charlotte Bay', 1933-36: 87.

[31] Ibid.: 88.

[32] Chase: personal communication. See Chase, *Which way now?* 1980b: 238, and photographs of dance festival performers, facing p. 238.

[33] 'The masked dancers of I'wai'i. A remarkable hero cult which has invaded Cape York Peninsula', 1956b: 18.

[34] At the time *Dix-sept ans chez les sauvages* was published Merland was a resident of Nantes.

[35] Reproduced here as Appendix I.

[36] 'Aborigines of Princess Charlotte Bay', 1933-36: 112.

[37] *The Times*, 21 July 1875. See Appendix VI.

CHAPTER 8

[1] James Morrill had a similar view of the cause of conflict where he lived with Bindal people in the region to the south of Townsville. He writes that 'it is about their wives that all their wars, fights and feuds occur' but that the wars are not 'of a very sanguinary nature' (Bowen Historical Society, *The story of James Morrill*, n.d.: n.p.).

[2] 'Science and sensibility on a foul frontier: at Flinders Island, 1935', 2005: 157 n. 46. The quote is from Warner, *A black civilization: a social study of an Australian tribe*, 1958 [1937]: 155. The Aboriginal people of north-east Arnhem Land now use the term 'Yolgnu' rather than 'Murngin' to refer to themselves. For both the pre-contact situation and the radically changed circumstances of resettled countrymen groups at Lockhart River in the 1970s, Chase devotes considerable analysis to intergroup conflict, its causes, the mechanisms for its regulation and in some cases its escalation, (*Which way now? Tradition, continuity and change in a North Queensland Aboriginal community*, 1980b).

[3] My thanks to Dominique Smith for this reference from Virgil to the legendary warrior maiden Camilla, who leads the Volscians into battle: 'If she ran full speed/ Over the tips of grain unharvested/ She would not ever have bruised an

ear, or else/ She might have sprinted on the deep sea swell/ And never dipped her flying feet.' (Virgil, *The Aeneid*, trans. Robert Fitzgerald, 1984: 225, Book 7.)

[4] Personal communication.

[5] See also Pizzey, *A field guide to the birds of Australia*, 1980, on these bird species.

[6] Thomson: personal communication.

[7] *Which way now?* 1980b: 280.

[8] Chase: personal communication.

[9] Chase notes in his ethnographic commentary that this practice is well recorded.

CHAPTER 9

[1] 'Australian Aborigines in a rich environment', 1987: 80. Chase and Sutton's article provides detailed information about resource availability across the year in terms of broad food types, but including a range of particular plant species, and about the pattern of resource exploitation for Umpila people of the Nesbit River region.

[2] Chase: personal communication; Wilson and Swan, *A complete guide to reptiles of Australia*, 2003: 368, 376.

[3] Charles Dessalines d'Orbigny (1806–1876), a geologist and the author of *Dictionnaire universel d'histoire naturelle* (1839–1849).

[4] Wilson and Swan, *A complete guide to reptiles of Australia*, 2003: 20.

[5] 'Aborigines of Princess Charlotte Bay, North Queensland', 1933–36: 109.

[6] The word *échidné* ('echidna') did exist in French but Merland uses the word *hérisson* ('hedgehog'). The Kuuku Ya'u term is *kaa'uma*.

[7] This is presumably the Sulphur-crested Cockatoo (*Cacatua galerita*) whose crest, not head, is yellow.

[8] Ostriches are an introduced species in Australia. Merland is referring to emus or cassowaries or both (see below).

[9] Personal communication.

[10] *Birds of Cape York Peninsula*, 1935a: 27.

[11] 'The Sandbeach People and dugong hunters of Eastern Cape York Peninsula', 1998: 213 n. 22.

[12] Chase: personal communication.

[13] 'The joking relationship and organized obscenity', 1935b: 481 n. 26. In Thompson's word list 'piado' and 'mampa' are *pi'athu* and *maampa* (*Lockhart River "Sand Beach" Language: an outline of Kuuku Ya'u and Umpila*, 1988b).

[14] Chase suggests that although there are marsupial mice in the area, Pelletier is probably thinking of bandicoots, *kulpa* in the local languages, which are plentiful, and will come out of the scrub on to the beaches at night (personal communication).

[15] Aeneas's faithful companion.

[16] 'Four Aboriginal legends from Cape York, northern Queensland, Australia', 1967: 93–4. A similar version of this myth, but with Emu and Bush Turkey, is known to Aboriginal people far from Cape York, in the north-eastern Gibson Desert (retold by Nicolas Rothwell, *Another country*, 2007: 272–3).

[17] *Birds of Cape York Peninsula*, 1935a: 23.

[18] Ibid.: 24.

[19] Ibid.: 23.

[20] Pizzey, *A field guide to the birds of Australia*, 1980: 21, 22.

[21] Personal communication.

[22] See Chapter 3 for comments about food prohibitions.

[23] Chase: personal communication.

[24] *A field guide to the birds of Australia*, 1980: 90.

[25] *Birds of Cape York Peninsula*, 1935a: plate V.

[26] Ibid.: 25.

[27] Thompson, Chase: personal communication.

[28] 'The hero cult, initiation and totemism on Cape York', 1933a: 530.

[29] *A field guide to the birds of Australia*, 1980: 91.

[30] 'Aborigines of Princess Charlotte Bay', 1933–36: 107.

[31] 'Australian Aborigines in a rich environment', 1987: 79.

[32] Chase: personal communication.

[33] 'Australian Aborigines in a rich environment', 1987: 79.

[34] See Appendix IV. Cf. diagrams in Thomson ('The dugong hunters of Cape York', 1934b: figs 4–9).

[35] 'Aborigines of Princess Charlotte Bay', 1933–36: 108.

[36] Some of these are reproduced in Hafner, 'Images of Port Stewart: possible interpretations', 2005: 224–5.

[37] Rigsby and Chase, 'The Sandbeach People and dugong hunters of Eastern Cape York Peninsula', 1999: 209.

[38] 'Australian Aborigines in a rich environment', 1987: 79.

[39] Chase: personal communication.

[40] *Lockhart River "Sand Beach" Language*, 1988b: 72.

[41] 'The dugong hunters of Cape York', 1934b: 248–9.

[42] *Which way now? Tradition, continuity and change in a North Queensland Aboriginal community*, 1980b: 261.

[43] Merland does not use the word 'dugong', a word of Malay origin, but refers to them as 'cachalots', a French (and English) word for cetaceans such as sperm whales with teeth in their bottom jaw.

[44] 1934b.

[45] This description of the dugong is summarised from Lawler, Marsh, McDonald and Stokes (CRC Reef Research Centre), *Dugongs in the Great Barrier Reef: current state of knowledge, April 2002*, 2002. Brochure accessed at CRC Reef website, 18 January 2009: http://www.reef.crc.org. au/publications/brochures/dugong_2002.pdf. The authors make the following comment about the relationship between indigenous Australians living in coastal regions of northern Australia and the dugong: 'Some Aboriginal people regard dugongs as a vital part of their Aboriginality. It is widely recognised that dugong meat and oil are among the most valuable traditional foods of coastal Aborigines and Torres Strait Islanders in northern Australia. Hunting can be carried out under permit in the Great Barrier Reef Marine Park except in Preservation Zones.'

[46] Chase: personal communication.

[47] 'The dugong hunters of Cape York', 1934b: 255–6.

[48] Chase notes that the dugong rope, a thick two-strand rope, was called *kupuy* after the term for the beach hibiscus whose inner bark was used to make it. The last of these ropes was made at Lockhart River in the late 1970s for the Queensland University Museum as part of a complete canoe kit. The dugong rope Thomson obtained is held in the Thomson Collection at Museum Victoria.

[49] 'The dugong hunters of Cape York', 1934b: 256. See also West, *Aboriginal string bags, nets and cordage*, 1999: 17–20 and 25–29 for discussion of

ropemaking techniques practised in the north-eastern Cape York region, together with photographs by Donald Thomson of ropemaking (plates 9a, 9b, 9c).

[50] 'The dugong hunters of Cape York', 1934b: 246.

[51] Rigsby and Chase, 'The Sandbeach People and dugong hunters of Eastern Cape York Peninsula', 1999: 207. For 'owner of the canoe' Thompson also recorded the term *tangunamu* from his informant Dorothy Short (personal communication).

[52] 'The dugong hunters of Cape York', 1934b: 245.

[53] Ibid.: 247.

[54] *Which way now?* 1980b: 260.

[55] 'The dugong hunters of Cape York', 1934b: 249.

[56] 'Cultural continuity: land and resources among East Cape York Aborigines', 1980a: 86. Chase describes how a large quantity of meat can be distributed rapidly through the community, starting with a major distribution to very close kin who will in turn make their own distributions according to kinship ties. See also Chase, *Which way now?* 1980b: 260–1.

[57] Sutton has recorded *piinti* for 'turtle pass season, when mated pairs are floating together' (personal communication). Thompson was told the word *paynti* by Donald and Beatrice Hobson for 'yellow turtle egg, no shell'. They supplied *wuympa* for 'white turtle egg with shell' (personal communication).

[58] 'The dugong hunters of Cape York', 1934b: 246.

[59] Ibid.

[60] 'Aborigines of Princess Charlotte Bay', 1933–36: 170.

[61] *Lockhart River "Sand Beach" Language*, 1988b: 117.

[62] 'Aborigines of Princess Charlotte Bay', 1933–36: 170. Sutton (personal communication) has recorded the very similar *i'ira* for the loggerhead turtle, not the Leathery Sea Turtle, in the Umpila avoidance register, or 'One Side Talk' (see Chapter 4, n. 10). He has recorded *i'ira* in 'Main Talk' for a species of mangrove, as has Thompson for the mangrove species *Bruguiera gymnorhiza* (personal communication).

[63] Personal communication.

[64] Six of the world's seven species of marine turtle are found in the Great Barrier Reef World Heritage area. In addition to those already mentioned, there are the Olive Ridley Turtle (*Lepidochelys olivacea*) and the Flatback Turtle (*Natator depressus*), but today the latter two species are rarely seen (Dobbs

2001: 5). The common name for Hale and Tindale's Leathery Sea Turtle is the Leatherback Turtle.

[65] 'The dugong hunters of Cape York', 1934b: 243.

[66] Ibid.: 245.

[67] 'The Sandbeach People and dugong hunters of Eastern Cape York Peninsula', 1998: 208.

[68] 'The dugong hunters of Cape York', 1934b: 246.

[69] It seems that this was Night Island because, in his final chapter, Merland tells us that the place where Pelletier was sighted by the crew of the *John Bell* was this same island, and we know from Aplin's report of his recovery that Pelletier was found in the vicinity of Night Island (Aplin manuscript, Letter to the Colonial Secretary, Somerset, 11 May 1875). See Chapter 11 n. 2.

[70] Diogenes of Sinope was a Greek philosopher (fourth century BC) who was one of the founders of the Cynic sect.

[71] Baron Léon Brisse (1813–1876) was a gastronomic expert and author of *Les 366 menus du Baron Brisse avec 1200 recettes et calendrier nutritif*, a book which appeared in multiple editions, the first in 1867.

[72] 'The dugong hunters of Cape York', 1934b: 247.

[73] See Thomson's photographs of a dugong cooked on the beach in this manner (ibid.: plate 30, fig. 2 and in *Kinship and behaviour in North Queensland*, 1972: 55).

[74] 'Aborigines of Princess Charlotte Bay', 1933–36: 130–1.

[75] 'The dugong hunters of Cape York', 1934b: 249.

[76] Rigsby and Chase, 'The Sandbeach People and dugong hunters of Eastern Cape York Peninsula', 1998: 209.

[77] Thomson, 'The dugong hunters of Cape York', 1934b: plate XXXI, fig. 1, provides a photograph of a turtle bladder, *wäkäntim* [*wakantim*] used for storing dugong and turtle oil. Thompson recorded the expressions *wakan nganu puuyana* or *wa'angu puuyana* for 'you blow up the bladder' from his informants Dorothy Short and Maria Butcher (personal communication).

[78] 'The dugong hunters of Cape York', 1934b: 250.

[79] 'Aborigines of Princess Charlotte Bay', 1933–36: 114–5.

[80] 'Ceremonial presentation of fire in North Queensland', 1932: 162–3.

[81] 'The fishermen and dugong hunters of Princess Charlotte Bay', 1956a: 35–6. The Donald Thomson Collection. Reproduced with the permission of the Thomson family and Museum Victoria.

CHAPTER 10

[1] The report in *The Times* records that Pelletier himself made two canoes (21 July 1875). See Appendix VI.

[2] See Thomson's description of the canoe's construction below.

[3] Thompson has recorded both this word and *yi'achinamu* as an alternative form from his informants (personal communication).

[4] 'The dugong hunters of Cape York', 1934b: 242–3. Clair Hill has recorded the term *kutinamu* for 'skipper, stern-GENITIVE', while Thompson has recorded *kutikuunchi* and *kutinamu* as alternatives (personal communication).

[5] 'The Sandbeach People and dugong hunters of Eastern Cape York Peninsula', 1998: 207.

[6] Chase: personal communication.

[7] 'The dugong hunters of Cape York', 1934b: 257.

[8] Ibid.: 258.

[9] 'Aborigines of Princess Charlotte Bay', 1933–36: 98–107.

[10] The peg, when fixed to the end of the spearthrower (see n. 13 below), varies in length from two to four centimetres (Chase: personal communication).

[11] See note 13 below.

[12] 'Aborigines of Princess Charlotte Bay', 1933–36: 99–100. They go on to describe how these ornaments, made only on Cape York, were also valued articles of trade: 'By slow degrees they may pass south-east as far as Cooper Creek in South Australia, where they are highly prized as neck ornaments to be worn by young male initiates. The Yendruwunta [Yandruwandha] of Cooper Creek have no knowledge of their origin, save that they come from the north.' (Ibid.: 101) The article also contains photographs of spearthrowers and their manufacture.

[13] Merland's description of the projection of the spearthrower is not accurate. The two-handed throwing action he describes does not correspond to the typical projection of the spear using the spearthrower where both the spear and the spearthrower are held by one hand only (some men use the left hand, and the thrower is made with a reverse twist in its blade so the spear lies on the correct side when held in position). The peg at the end of the spearthrower fits into the depression at the distal end of the spear, and the angle that it makes to the spearthrower is fixed. Sometimes it lies back a little in relation to the blade of the spearthrower but mostly it is at right angles. The peg is not loose, and

cannot change its position (Chase: personal communication). Furthermore it is bound to the end of the spearthrower, not to the 'arrow', with resin and twine (see Hale and Tindale's description above). Hale and Tindale include a photograph of a Flinders Island man holding a spear and spearthrower poised ready to throw ('Aborigines of Princess Charlotte Bay', 1933–36: 99, fig. 82).

[14] Chase: personal communication.

[15] 'The dugong hunters of Cape York', 1934b: 250.

[16] Ibid.: 258.

[17] Today the traditional skills of basket weaving are practised and taught by several senior women of the Lockhart River Community and their work is collected by art galleries and museums. Examples of the work of the Lockhart River artists Dorothy Short, Elizabeth (Queen) Giblet and Evelyn Omeenyo can be found in various publications. See Demozay (comp.), *Gatherings: Contemporary Aboriginal and Torres Strait Islander art from Queensland Australia*, 2001: 81, 159, 186–87; Butler, *Our way: contemporary Aboriginal art from Lockhart River*, 2007: 52; Queensland Art Gallery, *Story place: indigenous art of Cape York and the rainforest*, 2003: 127; Demozay (comp.), *Gatherings II: Contemporary Aboriginal and Torres Strait Islander art from Queensland Australia*, 2006: 96–97. Trish Johnson writes about Dorothy Short's weaving skills:

> Today Short has rejuvenated the practice of weaving baskets (*puunya*) using traditional grasses and dyes, and is one of only a few women in the community proficient in the technique. Each basket takes a few weeks to make, beginning with the arduous task of collecting the slender long green watul grass (*Lomandra longifolia*). After the grass has been dried, it is placed in a pot of boiling water coloured with the natural dyes released from various leaves or roots. Plants such as the wuyku produce a yellow dye. Short learnt the technique of weaving by watching her aunties and other old ladies weave various-sized baskets and bags for different functions. (Queensland Art Gallery, *Story place*, 2003: 124.)

See also West 1999: Chapter 3 on bags and weaving.

[18] 'Aborigines of Princess Charlotte Bay, 1933–36: 137.

[19] These pleated palm spathe baskets used as cradles are described in Chapter 3.

[20] 'Australian Aborigines in a rich environment', 1987: 79–80.

[21] See the introductory essay and Chapter 5 for discussion of this misconception on the part of Merland.

Chapter 11

[1] In the French scientific discourse of the time the noun '*Australiens*', 'Australians', was used to refer to Australian Aborigines.

[2] This episode is described in Chapter 9. The island was Night Island. But there is a discrepancy here between what Merland says and what Aplin notes in his report, namely that Pelletier was found 'at a spot opposite Night Isld'. (Aplin manuscript, Letter to the Colonial Secretary, Somerset, 11 May 1875). And the report in *The Times* states that Pelletier was found on the mainland while the *John Bell* was lying at anchor off Night Island (21 July 1875). Ottley's letter supports the location as being Night Island but it was written long after the event: 'We were informed that when the pearling schooner John Bell put in at Night Island for wood and water, it was observed that there was a white man amongst a number of blacks.' (Ottley manuscript, see Appendix V.)

[3] One undocumented source reports that the crew of the *John Bell* were Polynesians (Prideaux, *Somerset, Cape York Peninsula, 1864–1877, from spear to pearl-shell*, 1988: 144).

[4] Merland included this and two subsequent letters Pelletier wrote to his family at different stages of his journey back to France as an appendix to *Dix-sept ans*. The facsimiles, approximate transcriptions and translation are included here as Appendix III.

[5] In fact what is written is in English, namely 'Somerset Cape York' and below it the date '13 May 1875'. Merland misread the English 'May' for the French 'mars'. But this supports his observation that this is not Pelletier's handwriting, and the mismatch between the handwriting of the place and date and that of the body of the letter is quite evident. Aplin's typed report from Somerset about Pelletier's recovery is dated '11th May 1875' (Aplin manuscript, Letter to the Colonial Secretary, Somerset, 11 May 1875).

[6] In fact Pelletier was taken to Sydney from Somerset on the mail steamer *R. M. S. Brisbane*.

[7] Georges-Eugène Simon. See the introductory essay for discussion of this episode.

[8] An enquiry to the Archives historiques of the French Ministère des Affaires Etrangères has failed to find any report about Pelletier in Simon's dispatches from Sydney in the relevant volume of 'Correspondence Consulaire et Commerciale' of the French Consulate of Sydney. *La Presse* of 31 August 1875 reported that the Minister of the Navy had just had two photographs of Pelletier passed on to Pelletier's parents.

[9] In fact it is dated 11 July.

[10] In fact it was written from Rio de Janeiro (see Appendix III), and Merland notes later in this chapter that Pelletier left Noumea on 7 August.

[11] The disembarkation roll of the *Jura* lists the soldier's name as Charles Barthélemy Marchand (my thanks to Véronique Guilbaud for supplying this information).

[12] *Bulletin français*, 23 July 1875, 'Dix-sept ans chez les sauvages'.

[13] An eyewitness account of the homecoming of Narcisse Pelletier was described in a letter to *La Presse* of 9 January 1875 by a carpenter of Saint-Gilles.

[14] The church records of the Diocese of Luçon confirm that Pelletier was baptised on 3 January 1844 (extract from the records of the Diocèse de Luçon supplied by Véronique Guilbaud).

APPENDIX I

[1] Edouard Garnier (1821–1887) was a poet, musical critic and composer of the city of Nantes (*Dictionnaire de biographie française,* 1980, Fasc. 85: 478–9).

[2] Thomson gives the words of the second song (see Appendix IV) as '*Yunthu kalinan, kalinan. Yunthu kalinan, kalinan. Para kalinan, kalinan. Para kalinan, kalinan*': 'Waterlily root carry-we, carry-we. Waterlily root, carry-we, carry-we. White man carry-we, carry-we. White man carry-we, carry-we' (personal communication).

[3] Chase: personal communication.

[4] This recalls Merland's comment in Chapter 7 that, with rare exceptions, the words of the songs are not of the language of the people with whom Pelletier lived and that the meaning of the songs was not understood.

[5] Personal communication.

[6] The field of ethnomusicology was unheard of in 1876 and Garnier's lack of knowledge about non-European music is plain from his discussion.

[7] 'The hero cult, initiation and totemism on Cape York', 1933a: 467–8.

[8] Ibid.: 468. See Chase, 'Anthropology through a biological lens', 2005, and Chase's ethnographic commentary for discussion of Thomson's evolutionary perspective.

[9] 'The hero cult, initiation and totemism on Cape York', 1933a: 469.

[10] Thompson: personal communication.

[11] The hero cult, initiation and totemism on Cape York', 1933a: 469.

[12] Or Choctaw.

[13] Garnier's note: 'Places filled with huge expanses of still waters, clear and deep, and bordered with cypress, lianas and a dense vegetation of age-old trees, in a landscape whose character is solemn and piercingly sad.'

[14] The word Garnier gives is 'Taïques'.

[15] Barbara Thompson reported that she sang songs to herself at night in order not to forget her own language when living with the Kaurareg on Prince of Wales Island (Moore, *Islanders and Aborigines at Cape York*, 1978: 143), but Pelletier did not himself report that he acted in this way.

APPENDIX III

[1] I have transcribed these letters to mirror Pelletier's spelling and punctuation as closely as possible. These are highly idiosyncratic but they are basically understandable in the first letter and become progressively closer to correct French by the third. The translations into English can give a sense of the peculiarities of the grammar but not of the incorrect spelling. Bouchon (*Un Mousse oublié. Narcisse Pelletier, Vendéen*, 1997: 34, 36–37) and Pécot (*Pelletier, Chez les sauvages. Dix-sept ans de la vie d'un mousse vendéen dans une tribu cannibale 1858–1875*, ed. Philippe Pécot, 2001: 117–121) also offer transcriptions of the letters that differ slightly from these.

APPENDIX V

[1] The letter is held in the Archives of the Royal Historical Society of Queensland and is reproduced here with their permission. It was transcribed by a Mr Davies, Secretary of the Society, who included it in an address he gave to a meeting of the Society entitled 'Story of Narcisse Pelletier as related by Sir John Ottley R. E. K. C. I. E.'. The version reproduced here is a typescript of Dodd's address, corrected by hand in places, of the pertinent section of Ottley's letter. The extract preserves the spelling and punctuation of the original typescript. The rest of Ottley's letter with H. J. Dodd's comments about its contents and his own opinion about them concerns the theory discussed in the

introductory essay that the 'Mystery Man' of Staaten River was Pelletier.

[2] Ottley, writing almost 50 years later, says that he has forgotten the name of the ship, but he has also misremembered the place of Pelletier's embarkation, which was Somerset, not Thursday Island.

[3] This statement does not appear in the *Times* article. Even though, as explained in the introductory essay, Sir Arthur Hamilton-Gordon largely based his article on Ottley's own information, Ottley seems to have little knowledge of its contents.

[4] Presumably this should read 'près de l'isle d'Yeu', in English 'near the island of Yeu'.

[5] Merland's account only mentions one boat in which the men escaped.

[6] It is strange that Ottley, so interested in Pelletier and his story, had not followed up the fate of the *Saint-Paul* which, by 1875, was well known, or that he, and those on board the *Brisbane*, had no definite knowledge of it when news of the story had travelled around the world after the rescue mission carried out by the *Styx*.

[7] This is slightly different from Merland's version in which Pelletier said that after he realised he had been abandoned, he had taken a path in the direction of a mountain, spent the night under a tree, had continued on his way the next morning in a state of near collapse and then been found by the Aboriginal women.

[8] Unfortunately these sketches, tracings of his own originals, are not now held with this manuscript in the Archives of the Royal Historical Society of Queensland. Ottley had no children and the whereabouts of his personal papers, if they still exist, is unknown.

[9] Only Pelletier's right ear lobe was pierced.

[10] See Chapter 7 on scarification.

[11] Pelletier had no sisters and, when he left France in 1857, only two younger brothers. Ottley has misremembered the facts here or simply generalised. Pelletier had correctly informed Frazer or Aplin that the names of his brothers were Elie and Alphonse (see Aplin manuscript, Letter to the Colonial Secretary, Somerset, 11 May 1875).

BIBLIOGRAPHY

Anderson, Stephanie.
2006. Clichés of Australian Aborigines: Photography and raciology, Paris, 1885. In Louise Maurer and Roger Hillman (eds), *Reading images, viewing texts/Lire les images, voir les textes*, 13-30. Bern: Peter Lang (Transversales 14).

Armstrong, W. E.
1928. *Rossel Island: an ethnological study*. Introduction by A. C. Haddon. Cambridge: Cambridge University Press.

Auroux, Sylvain.
1989. La question de l'origine des langues: ordres et raisons du rejet institutionnel. In Joachim Gessinger and Wolfert von Rahden (eds), *Theorien vom Ursprung der Sprache*. Vol. 2, 122-150. Berlin: Walter de Gruyter.

Australian dictionary of biography, online edition: http://www.adb.online.anu.edu.au.

Australian Government, Department of the Environment and Heritage.
2004. Report, *Assessment of the Queensland east coast beche-de-mer fishery*.

Barrett, Charles.
1948. *White blackfellows. The strange adventures of Europeans who lived among savages.* Melbourne: Hallcraft.

Bartra, Roger.
1994. *Wild men in the looking glass: the mythic origins of European otherness*. Trans Carl T. Berrisford. Ann Arbor: University of Michigan Press.

Baudouin, Marcel.
1911. L'homme sauvage de Vendée. *Bulletins et Mémoires de la Société d'Anthropologie de Paris*, 6e série, t. 2: 156–158.
1986. *Saint-Gilles Croix-de-Vie, d'après les écrits de Marcel Baudouin. Miroir d'une mémoire*, (ed.) B. de Maisonneuve. Saint-Gilles Croix-de-Vie: Association de Recherche Historique Maritime et Sous-marine.

Boileau, Nicolas.
1966 [1674]. *L'art poétique* suivi de Horace, *Épitre aux Pisons* (ed. G. Picot). Paris: Bordas.

Bouchon, Jean-Paul.
1997. *Un Mousse oublié. Narcisse Pelletier, Vendéen*. Poitiers: Paréiasaure Editions.

Bowen, James and Margarita Bowen.
2003. *The Great Barrier Reef: history, science, heritage*. Cambridge: Cambridge University Press.

Bowen Historical Society. n.d.
The story of James Morrill. Compiled by 'The Bowen Independent' on behalf of the Society.

Bradley, Vera.
1995. *I didn't know that: Cairns and districts, Tully to Cape York, 1936–1946, service personnel and civilians*. Brisbane: Boolarong Press.

Broc, Numa.
1992. *Dictionnaire illustré des explorateurs français du XIXe siècle*. 4 vols (vol. 2, Asie; vol. 4 Océanie). Paris: Ed. du CTHS.

Broca, Paul.
1864 [1860]. *On the phenomena of hybridity in the genus Homo*, tr. and ed. C. Carter Blake. London: Longman, Green, Longman & Roberts for the Anthropological Society.

1866. Discours sur l'homme et les animaux. *Bulletins de la Société d'Anthropologie de Paris*, 2e série, 1: 53–79.

Butler, Sally.
2007. *Our way: contemporary Aboriginal art from Lockhart River*. St Lucia, Queensland: University of Queensland Press.

Chase, Athol.
1979. 'Thomson time'. *Aboriginal History* 3 (2): 109–110.
1980a. Cultural continuity: land and resources among East Cape York Aborigines. In N. C. Stevens and A. Bailey (eds), *Contemporary Cape York Peninsula*. Proceedings of a Symposium held at Queensland University of Technology, 29 October 1979, 83-88. Brisbane: Royal Society of Queensland.
1980b. *Which way now? Tradition, continuity and change in a North Queensland Aboriginal community*. PhD Thesis, University of Queensland.
1981. 'All kind of nation': Aborigines and Asians in Cape York Peninsula. *Aboriginal History* 5 (1): 7–19.
1984. Belonging to country: territory, identity and environment in Cape York Peninsula, Northern Australia. In L. R. Hiatt (ed.), *Aboriginal landowners: contemporary issues in the determination of traditional Aboriginal land ownership*, 104-122. Sydney: University of Sydney.
1988. Lazarus at Australia's gateway: the Christian mission enterprise in eastern Cape York Peninsula. In Tony Swain and Deborah Bird Rose (eds), *Aboriginal Australians and Christian missions: ethnographies and historical studies*, 121-139. Adelaide: The Australian Association for the Study of Religions.
1989. Perceptions of the past among north Queensland Aboriginal people; the intrusion of Europeans and consequent social change. In Robert Layton (ed.), *Who needs the past? Indigenous values and archaeology*, 169-179. London: Unwin Hyman.
2005. Anthropology through a biological lens. In Bruce Rigsby and Nicolas Peterson (eds), *Donald Thomson: the man and scholar*, 17-28. Canberra: The Academy of the Social Sciences in Australia.

Chase, Athol and Peter Sutton.
1987. Australian Aborigines in a rich environment. In W.H. Edwards (ed.), *Traditional Aboriginal society*, 68-95. Melbourne: MacMillan

Cilento, Sir Raphael and Clem Lack.
1959. *Triumph in the tropics: an historical sketch of Queensland*. Compiled and edited for the Historical Committee of the Centenary Celebrations Council of Queensland. Brisbane: Smith & Paterson Pty. Ltd.
1963. *Wild white men in Queensland*. Brisbane: Smith and Patterson for the Royal Historical Society of Queensland [originally published in *Journal of the Royal Historical Society of Queensland*, 1959, vol. 6 (1): 73–93].

Croix, Robert de la.
1957. *Mysteries of the Pacific*. Trans. James Cleugh. London: Frederick Muller.

Crowley, Terry and Bruce Rigsby.
1979. Cape York Creole. In Timothy Shopen (ed.), *Languages and their status*, 153-207. Cambridge, Massachusetts: Winthrop Publishers.

Dampier, William.
1968. *A new voyage round the world*. With an introduction by Sir Albert Gray and a new introduction by Percy G. Adams. New York: Dover Publications, Inc. [First edition 1697; this work is a reprint of vol. 1 of the seventh edition published in 1729].

Demozay, Marion (comp.).
2001. *Gatherings: contemporary Aboriginal and Torres Strait Islander art from Queensland Australia*. Southport, Queensland: Keeaira Press.
2006. *Gatherings II: contemporary Aboriginal and Torres Strait Islander art from Queensland Australia*. Southport, Queensland: Keeaira Press.

Dictionary of Australian artists online. http://www.daao.org.au/.

Dictionnaire de biographie française.
1980. 'Garnier, Edouard', Fasc. 85, Gacho-Gallou: 478–479.

Dobbs, Kirstin.
2001. *Marine turtles in the Great Barrier Reef World Heritage Area.* Townsville: Great Barrier Reef Marine Park Authority.

Encyclopaedia of Aboriginal Australia: Aboriginal and Torres Strait Islander history, society and culture.
1994. David Horton (gen. ed.). 2 vols. Canberra: Aboriginal Studies Press for the Australian Institute of Aboriginal and Torres Strait Islander Studies.

Finch-Hatton, Harold.
1885. *Advance Australia!: an account of eight years' work, wandering and amusement in Queensland, New South Wales and Victoria.* London: W. H. Allen & Co.

Flannery, Tim (ed.).
2002. *The life and adventures of William Buckley.* Melbourne: Text Publishing Company [first published in 1852 under the authorship of John Morgan].

Frith, Dawn W. and Clifford B. Frith.
2006 [c.1995]. *Cape York Peninsula: a natural history.* Photography by Kerry Trapnell. Malanda, Queensland.

Ganter, Regina.
1994. *The pearl-shellers of Torres Strait: resource use, development and decline 1860s-1960s.* Melbourne: Melbourne University Press.

Gaucher, Michel.
1969. *Saint-Gilles-Croix-de-Vie.* Fontenay-le-Compte: Amitiés Sablaises.

Gittins, Jean.
1981. *The diggers from China: the story of the Chinese on the goldfields.* Melbourne: Quartet Books.

Goodman, Jordan.
2005. *The Rattlesnake. A voyage of discovery to the Coral Sea.* London: Faber and Faber.

Gregory, Edmund.
1896. *Narrative of James Murrells' ("Jemmy Morrill") seventeen years' exile among the wild blacks of North Queensland and his life and shipwreck and terrible adventures among savage tribes; their manners, customs, languages, and superstitions; also Murrells' rescue and return to civilization.* Brisbane: Printed by Edmund Gregory [first published 1863].

Gribble, P. J.
1985. *What hath God wrought: the story of the electric telegraph, Queensland.* Brisbane: Telecom Australia.

Guillou, Jean. 1981.
Le naufrage du *Saint Paul* en 1858. *Société d'études historiques de la Nouvelle-Calédonie.* 1er trimestre. Bulletin No 46: 27–45.

Hafner, Diane. 2005.
Images of Port Stewart: possible interpretations. In Bruce Rigsby and Nicolas Peterson (eds), *Donald Thomson: the man and scholar,* 211-230. Canberra: The Academy of the Social Sciences in Australia.

Hagan, Denise (ed.).
2005. *Lockhart River Community Plan 2004–2008. Empowering the community – working together.* Lockhart River, Queensland: Lockhart River Aboriginal Shire Council.

Hale, Herbert M. and Norman B. Tindale.
1933–1936. Aborigines of Princess Charlotte Bay, North Queensland. *Records of the South Australian Museum* 5: 63–116 (Part 1), 117–172 (Part 2).

Harris, David R.
1978. Adaptation to a tropical rain-forest environment: Aboriginal subsistence in northeastern

Queensland. In N. Blurton-Jones and V. Reynolds (eds), *Human behaviour and adaptation*, 113-134. London: Taylor & Francis.

Haviland, John B., with Roger Hart.
1998. *Old Man Fog and the last Aborigines of Barrow Point*. Bathurst: Crawford House Publishing.

Hawtrey, Seymour H. C.
1901. The Lengua Indians of the Paraguayan Chaco. *Journal of the Royal Anthropological Institute* 31: 280–99.

Heaton, J. Henniker.
1879. *Australian dictionary of dates and men of the time ; containing the history of Australasia from 1542 to May 1879*. Sydney: George Robertson.

Hervé, G.
1911. Le sauvage de l'Aveyron devant les observateurs de l'homme (avec le rapport retrouvé de Philippe Pinel), *Revue d'anthropologie* 21: 383–98, 441–54.

Hill, Barry.
2003. Crossing cultures. *Meanjin* 62 (4): 116–20.

Holthouse, Hector.
1986. *Ships in the coral*, rev. ed. Sydney: Angus and Robertson.

Howard, Rod.
2006. *The fabulist: the incredible story of Louis de Rougemont*. Sydney: Random House Australia.

Hynes, R. A. and A. K. Chase.
1982. Plants, sites and domiculture: Aboriginal influence upon plant communities in Cape York Peninsula, *Archaeology in Oceania* 17 (1): 38–50.

Idriess, Ion.
1959. *The tin scratchers*. Sydney: Angus and Robertson.

Illustrated Sydney News New South Wales weather almanac.
1873–1881 (bound in one volume). Sydney: Gordon & Gotch.

Johnson, Trish.
2003. Dorothy Short. In Queensland Art Gallery, *Story place: indigenous art of Cape York and the rainforest*, 124-127. Brisbane: Queensland Art Gallery.

Jones, Rhys.
1988. Images of natural man. In Jacqueline Bonnemains, Elliott Forsyth and Bernard Smith (eds), *Baudin in Australian waters: the artwork of the French voyage of discovery to the southern lands 1800–1804*, 35-64. Melbourne: Oxford University Press in association with the Australian Academy of the Humanities.

Jukes, J. Beete.
1847. *Narrative of the surveying voyage of H.M.S. 'Fly'...during the years 1842–1846*, vol. 1. London: T. & W. Boone.

Kellaway, C. H. and Donald F. Thomson.
1930. Observations on the venom of a large Australian snake, *Pseudechis Australis* (Gray). 2. The venom yields and venom. *Australian journal of experimental biology and medical science* 7: 134–50.

Laade, Wolfgang.
1967. Four Aboriginal legends from Cape York, northern Queensland, Australia. *Archiv für Völkerkunde*. 21: 91–94.
1970. Notes on the boras at Lockhart River Mission, Cape York Peninsula, north-east Australia. *Archiv für Völkerkunde*. 24: 273–309.

Lack, Clem.
1967. The strange story of Narcisse Pelletier. *Local Government* 62 (September 1967): 20–22.

Lane, Harlan.
1976. *The wild boy of Aveyron*. Cambridge, Mass.: Harvard University Press.

Lawler, Ivan and Helene Marsh, Brenda McDonald and Tony Stokes (CRC Reef Research Centre).
2002. *Dugongs in the Great Barrier Reef: current state of knowledge, April 2002*. Townsville, Queensland: CRC Reef Research Centre Ltd.
http://www.reef.crc.org.au/publications/brochures/dugong_2002.pdf. Brochure accessed at CRC Reef website, 18 January 2009.

Letourneau, Charles.
1880. Sur un Français nommé Narcisse Pelletier, qui oublia sa langue chez les Australiens. *Bulletins de la Société d'Anthropologie de Paris*, 3e série, t. 3: 710–716.

Leys, Simon.
2005. *The wreck of the Batavia and Prosper*. Melbourne: Black Inc.

Liep, John.
1983.'This civilising influence': the colonial transformation of Rossel Island society. *Journal of Pacific History*, vol. 18 (1–2): 113–131.

Loney, Jack.
1993. *Wrecks on the Queensland coast, 1791–1992 (includes Great Barrier Reef, Coral Sea, Torres Strait, Gulf of Carpentaria)*. Yarram, Victoria: Lonestone Press.

Loos, Noel.
1982. *Invasion and resistance: Aboriginal-European relations on the North Queensland frontier 1861–1897*. Canberra: Australian National University Press.

Lumholtz, Carl.
1980. *Among cannibals. An account of four years' travels in Australia, and of camp life with the Aborigines of Queensland*. Canberra: Australian National University Press [first published in English in 1889].

MacGillivray, John.
1852. *Narrative of the voyage of H.M.S. Rattlesnake: Commanded by the late Captain Owen Stanley, during the years 1846–1850*. London: T. & W. Boone.

Mackaness, George.
1931. *The life of Vice-Admiral William Bligh*. Sydney: Angus and Robertson. 2 vols.

Maddock, Kenneth.
1972. *The Australian Aborigines: a portrait of their society*. Harmondsworth: Penguin.

Marlex, Bernard.
n.d. *La vie à Saint-Nazaire au 19e siècle*. No place or publisher given. Held in Ecomusée de Saint-Nazaire, n° d'inventaire 2149, cote 320.2 MAR.

Martin de Moussy.
1866. La religiosité est-elle un des caractères spéciaux du genre humain? *Bulletins de la Société d'Anthropologie de Paris* 2e série, t. 1:105–20.

Merland, Constant.
1876a. Narcisse Pelletier. *La Revue de Bretagne, de Vendée et d'Anjou*, t. 39: 253–272.
1876b. *Dix-sept ans chez les sauvages. Narcisse Pelletier. Notice par C. Merland avec portrait, fac-simile, musique et dessin d'armes*. Paris: E. Dentu.

Moore, David R.
1979. *Islanders and Aborigines at Cape York. An ethnographic reconstruction based on the 1848– 1850 'Rattlesnake' Journals of O. W. Brierly and information he obtained from Barbara Thompson*. Canberra, Australian Institute of Aboriginal Studies and New Jersey, U.S.A., Humanities Press inc.

Mullins, Steve.
1995. *Torres Strait: a history of colonial occupation and culture contact, 1864–1897*, Central Queensland University Press: Rockhampton, Qld.

Osborne, Hugh.
1959. 'Bits of the 'St Paul' are still there. But there have been other wrecks on Rossel'. *Pacific Islands Monthly*. September 1959: 53–55.

Pajot, Stéphane
1999. *Personnages Pittoresques de Nantes et de Loire-Atlantique*. Le Château d'Olonne. Editions d'Orbestier.
2002. *Nantes-sur-mer. Histoires de l'eau de la Loire à l'Atlantique*. Le Château d'Olonne. Editions d'Orbestier.

Pelletier, Narcisse.
2001. *Chez les sauvages. Dix-sept ans de la vie d'un mousse vendéen dans une tribu cannibale 1858–1875*. Ed. Philippe Pécot. Paris. Cosmopole. New edition.

Perocheau, Joël.
1994. *Dictionnaire historique des Vendéens célèbres additionné des incontournables*. Published by the author, 1994.

Peterson, Nicolas.
2005. Thomson's place in Australian anthropology. In Bruce Rigsby and Nicolas Peterson (eds), *Donald Thomson: the man and scholar*, 29-44. Canberra: The Academy of the Social Sciences in Australia.

Pizzey, Graham.
1980. *A field guide to the birds of Australia*. Illustrated by Roy Doyle. Sydney: Collins.

Poignant, Roslyn.
1993. Captive Aboriginal lives: Billy, Jenny, Little Toby and their companions. In *Captive lives: Australian captivity narratives*, Kate Darian-Smith, Roslyn Poignant, and Kay Schaffer, 35–57. London: Sir Robert Menzies Centre for Australian Studies, Institute of Commonwealth Studies, University of London.

Porset, Charles.
1979. Langues universelles, langues philosophiques, langues auxiliaires au XIXe siècle. Essai de bibliographie. *Romantisme* nos 25–26: 209–215.

Prideaux, P.
1988. *Somerset, Cape York Peninsula, 1864–1877, from spear to pearl-shell*. Brisbane: Boolarong Publications (for the author).

Pruner-Bey, Franz.
1865. L'homme et l'animal. *Bulletins de la Société d'Anthropologie de Paris* 1ère série, 6: 522–62.

Queensland Art Gallery.
2003. *Story place: indigenous art of Cape York and the rainforest*. Brisbane: Queensland Art Gallery.

Reid, Frank.
1954. *The romance of the Great Barrier Reef*. Sydney and London: Angus and Robertson.

Rigsby, Bruce.
1980. The language situation on Cape York Peninsula: past, present, future. In J. Wright, B. Mitchell and P. Watling (eds), *Reef, rainforest, mangroves, man*, 5-7. Cairns: Wildlife Preservation Society of Queensland.
1999. Genealogies, kinship and local group composition: old Yintjingga (Port Stewart) in the late 1920s. In J. Finlayson, B. Rigsby and H. Bek (eds), *Connections in native title: genealogies, kinship and groups* (CAEPR research monograph No. 13), 107-123. Canberra: Centre for Aboriginal Economic Policy Research, Australian National University.
2005. The languages of eastern Cape York Peninsula and linguistic anthropology. In Bruce Rigsby and Nicolas Peterson (eds), *Donald Thomson: the man and scholar*, 129-142. Canberra: The Academy of the Social Sciences in Australia.

Rigsby, Bruce and Athol Chase.
1998. The Sandbeach People and dugong hunters of Eastern Cape York Peninsula: property in land

and sea country. In Nicolas Peterson and Bruce Rigsby (eds), *Customary Marine Tenure in Australia*, 192-218. Sydney: University of Sydney, Oceania Publications (Oceania Monographs No. 48).

Rigsby, Bruce and Nicolas Peterson (eds).
2005. *Donald Thomson: the man and scholar*. Canberra: The Academy of the Social Sciences in Australia.

Rochas, Victor de.
1861. Naufrage et scènes d'anthropophagie à l'île Rossell [sic] dans l'archipel de la Louisiade (Mélanésie). *Le Tour du Monde*, 1861, second semestre: 81–94.

Rothwell, Nicolas.
2007. *Another country*. Melbourne: Black Inc.

Rouillé, Joseph.
1967. *De Vendée en Australie: l'aventure de Narcisse Pelletier mousse vendéen*. Dessins. H. Simon. Benet: Ed. du Marais.
1980. *Le sauvage blanc : de Vendée en Australie*. Nantes: Ed. Reflets du Passé.
2002. *La prodigieuse et véritable aventure d'un mousse vendéen*. La Mothe-Achard: Ed. Offset Cinq.

Roussière, Valentin.
1975. *A l'écoute de la Vendée*. La Roche-sur-Yon: S.A. Imprimerie Centrale de l'Ouest.

Ruhen, Olaf.
1963. *Mountains in the clouds*. London: Angus & Robertson; Adelaide: Rigby Ltd.

Sharp, Nonie.
1992. *Footprints along the Cape York Sandbeaches*. Canberra: Aboriginal Studies Press.

Stanner, W. E. H.
1965. 'Aboriginal territorial organization: estate, range, domain and regime', *Oceania* 36: 1–26.
1966. *On Aboriginal religion*. Oceania Monograph 11. Sydney: University of Sydney.

Sutton, Peter.
2005. Science and sensibility on a foul frontier: at Flinders Island, 1935. In Bruce Rigsby and Nicolas Peterson (eds), *Donald Thomson: the man and scholar*, 143-158. Canberra: The Academy of the Social Sciences in Australia.
2008a. After consensus. *Griffith Review*, Spring 2008, 'Hidden Queensland': 199–216.
2008b. Stories about feeling: Dutch-Australian contact in Cape York Peninsula, 1606–1756. In Peter Veth, Peter Sutton and Margo Neale (eds), *Strangers on the shore: early coastal contacts in Australia*, 35-59. Canberra: National Museum of Australia Press.

Tennant, Kylie. 1959. *Speak you so gently*. London: Victor Gollancz Ltd.

Thompson, David A.
1985. *'Bora is like Church'*. Sydney: Australian Board of Missions. Revised edition [originally published in 1982].
1988a. Bora, church and modernization at Lockhart River, Queensland. In Tony Swain and Deborah Bird Rose (eds), *Aboriginal Australians and Christian missions: ethnographies and historical studies*, 263-276. Adelaide: The Australian Association for the Study of Religions.
1988b. *Lockhart River "Sand Beach" Language: an outline of Kuuku Ya'u and Umpila*. Work Papers of SIL-AAIB, Series A Volume 11. Darwin: Summer Institute of Linguistics.
1995. *'Bora belonga white man': Missionaries and Aborigines at Lockhart River Mission*. MA thesis, University of Queensland. Revised edition.

Thomson, Donald F.
1932. Ceremonial presentation of fire in North Queensland: a preliminary note on the place of fire in primitive ritual. *Man* 32: 162–166.
1933a. The hero cult, initiation and totemism on Cape York. *Journal of the Royal Anthropological Institute* 63: 453–537.
1933b. Notes on Australian snakes of the genera *Pseudechis* and *Oxyuranus*. *Proceedings of the Zoological Society of London* Part 4: 855–860.
1934a. Across Cape York Peninsula with a pack team. *Walkabout* 1: 21–31.
1934b. The dugong hunters of Cape York. *Journal of the Royal Anthropological Institute* 64: 237–262.

1935a. *Birds of Cape York Peninsula. Ecological notes. Field observations, and catalogue of specimens collected on three expeditions to North Queensland.* Melbourne: H. J. Green, Government Printer.
1935b. The joking relationship and organized obscenity. *American Anthropologist* 37: 460-490.
1956a. The fishermen and dugong hunters of Princess Charlotte Bay. *Walkabout* 22(11): 33–36.
1956b. The masked dancers of I'wai'i. A remarkable hero cult which has invaded Cape York Peninsula. *Walkabout* 22(12): 17–19.
1966. Masked dancers of the crocodile cult. *Hemisphere* 10(8): 24–28.
1969. Cape York. Nature's gateway to Australia. *Walkabout* 35(7): 14–17.
1972. *Kinship and behaviour in North Queensland. A preliminary account of kinship and social organisation on Cape York Peninsula.* Foreword, afterword and editing by H.W. Scheffler. Australian Aboriginal Studies No. 51. Canberra: Australian Institute of Aboriginal Studies.
1983. *Children of the wilderness.* South Yarra, Vic.: Currey O'Neil Ross.

Trogoff, Maurice.
2002. *Mémoires sauvages.* Le Faouët: Liv'Éditions.

Tylor, Edward Burnett, Sir.
1871. *Primitive culture: researches into the development of mythology, philosophy, religion, language, art and custom.* 2 vols. London.

University Gallery, University of Melbourne.
1983. *Mortuary objects from North East Arnhem Land and Cape York Peninsula: the Donald Thomson Collection. August 3 – September 16, 1983.* Parkville, Vic.: University Gallery, University of Melbourne.

Virgil.
1984. *The Aeneid*, trans. Robert Fitzgerald, London: Harvill Press.

Voltaire.
1975 [1775]. *Zaïre.* Ed. Eva Jacobs. London: Hodder and Stoughton.

Warby, John.
2000. *You – me mates eh! : a personal story of reconciliation and change among the Aboriginal people and missionary staff of Lockhart River Mission, Cape York Peninsula 1924 – 1960.* Rev. ed. North Rockhampton, Qld.: John Warby.

Warner, Lloyd.
1958 (1937). *A black civilization. A social study of an Australian tribe.* Rev. ed. New York: Harper and Brothers.

West, Alan L.
1999. *Aboriginal string bags, nets and cordage.* Melbourne: Museum Victoria.

White, Hayden.
1972. The forms of wildness: archaeology of an idea. In Edward Dudley and Maximillian E. Novak, *The wild man within: an image in Western thought from the Renaissance to Romanticism*, 3-37. University of Pittsburgh Press.

White, Patrick.
1977 [1976]. *A fringe of leaves.* Harmondsworth: Penguin.

Who was who, 1929–1940.
1967. Second edition, vol. 3. London: A. and C. Black.

Wilbert, Johannes. n. d. 'Lengua', *World culture encyclopedia.*
http://www.everyculture.com/South-America/Lengua.html. Accessed 15 January 2007.

Wilson, Steve and Gerry Swan. 2003. *A complete guide to reptiles of Australia.* Frenchs Forest. N.S.W.: Reed New Holland.

Woods, J. T.
1964. C. D'Oyly H. Aplin, First Government Geologist for the Southern District of Queensland. *Memoirs of the Queensland Museum*, vol. 14, part 4, 107–114.

Newspaper And Magazine Articles in English

The Age, 28 May 1875, 'Rescued from the blacks'.

Brisbane Courier, 24 May 1875, 'The narrative of Narcisse Pelletier'; 26 May 1875, 'Distinguished arrival, by mail steamer'; 4 December 1865, 'Two Chinamen rescued after a residence of seven years with the blacks'; 6 December 1875; Supplement, 16 December 1875.

The Bulletin, December 7 1960, 'The case of the shipwrecked Chinaman' (correspondent Olaf Ruhen).

Canberra Times, 16 May 1992, 'Salvation came in being castaway on an island' (correspondent Robert Willson).

The Capricornian, 22 May 1875, 'Shipping news'; 5 June 1875, 'The narrative of Narcisse Pelletier'.

Cooktown Courier, 22 May 1875, 'A Chinese lady'.

Cooktown Herald and Palmer River Advertiser, 19 May 1875, 'Shipping Intelligence'; 'Our late visitor'; 'A Chinese lady'.

Courier Mail, 27 December 1995, 'Cabin boy's tale of tribal survival' (correspondent Lawrie Kavanagh).

Cummins & Campbell's Monthly Magazine, April 1935, 'Narcisse Pellatier. A castaway in the far North' (correspondent 'Viator'); December 1948, 'Cape York's 'wild white man' (correspondent William H. MacFarlane).

Daily Northern Argus, 21 May 1875, 'Shipping Intelligence'.

Holy Name Monthly, October 1969, vol. 38(9), 'Perilous passage: he preferred the bush myalls to civilised mankind' (correspondent Francis Murray).

Illustrated Australian News for Home Readers, 12 July 1875, 'Sir Arthur Hamilton Gordon, Governor of Fiji'.

Melbourne Herald, 21 March 1961, 'Boy's 16 years with natives'.

New York Times, 14 April 1859, 'Shipwreck, butchery and cannibalism'; 3 August 1875.

Port Denison Times, 25 November 1865, 'Two Chinamen rescued after a residence of seven years with the blacks'.

Queenslander, 29 May 1875, 'Shipping Intelligence'.

Records of the Blue Mountains, March 1924, 'A renegade: the romantic case of Pellatier'.

Rockhampton Bulletin, 21 May 1875, 'Shipping Intelligence'; 31 May 1875, 'The narrative of Narcisse Pelletier'.

Smith's Weekly, 25 February 1922, 'The Mystery Man of Staaten River'; 17 November 1923, 'The Mystery Man of Staaten River. Australia's only white "Aboriginal" who is living with the blacks in far North Queensland'.

Sydney Evening News, 22 May 1875, 'Story of the French boy rescued from the blacks'.

Sydney Mail, 22 May 1875, 'Recovery of a shipwrecked boy'; 29 May 1875, Narcisse Felletier [sic]. A Frenchman who has lived seventeen years among cannibals'.

Sydney Morning Herald, 26 May 1875, 'Shipping'; 27 May 1875, Narcisse Pelletier. A Frenchman who has lived seventeen years among cannibals'; 9 June 1875, 'Photographs of Narcisse Pelletier'.

Sydney Shipping Gazette, 3 January, 1859, 'The loss of the St. Paul'; 24 January 1859, 'Wreck of the St. Paul from China'.

Sydney Sun, 5 August 1974, 'Cabin boy became a native warrior'.

The Times, 21 July 1875, 'Seventeen years among savages'.

Town and Country Journal, 29 May 1875, 'Extraordinary story of the French boy rescued from the blacks'.

The World's News, 17 November 1923. 'Away out on the Barrier. Where the dead ships lie' (correspondent A. Meston).

NEWSPAPER ARTICLES IN FRENCH

Bulletin français, 23 July 1875, 'Dix-sept ans chez les sauvages' (correspondent Louis Bloch).

Journal des débats politiques et littéraires, 26 December 1875.

Journal des Sables, 6 June 1954, 'Un marin vendéen chez les nègres' (correspondent Camille Millet).

Journal illustré, 8 August 1875, 'La capture de Narcisse Pelletier' (correspondent Aristide Roger).

La Presse, 28 July 1875; 29 July 1875; 31 August 1875; 2 September 1875; 9 January 1876.

La Presse illustrée, 7 August 1875, 'Narcisse Pelletier: Le Robinson français'.

Univers illustré, 7 August 1875, 'Pierre Pelletier: Le sauvage d'Australie', (correspondent X. Dachères).

MANUSCRIPTS/UNPUBLISHED MATERIAL

Aplin, Christopher D'Oyly.
Report on the pearl fisheries of Torres Strait, Somerset, 3 March 1875. Queensland State Archives Item ID313071, Letterbook No: 263–271.
Letter to the Colonial Secretary, Somerset, 11 May 1875. Dixson Library, DL MSQ 589, Somerset Letterbook. 53/75 ff. 292–3 (also Queensland State Archives Item, ID313071, Letterbook).

Baudouin, Marcel.
Carnet de notes du Docteur Marcel Baudouin sur Narcisse Pelletier. Fonds Marcel Baudouin, Musée de l'Abbaye Sainte-Croix, Les Sables d'Olonne.

Hamilton-Gordon, Arthur.
'Seventeen years among the savages'. Correspondence and Papers of Arthur Hamilton-Gordon, 1st Baron Stanmore. British Library, Manuscripts. Add. 49271, Stanmore papers. Literary collection of Lord Stanmore. Item 5, ff. 195–206.

Hôpital Beaujon, Paris.
Registre des entrées, 1875, 1 Q 2/110. Archives de l'Assistance Publique-Hôpitaux de Paris.

Jura.
Extrait du rapport médical du *Jura* (rapports médicaux XIII -9), Service Historique de la Défense, Département 'Marine', Toulon.

MacFarlane, W. H.
Early days of Thursday Island, Book 6, c.1925, MS 2616/1, Item 7, Australian Institute of Aboriginal and Torres Strait Islander Studies Library.

McFarlane, Samuel.
Letter to Joseph Mullens, Foreign Secretary of the London Missionary Society, Somerset, 12 May 1875. School of Oriental and African Studies Library, University of London. CWM/Papua/Incoming Correspondence/Box 1 1872-1876.

Ottley, John.
Letter to H. J. Dodd dated 30 May 1923 including 'Story of Narcisse Pelletier'. Royal Historical Society of Queensland Library.

NOTE ON THE TRANSLATION

In presenting this translation of Merland's *Dix-sept ans chez les sauvages* to readers more than a century after the book was first published, I felt that it was important to annotate Pelletier's account of his life with Uutaalnganu people so as to amplify, clarify or correct specific points raised in it in order to provide a fuller understanding of the society and environment it portrays in the period just before European incursion by land and sea began in earnest in north-east Cape York Peninsula. I have used various anthropological, linguistic and other sources to do this. The annotations include excerpts from Athol Chase's published and unpublished work in particular, together with excerpts from the work of David Thompson, Bruce Rigsby and Peter Sutton, all of whose research relates, or has related to, the *Pama Malngkana*, as well as excerpts from the work of earlier writers such as Donald Thomson. Responsibility for the way in which I have drawn on these works is mine alone, but I hope the annotations, which can only give a glimpse of the original sources, will encourage readers to seek them out in order to gain a deeper perspective on the history, culture and languages of the Aboriginal people of north-east Cape York Peninsula.

Johnson Butcher, Uutaalnganu and Kaanju affiliation, at Lockhart River (c. 1973). Courtesy of Athol Chase.

Alick Sandy, Uutaalnganu affiliation, spearing fish at Cape Direction (c. 1972). Courtesy of Athol Chase.

Lockhart men cutting up a dugong while their relatives wait for shares, Lockhart River(1972). Courtesy of Athol Chase.

At Chinchanyaku, the camping place opposite Night Island, where, on 11 April 1875, Pelletier was taken aboard the *John Bell* (1989). Courtesy of Athol Chase.

Uutaalnganu men camping at the Lockhart River (c. 1975). Courtesy of Athol Chase.

Alick Naiga, Uutaalnganu and Kaanju affiliation, making a traditional fishing spear (1973). Courtesy of Athol Chase.

Uutaalnganu and Umpila men digging eggs from a scrub turkey mound at Chester River in Umpila country (1975). Courtesy of Athol Chase.

Johnson Butcher and Alick Sandy opening coconuts at the old Lockhart mission site (1974). Courtesy of Athol Chase.

Tiki, firestick with decorated sheath. Courtesy of the National Museum of Australia, photographer George Serras.

Ulku, palm leaf water carrier. Courtesy of the artist Elizabeth (Queen) Giblet. Collection of the National Museum of Australia, photographer George Serras.

L–R: George Rocky (Umpila affiliation), anthropologist Athol Chase, Alick Naiga, Lockhart River (1973). Courtesy of Athol Chase.

Alick Sandy with young Uutaalnganu children, Lockhart River (1974). Courtesy of Athol Chase.

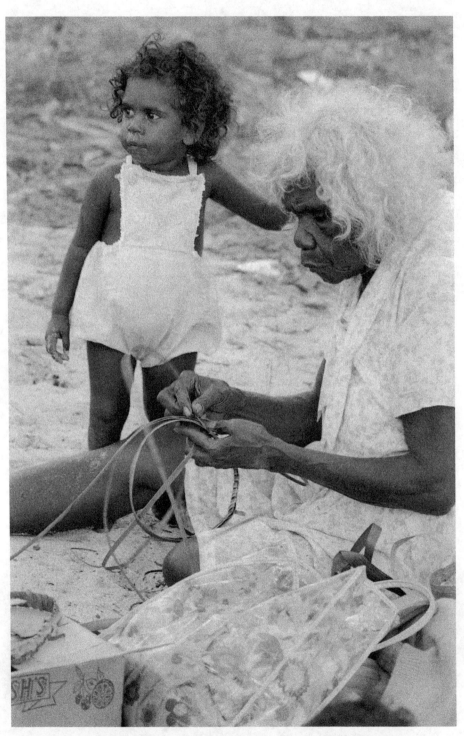

Margaret Temple, Uutaalnganu affiliation, weaving a pandanus leaf basket, with her granddaughter, Lockhart River (1973). Courtesy of Athol Chase.

CPSIA information can be obtained
at www.ICGtesting.com
Printed in the USA
LVHW082315041222
734539LV00022B/208